THIS BEAUTIFUL TABLE for outdoor buffets is elegant enough to use indoors, too. It folds into a 7-in. width for storage. See plans for it, and another table, on page 137

ADD A HEARTH-WARMING and heart-warming fireplace to your home. With a freestanding prefab unit, it's a relatively easy project. See page 67

INVEST A FEW DAYS' WORK in a summer of fun. Above-ground pools are simple to erect and relatively low in cost. See page 62 for information on selecting the best pool for your needs, and tips on setting it up

PERSONALIZE YOUR TREE with your own sparkling decorations this year. Blend strips of walnut and birch, aluminum and brass into delicate baubles. See page 188

MAKE A HANDSOME platform bed! Choose this king-size one with movable end tables, or an easy-to-build single sleeper. You'll find plans on page 128

BUILD THIS ROLL-ABOUT STACK of swinging trays. It provides a lot of storage in a small space, and is a novel and fascinating piece of furniture. See page 141

LET THE SUN SHINE IN! A skylight can turn a room into a bright and cheerful haven on the dreariest of days. See page 58 to learn exactly how to install a skylight

EVERYDAY OBJECTS take on a striking new appearance when made of laminated wood. An article on page 132 has plans for six handsome laminated projects.

Popular Mechanics
Do-It-Yourself Yearbook

1978

Exciting new products
- for your home
- for your shop
- gear for outdoorsmen
- the best of the new tools
- what's new for photographers
- newsmakers in electronics

Great projects of the year
- to improve your home
- shop know-how
- challenging craft projects
- how-to in the great outdoors
- photo projects
- electronics know-how
- projects just for fun

Popular Mechanics, 250 W. 55th St., New York, N.Y. 10019

EDITOR
  Clifford B. Hicks

ART DIRECTOR
  Ralph Leroy Linnenburger

MANAGING EDITOR
  Paul Hilts

ASSOCIATE EDITOR
  Anne T. Cope

CONTRIBUTING EDITORS
  Ed Nelson
  David Paulsen
  Benjamin Lee

STAFF ARTISTS
  Marion Linnenburger
  Sue Sevick

ASSISTANT EDITOR, Production
  Shari Green

EDITORIAL ADVISORY BOARD, *Popular Mechanics*

  John Linkletter, *Editor*
  Sheldon Gallager, *Executive Editor*
  Daniel C. Fales, *Managing Editor*
  Wayne C. Leckey, *Special Projects Editor*
  William T. McKeown, *Outdoors Editor*

ISBN 0-910990-67-0

Library of Congress Catalog Number 77-84921

© 1978, The Hearst Corporation
All Rights Reserved

*No part of the text or illustrations in this work
may be used without written permission by
The Hearst Corporation.*

Printed in the United States of America

CONTENTS

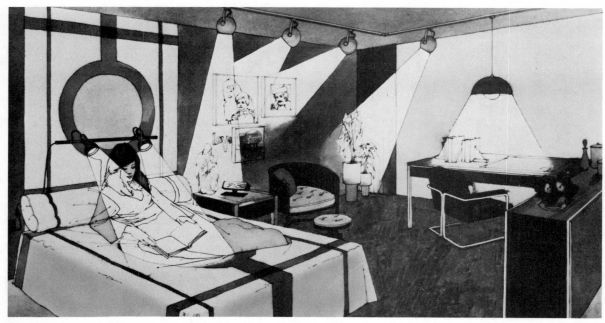

Lightcraft's spheres will concentrate light where you need it most

Skillful lighting makes a room look great

BY MIKE McCLINTOCK

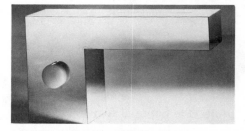

■ LIGHTING CAN MAKE a good room look great and a great room look spectacular. It's the finishing touch that should combine beauty and efficiency, but it usually gets little attention because outlets may not be in the right place or there may not be enough of them. So you wind up putting lamps where you *have* to instead of where you'd *like* to. But more wiring (in the right place) is only part of the solution. The real trick lies in planning how you'll be using the room (including what you'll be doing and where) and picking the best kind of light or combination of lights for those situations.

To begin with, most rooms need some kind of general lighting. This can be high-intensity light in a kitchen or bathroom or soft overall light in a living or dining room. The question is how to illuminate the whole room without putting a 200-watt bulb in the middle of the ceiling. Track

Simple G-lamps provide flexible general lighting in the kitchen

Yes, believe it or not, they're all lamps. The ones on the opposite page (left) and the grow light (above, middle) are among the unique fixtures made by George Kovacs Lighting, 831 Madison Ave., New York, NY 10021. The grow lamp comes in two different sizes. Kovac's lamps range from conventional shapes to geometric designs. Track lights (other photos above) can floodlight, pinpoint a spot on the wall, and reflect light from silver-coated bulbs gently over an entire area. You can get bulbs (in a variety of sizes) that are frosted, clear or darkened

TRACK LIGHT HARDWARE

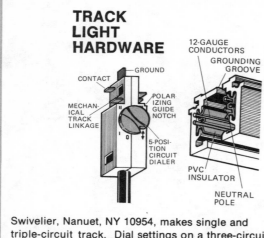

Swivelier, Nanuet, NY 10954, makes single and triple-circuit track. Dial settings on a three-circuit system will activate any combination of lamps

Snap-in wiring

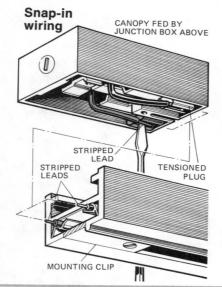

Rotating connectors

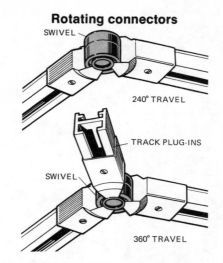

Lightcraft, 5691 Rising Sun Ave., Philadelphia, PA 19120, features these connectors (and a six-point swivel) to track in any direction

Lightolier, 346 Claremont Ave., Jersey City, NJ 07305, makes over 35 lamps. Canopy boxes, wired at the ceiling, act as plugs for the track sections

lighting is one answer for two good reasons. Wiring one junction box in the ceiling can feed a whole series of tracks. You can hang fixtures from them that will throw exactly the light you want.

Track lighting frees you from the limitation of having one outlet box near every source of light. It also lets you make a mistake or change your mind. When you sink a lot of money into an elaborate center-ceiling fixture that's it. The light is going to stay there. But if you don't like the way your tracks look, just unplug them from the supply box and make a different arrange-

ment. You can also slide fixtures along the track, bunch them at either end, or put different fixtures (throwing different kinds of light) on different tracks altogether. The possibilities are endless and they're all up to you.

The system starts at the feed box. It's a small box, matching the contour and style of the track, that sits on the ceiling and connects to the junction box above it. Once this is installed, wiring the rest of the system is literally a snap. Since conductors run the full length of the track, power is available at each end. There are caps (made to close off one end if you're hanging only one

WIRING MADE SIMPLE

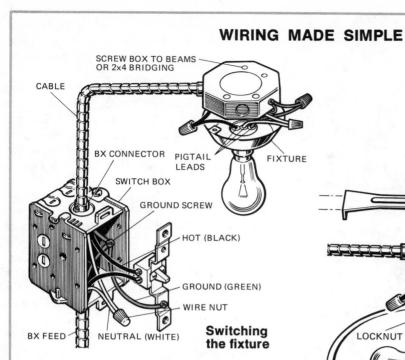

SCREW BOX TO BEAMS OR 2x4 BRIDGING

CABLE

BX CONNECTOR

SWITCH BOX

GROUND SCREW

PIGTAIL LEADS

FIXTURE

HOT (BLACK)

GROUND (GREEN)

WIRE NUT

BX FEED   NEUTRAL (WHITE)

Switching the fixture

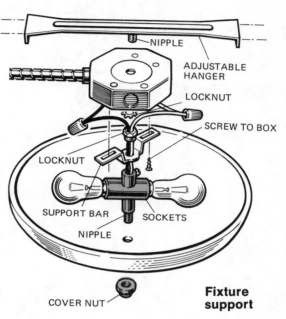

NIPPLE

ADJUSTABLE HANGER

LOCKNUT

SCREW TO BOX

LOCKNUT

SUPPORT BAR   SOCKETS

NIPPLE

COVER NUT

Fixture support

A full cellar or open attic gives you easy access to string your wires and make all of the electrical connections. It's harder if you have to work from inside a finished room. An electrician's fish tape (a spring-tempered length of flat steel ribbon) is inserted down through holes in the ceiling or floor framing and maneuvered until you get to the source of the cable. You may need to make an extra hole in the wall to clear the tape from an obstruction. To pull the cable up (Romex will come easier than BX), splice the exposed leads around the hook at the end of the ribbon. Then wrap the connection with tape and haul away. Here are wiring connections for single and dual-control switches and a typical ceiling box supported between the beams. Carefully study all the necessary wiring before you begin the job

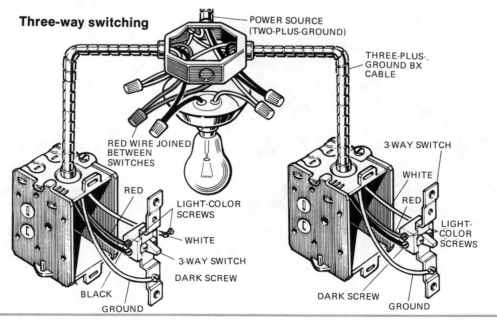

Three-way switching

POWER SOURCE (TWO-PLUS-GROUND)

THREE-PLUS-GROUND BX CABLE

RED WIRE JOINED BETWEEN SWITCHES

RED

LIGHT-COLOR SCREWS

WHITE

3-WAY SWITCH

DARK SCREW

BLACK

GROUND

3-WAY SWITCH

WHITE

RED

LIGHT-COLOR SCREWS

DARK SCREW

GROUND

The soft square (top) comes in three sizes and colors for use in track lighting. It is made by Lightcraft. Kovacs carriers an array of interesting shapes and sizes plus unique imports like the Swedish gooseneck

track) and connectors (elbows and straights) that let you plug one track into another and continue the system in any direction. It's a job you can do by yourself, too.

Measure from a side wall and snap a line where the track will be. Small mounting clips are screwed into the ceiling and tracks slip onto them. These clips make installation easy and space the track about ¼ in. off the ceiling to absorb the margin of high or low spots that could make the track uneven.

more work, more rewards

Companies like Swivelier offer two kinds of track. Most basic and easiest to install is a single-circuit track fed with a standard three-wire cable (hot, neutral and ground). You can control it with two or three-way switches. That means either a switch in one central location or switches at opposite ends of the room so you can turn on the light as you enter at one end and turn it off as you leave from the other. All lamps on this track will go off and on at the same time. But they also make three-circuit track with hardware to match (page 6). This system links three separately switched circuits with each length of track. It's ideal in a large room where you can install continuous tracks to cover the entire area.

Say you have six lamps along a 30-ft. wall. You may have pictures hung at one end that need "wall-washing" fixtures; lamps that flood the wall—and only the wall—with light. A stereo cabinet at the other end needs a spotlight for high visibility. You might want softer light on a couch in the center of the wall. With three-circuit track you can control each area independently. And if you decide to move the couch to the other end of the room, you can move the fixtures with it as though the wiring were specially designed to accommodate the brand-new setup.

the light you can't see

This sounds impossible, but it's the special effect you get from a newly developed fixture. You can look directly into this light from six inches away without squinting. It throws a wide beam of clean white light, but you can't see where the beam is coming from. The effect is both dramatic and mystifying. Objects appear to be lighting themselves. The light source is a clear bulb with a silver bowl covering half its outer skin. Light bounces up into a mottled, high-purity, aluminum bowl and is diffused down onto the room. The fixture, generally referred to as "no-glare," is shown in the left center of page 5.

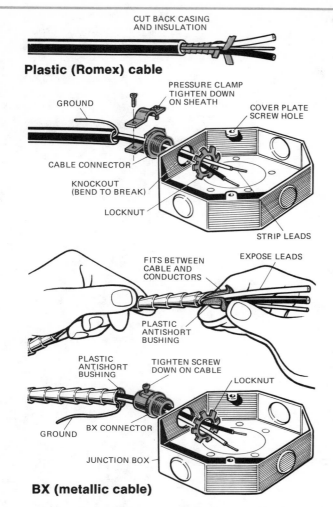

CUT BACK CASING
AND INSULATION

Plastic (Romex) cable

GROUND

PRESSURE CLAMP
TIGHTEN DOWN
ON SHEATH

COVER PLATE
SCREW HOLE

CABLE CONNECTOR

KNOCKOUT
(BEND TO BREAK)

LOCKNUT

STRIP LEADS

FITS BETWEEN
CABLE AND
CONDUCTORS

EXPOSE LEADS

PLASTIC
ANTISHORT
BUSHING

PLASTIC
ANTISHORT
BUSHING

TIGHTEN SCREW
DOWN ON CABLE

LOCKNUT

GROUND

BX CONNECTOR

JUNCTION BOX

BX (metallic cable)

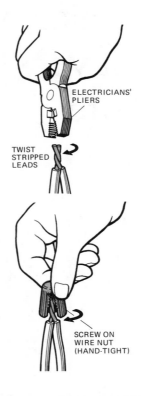

ELECTRICIANS'
PLIERS

TWIST
STRIPPED
LEADS

SCREW ON
WIRE NUT
(HAND-TIGHT)

The safe way to install and wire lighting is defined in the National Electrical Code. It's no more complicated than haphazard, on-the-spot methods, so follow these code-approved methods for a better, safer job.

Choose copper conductors. Use UI-approved, sheathed, copper wiring. It can be packaged in armored metallic cable (type AC) or thermoplastic cable (type TW or THW). These symbols are embossed on the cable's outer surface. For 15-ampere circuits, use No. 14 gauge and heavier No. 12 gauge for 20-amp. circuits. Each should have a third grounding wire. Specifying "fourteen-two, with ground" is the right way to give your order to the electrical supply house or hardware store.

Watch your colors. When you're joining new conductors to existing ones, always connect black to black, white to white and the bare or green wire to its counterpart. This is important because in house wiring the white always acts as the grounded neutral conductor, the black as the hot, ungrounded conductor, and the bare or green as the safety grounding conductor that protects you from getting a shock.

Don't break the chain. If you have to install a new junction box or take a new line out of an existing one, be sure to attach the grounding wire to the metal box. If two or more sets of conductors are spliced in the box, connect the two grounding wires together *in addition* to attaching them to the metal frame. One break in the line can cancel out the safety factor on the whole circuit.

Always switch the black. Always run the black (hot) conductor through the switch, never the white. If you switch the white instead, the fixture on the circuit will be a permanent, hot, shock hazard—even when the switch is off.

Attach the white to the shell. When you wire to a permanent lamp fixture, connect the white (neutral) to the screw on the metal shell of the lightbulb socket. If the lamp is already fitted with "pigtail" leads, join the white wires with a wire nut as shown above.

Try three-way switching. To control one light from two different locations, you'll need two three-way switches and special cable known as "fourteen-three, with ground." Our diagrams on page 7 will show you how to connect the wires.

No multiple choice. If you have any doubts about which wire goes where, don't guess. Turn over the job to a licensed electrician and you'll keep your peace of mind.

A fire alarm may save your life

BY MORT SCHULTZ

Sixty percent of fires in the home occur when people are sleeping. Fire detectors can awaken you and give you a chance to escape before the fire spreads

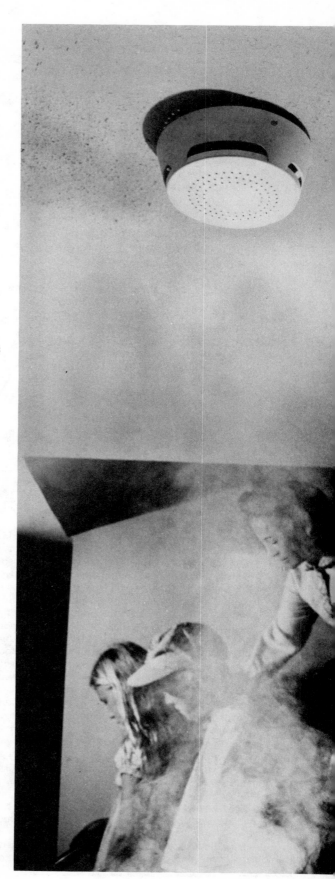

■ IN FAIRFAX, VA, smoke from a smoldering fire caused a family of five to suffocate as they slept in their expensive two-story home.

Commenting on the tragedy, Fairfax assistant fire chief William Bittle said, "It doesn't seem right spending $80,000 on a house, but not $50 for safety."

The $50 Chief Bittle was referring to would have bought the family an automatic warning device that would have sounded an alarm moments after the fire started, awakening them and giving them time for escape.

In Freehold Township, NJ, a 15-year-old boy and his grandmother perished when fire swept a two-story home during the night. The boy died in a leap from a second-story window trying to escape. The woman was asphyxiated by smoke.

"There is no doubt in my mind that if there had been a fire or smoke detection device in the home we could have possibly saved the lives of two people," Fire Marshal Frank Wilgus says.

300 fires an hour

The dramas in Fairfax and Freehold are duplicated every day of the week. According to the National Commission on Fire Prevention and

Control, statistically there is the likelihood that nationally within the next hour 300 fires will break out. This figure translates into a mind-boggling 2,628,000 fires a year.

The Commission reports that annually in this country alone fire kills 12,000—more than 6000 of them in home fires—injures 300,000 and destroys $11 billion in property.

Every day one fire official or another is reminding us that this terrible toll in lives and suffering could be substantially reduced if homeowners planned for fire as carefully as most do, say, for vacation.

But most people don't. Fewer than two million of the nation's 70 million residences are presently equipped with fire-detection devices. This is particularly tragic when you realize that 9 out of 10 deaths from fire occur at home, but that an estimated 8 of every 10 of them could be saved if homes were equipped with detection alarms.

Joe Erdmann and his wife and daughter today swear they owe their lives to such a device. About 2 a.m. Erdmann was awakened abruptly by a raucous blast from the smoke detector outside the bedroom area in his Neenah, WI, home.

A wisp of smoke from a fire smoldering in the kitchen had set off the alarm, giving Erdmann time to evacuate his family and extinguish the flames. "Thanks to that smoke alarm we were able to save our lives and our home," he says.

The two basic types of home fire detectors are smoke and heat. A smoke detector detects particles of combustion. A heat detector detects high temperature or a high rate-of-temperature rise.

inexpensive protection

When activated, both types emit a leather-lunged horn blast of at least 80 decibels for at least four minutes that will arouse the soundest sleeper.

Some fire experts suggest a system combining both heat and smoke detectors where maximum protection is desired and cost is no object. However, many now feel that the newer, more sensitive smoke detector that does not require heat buildup to function offers early-warning protection at a modest price—and should become just as common a household appliance as a toaster, food mixer or hair dryer.

For the average home, an elaborate setup is not needed. The National Fire Protection Assn. advises that "some very real protection is possible with one smoke detector on each floor or one smoke detector placed between the bedroom and the rest of the house."

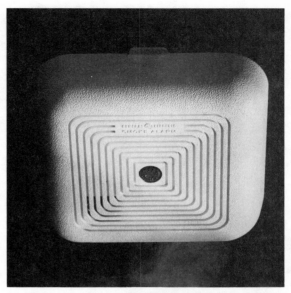

Many detectors come in a choice of battery or plug-in models such as the GE model shown in the top two photographs. The battery-powered type is handy for ceiling mounting where no power source may be near. The battery models also require a weak-battery warning indicator. The bottom photo shows the handsome Gillette photoelectric model. It's also available in battery and plug-in versions

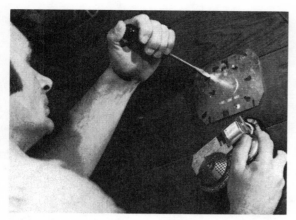

Installation is easy, as typified by this Honeywell mounting sequence. The base plate is first screwed to the wall or ceiling

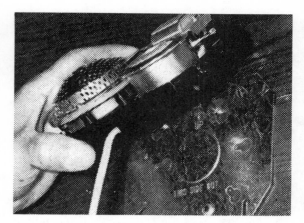

Next the sensor unit is attached to the plate as shown in the photo above. Alarms are best mounted high on the wall or ceiling as smoke rises

smoke sensors work far away

The most important necessity when fire starts is to give a home's occupants ample warning of danger so they can escape. Smoke detectors do this.

"Smoke detectors by their very nature can monitor smoke far from the point of origin because smoke moves, rising up to the ceiling and up stairways," Richard B. Bright states. He is senior research engineer of a special fire-protection project being conducted by the U.S. Bureau of Standards.

A reliable smoke alarm costs about $30 to $50. If you deploy more than one, they can be wired together in series so if smoke activates one alarm, the alarms in other areas will sound off, too.

It is at night that alarms earn every penny you spend for them. Sixty percent of fires in the home occur when people are sleeping.

The National Fire Protection Assn. points out that most people who die in home fires are not the victims of flames, but inhale smoke and poisonous gases that rise ahead of the flames.

"Victims suffocate to death in the middle of the night, asleep, never knowing what happened," the association points out. "Many die upstairs from a downstairs fire that never burns a thing on the second floor."

The danger of death by suffocation has reached a point of crisis because of widespread use in homes of synthetic materials, such as polyvinyl chloride. Synthetics are used in furniture, carpeting, drainpipes, shower curtains and other furnishings. When they begin to smolder, deadly chemical gases are given off.

how detectors work

"Flame is the last on the list of killers during fire," the National Fire Protection Assn. informs us. "Most people die from lack of oxygen, hot air or gases, and from smoke—often before they can awaken."

Smoke detectors are designed to sniff out fumes and warn people of danger before they are overcome. There are two basic types of smoke detectors for the home: photoelectric and ionization.

Photoelectric smoke detectors contain a small light source. When smoke enters the enclosure that surrounds the unit, the light beam is disrupted by smoke particles, causing light to be reflected to a photoelectric cell. This triggers the alarm.

An ionization smoke detector employs a small amount of radioactive material, which is less than the amount used on luminous watch dials. The material ionizes the air in a small pocket, causing a faint electric current. This current triggers the alarm when it's disturbed by fine smoke particles.

Both types work well and are approved by fire safety experts. Many are made by well-known reliable manufacturers such as General Electric, Honeywell, NuTone, Walter Kidde, Gillette, Norelco, Emhart, Teledyne, Master Lock, Pittway, BSR-Metrotec and Pyr-A-Larm. Whatever unit you select, it is important that it carry the UL (Underwriters Laboratories) or FM (Factory Mutual) label. This is your assurance the device has been tested by an independent agency and has met rigid standards.

The final step is installing the cover. This snaps on the sensor unit. The detector should now be given a thorough test using the self-testing controls

battery or plug-in?

You have a choice of battery or plug-in power. Each has its advantages. Battery-powered alarms are handy where there is no nearby wall outlet to plug into, especially since such sensors should usually be mounted high—on the ceiling or near the top of a wall—to intercept rising smoke and fumes. They also eliminate the possibility that a chance power outage could cause the units to fail to sound off.

But batteries require periodic checking and replacement—a vital precaution to insure proper operation. Any unit you consider should have an automatic indicator, visual or audible, to warn when batteries are low and need replacement. Both battery and house-wired units should also have test buttons because frequent testing is important to insure that the devices are operating correctly.

House-powered alarms eliminate the need for battery changing but require a source of current. If there's no convenient outlet, or you don't want the power cord to show, you may want to connect directly into your house wiring—a neat

Two basic types of smoke detectors are diagrammed in simplified form at the right. In the photoelectric alarm, a small light beam, constantly on, shines across a darkened chamber. If fire occurs, smoke particles enter the chamber, act as tiny reflectors and divert part of the light to the photocell detector. The photocell senses the light and sounds an alarm. In the ionization detector, ionized air molecules gravitate toward oppositely charged electrodes, setting up a tiny current flow. Entering smoke particles slow the ion flow, producing a current drop that triggers the alarm. Units which combine smoke detectors with heat detectors offer maximum protection

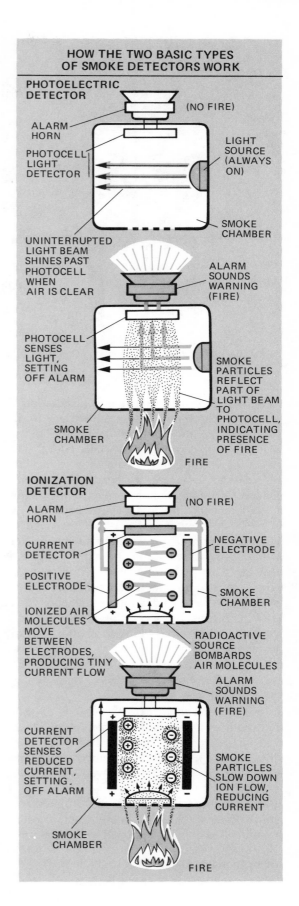

HOW THE TWO BASIC TYPES OF SMOKE DETECTORS WORK

PHOTOELECTRIC DETECTOR

(NO FIRE)

ALARM HORN

PHOTOCELL LIGHT DETECTOR

LIGHT SOURCE (ALWAYS ON)

SMOKE CHAMBER

UNINTERRUPTED LIGHT BEAM SHINES PAST PHOTOCELL WHEN AIR IS CLEAR

ALARM SOUNDS WARNING (FIRE)

PHOTOCELL SENSES LIGHT, SETTING OFF ALARM

SMOKE PARTICLES REFLECT PART OF LIGHT BEAM TO PHOTOCELL, INDICATING PRESENCE OF FIRE

SMOKE CHAMBER

FIRE

IONIZATION DETECTOR

(NO FIRE)

ALARM HORN

CURRENT DETECTOR

NEGATIVE ELECTRODE

POSITIVE ELECTRODE

SMOKE CHAMBER

IONIZED AIR MOLECULES MOVE BETWEEN ELECTRODES, PRODUCING TINY CURRENT FLOW

RADIOACTIVE SOURCE BOMBARDS AIR MOLECULES

ALARM SOUNDS WARNING (FIRE)

CURRENT DETECTOR SENSES REDUCED CURRENT, SETTING OFF ALARM

SMOKE PARTICLES SLOW DOWN ION FLOW, REDUCING CURRENT

SMOKE CHAMBER

FIRE

Easy-to-handle all-purpose extinguishers like this BernzOmatic are handy for home use, especially in the kitchen, shop and garage

Portable fire ladders can offer an emergency escape route from upper-floor windows. Most hook over the sill or lock across the window frame

though slightly more expensive installation. If you do plug into an existing outlet, be sure it's permanently "hot" and not one controlled by a wall switch that could accidentally cut off power. As for a power outage knocking out an alarm before it can sound off, most experts believe the chances of this happening are extremely slim.

Until recently, photoelectric detectors tended to be house-powered because of the need for adequate current to operate the always-on light source. Now at least one company, Gillette, is bringing out a low-drain battery-operated version for those who want the convenience of cordless installation. And another maker, Master Lock, is offering an ionization-type model that works on house current but has a battery backup power supply. So you have a wide range of systems to select from.

new laws require alarms

As of this writing, there are already 12 states that require all new homes to be equipped with wired-in smoke detectors. The Federal Housing Administration requires the same for all new homes before an FHA-approved mortgage is issued.

Keep in mind also that some insurance companies offer a reduction in homeowner insurance premiums if a home is equipped with fire alarms.

where to locate alarms

The most critical spots in a house where smoke detectors should be placed are bedroom areas. The National Bureau of Standards suggests that at least one detector should be placed on the ceiling or wall of a hallway outside *each* group of bedrooms. If the hallway is more than 30 feet long, a detector should be installed at each end.

If your home has bedrooms on a second (or third) floor, place an alarm at the head and foot of the stairway. A smoke detector should also be installed at the head of a stairway leading to the basement.

Being awakened in the middle of the night by a fire alarm is one thing. Knowing what to do is another. It is ludicrous to install fire detectors and then keep members of the family in the dark about how to act when an alarm goes off.

For example, there have been cases where small children have been frightened to the point of panic by the raucous blast in the middle of the night and have hidden in a closet. Kids should be made acquainted with the noise emitted by alarm units (use self-testing controls) and told what to do when they hear it—not once or twice, but many times.

Richard Strother, who is associate administrator of the National Fire Prevention and Control Administration, points out that as part of a sound fire expectation program families should have an escape plan and practice using it.

"When a smoke alarm awakens you, you'll be groggy and won't be able to think well," he says.

safety pointers

Here are points to keep in mind when putting together your evacuation plan and teaching it to your family:

■ Every family member should have at least two escape routes from his or her bedroom. Make sure windows open easily if they are to be used.

■ If a means of escape is to be a window high above the ground, you can buy special escape ladders that hook to the windowsill. People who are to use the ladder should know where it is stored and how to employ it. Store the ladder in the same room where it's to be used.

■ If there are *no* smoke detectors in the home, sleep with the bedroom door closed. It holds back smoke and gives you more escape time.

When fire strikes, test the door by running your hand over it. If it is hot, use an alternate escape route. If cool, brace your shoulder against the door and open it cautiously. Be ready to slam it shut if smoke or heat come in. If the hallway is clear, you can use your primary exit of escape.

■ If the bedroom area is equipped with a smoke detector, sleep with doors *open*. One reason is to allow smoke from a fire starting in a bedroom to reach the detector.

■ Establish a meeting site outdoors and count heads to determine if everyone is safe.

■ Practice your escape plan with other members of the family over and over again until everyone is thoroughly familiar with it.

The order of procedure to follow when a detector sounds off is: (1) evacuate; (2) call the fire department; (3) if the fire is small, fight it if your home is equipped with fire-extinguishing equipment.

types of extinguishers

Fire extinguishers come in three basic types, designated as "A," "BC" and "ABC." These designations refer to the class of fires each is designed to fight.

The "A" type of extinguisher is filled with water and is effective on ordinary combustible materials such as wood, paper, drapes and upholstery. These are about all it is good for, however, and for this reason the "A" type is seldom purchased nowadays as an all-round household extinguisher. *Never, never* spray water on an electrical fire or flammable liquids (cooking grease, gasoline, oil). On an electrical fire, the conductive stream could cause a lethal shock. On flammable liquids, it will just blast flaming material all over the place.

The "BC" extinguisher is filled with dry chemical or carbon dioxide and is used where water can't be—on flammable liquids and electrical fires. The "C" means it can be safely used on electrical fires without danger of electrocution. One advantage of CO_2 over dry chemical is that it leaves no residue—you can put out a flaming piece of meat and still eat the meat.

"BC" extinguishers are handy around kitchens and cars because of their ability to fight grease and oil fires, but they're still limited—they can't handle the conventional "A"-type household fire of wood, paper or cloth. For this reason, the so-called multi-purpose "ABC" extinguisher is recommended by most fire safety experts for general household use. It is filled with a dry chemical agent and is effective against all home fires.

work fast

Don't become overconfident, however, just because you have an extinguisher that will fight anything. The typical small-size, home-type dry-chemical extinguisher is exhausted in 8 to 10 seconds. Not much time, so you have to work fast, carefully and without panic. Two important tips that can extend your firefighting range are: 1. If the fire is electrical in origin, turn off the power as soon as it is safe to do so. It can then be fought as a conventional "A"-type fire—with plain water if necessary. Just be sure the power is really off. 2. If the fire is feeding on ordinary combustibles, it is wise to water it down as soon as the flames have been extinguished to prevent rekindling. This may save the day if your extinguisher is empty and the fire starts up again.

beware of old tanks

The old soda-acid fire extinguisher is now considered obsolete, ineffective and possibly dangerous. It is no longer being sold, but some may still be found in homes. The Fire Equipment Manufacturers Assn. strongly urges that such units be discarded—but *not* just thrown out. They should be taken to an authorized extinguisher service center for careful disassembly. (If discarded in trash, they could be unintentionally activated when turned upside down, and an old corroded tank could blow up like a bomb.)

One of the most important bits of advice is this: In case of fire in your home, keep cool. Think! The fire alarms you've put into your home have given you sufficient escape time. Don't blow it by becoming panicky.

Here come the '78s!

Detroit gives birth to a diesel, and Chrysler multiplies the
midgets in its family. Most of the larger models are out in
de-fatted versions. We're in for some basic changes in American motoring

BY ED NELSON

■ AUTOMOTIVE INNOVATION picked up speed in the 1978 models—a surprising development after a '77 model year that reporters called "revolutionary."

Ford's long-awaited little Fiesta perhaps made the top new-car news, along with the new Fairmont and its Lincoln-Mercury sibling, the Zephyr.

Chrysler proclaimed Detroit's "first 1978 models" back in April, 1977, then sparked the new model season with two subcompacts, Chrysler Sapporo and Dodge Challenger. They were bigger than two already in the inventory—the Plymouth Arrow and Dodge Colt. All four came from Japan's Mitsubishi Motors; Chrysler apparently still couldn't produce a home-grown subcompact.

But as the calendar underwent its own changeover, from '77 to '78, Chrysler set the introduction of U.S. subcompacts: Dodge's Omni and Plymouth's Horizon.

what's in a name?

Dodge spokesmen noted that "omni-" meant "all," but others muttered that the name was a case of saying nothing by trying to say everything—in one word.

Omni is a front-drive subcompact with transverse engine. Partisans hailed the flat floor and front legroom. They scoffed at other U.S. entries as mere "shrinks," de-fatted versions of bigger cars. Indeed, nothing of Omni's character had come from the States. Whether that ensured acceptance wasn't clear.

Those "first 1978 models" were the mid-size Dodge Diplomat and Chrysler LeBaron. As the model year began, each got a wagon. The same season saw the end of Dodge's Royal Monaco nameplate along with Plymouth's Gran Fury, and Chrysler's Newport sedan and Town and Country wagon.

Dodge showed the specialty Magnum XE instead, its rectangular headlights with covers both transparent and retractable. Its grille carries out the body color. The XE looked like a thinly disguised Monaco with about five percent more side glass. Essentially the same car is also called the Dodge Charger SE.

Observers found Ford's front-drive Fiesta, smaller than VW's Rabbit, appealing, "miles ahead of . . . Chevette and Pinto." It ran well and promised easy maintenance. Visually, the boxy Maverick replacement drew little attention. Before U.S. introduction, a reporter drove one across country without drawing any comment.

Federal fuel-economy pressure aimed the same way. A manufacturer's cars are to meet economy goals as a fleet average, and the thrifty Fiesta will help Ford. But, starting with 1980 models, Detroit can't include "captive" imports in its fleet. Fiesta would take sales from domestic Ford economy cars that *would* help the average. So an American Escort, now expected as an '81 model, is a natural under whatever name to take over.

Fairmont and Zephyr lines include a coupe, four-door sedan, and wagon. Sporty coupes are expected for '78½. Ford dropped Mavericks and Comets.

half-time engine

In search of fuel economy, Ford was the first to use a "valve selector" by Eaton Corporation. Its solenoids close selected valves to disable cylinders in light-load driving. (Eaton engineers first called it a "valve disabler, but the term had none of the affirmative ring that Detroit likes.) On some '78 Ford trucks, it closes exhaust and intake valves on half the cylinders in idling or steady-speed cruising. Fuel savings can reach 40 percent. What began as a truck innovation is likely to move to cars soon.

At General Motors, the big news was Old's U.S.-built diesel passenger car. The diesel is an extra-cost option—around $1000—for Delta 88s and 98s. It is based on Olds' cast-iron 350-CID V8, the casting far heavier to contain the 22:1 compression ratio.

Diesel 0-to-60 time is about 30 per cent longer than the time for a comparable gasoline-engine car. A GM engineer concedes, "It's not a screamer, by any means, but a perfectly acceptable car for the family.'' GM says diesel fuel generally saves about 7 cents a gallon over unleaded gas. With expected fuel consumption, that saves about $30 in 10,000 miles.

A turbocharged V-6 engine—a production version of the 1976 Indianapolis pace car's engine—drives Buick's '78 Regal Sport Coupe.

Stiffer suspension and a steering ratio about seven percent faster help Sport Coupe handling. The turbocharger is reminiscent of one on a 'charged Corvair of the early 1960s. It uses exhaust gas to drive a compressor that, on demand, rams a larger air-fuel charge into Regal combustion chambers. Steel-belted radials are standard.

Buick sought to divorce the notchback Regal from the Century line. The '78 Regal is about 80 pounds heavier and 4 in. longer. But the frame's the same. It's also used for the Century, the Chevrolet Malibu and Monte Carlo, the Olds Cutlass and Cutlass Supreme, and Pontiac's LeMans and Gran Prix.

At Chevrolet, the Vega nameplate died; surviving models were offered as Monzas. Corvette got a new fastback design with more rear-end glass. And the Z-28 returned to the Camaro lineup. Pontiac's Astre also died, with its 2-door wagon joining Sunbird.

denials from AMC

Principal news from American Motors was in the denials that it was ending auto production. AMC car sales (except for Jeep)—poor in 1976—were even worse in 1977. Observers said AMC had only one auto specialty: small cars. With the whole industry racing in that direction, AMC's domination evaporated.

But if AMC cars are heading to the end of the road, the company chose a unique man to lead it in that direction. Gerald C. Meyers, only 48, was the moving force behind AMC's subcompact Gremlin and later the Pacer, both born on shoestring budgets.

In any case, the Hornet name died for 1978. Models were renamed AMX, with the top of the line called Concord. Gremlin was due for major restyling for '79.

Volkswagen also took a hand in the Diesel game, but played it hesitantly. Early claims hailed the fuel economy and exhaust-emission control in the diesel Rabbit. Then VW began delaying the planned introduction. When dealers finally got cars, advertising support was minimal. VW said that was because sales were so good and supply so short.

U.S. auto problems went beyond finance and government. Growing evidence of turning back odometers as a used-car sales practice generated wide cynicism about cars. A careful study that found 24 percent of car repairs unneeded, wasting 32 cents of each repair dollar, contributed further. Surveys showed public disenchantment was booming.

The biggest flap came over GM's use of 350-CID Chevy engines in Olds, Buick, and Pontiac cars. The blow-up came when an Illinois Olds owner was sent to a Chevy dealer for an alternator belt. Owners across the country began checking under the hood. Soon 20-odd states and about that many other parties sued GM.

The company had promoted each division's product as special, suggesting buyers could do better buying from higher cost divisions. When the Big Switch became known, GM said the differences were unimportant. ''It didn't occur to us that people would be so interested in where an engine was built,'' said Tom Murphy, GM chairman.

The company offered to trade engine-switch cars for new, or give long power-train warranties. Stockholders asked Murphy what the program would cost the company. He shrugged it off as ''a couple of cents a share,'' but one stockholder demanded, ''How many millions?'' That question was dealt with in a one-word answer: ''Twelve,'' Murphy said.

when are trades 'even'?

Owners who thought the offer amounted to ''Bring in your unsatisfactory car and get a new one'' were soon disappointed. If they chose the exchange, they were also to pay 8 cents for each mile on the old car. Plus an amount—sometimes almost $1000—for ''wear and tear.'' GM seemed to feel its position vindicated when 9 of 10 owners rejected the ''trade.''

GM may have felt burned by the uproar. In any case, Chevrolet took pains to make a formal announcement when it began equipping Chevettes with automatic transmissions from France.

The wide use by other divisions of the Chevy 350 was natural under GM's ''commonality'' principle, in which cars share parts with cars from other divisions. The principle doesn't completely square with each division's claim to special quality, or with the company's claim that divisions compete bitterly.

But the diesels and the midgets are the big news of the year. They portend basic changes in the pattern of American motoring.

20 tips on buying a used car

■ NEW CARS COST too much, and so do used lemons. So the trick is to find a used car that's as good as new and a few thousand dollars less expensive. Impossible? Not if you can remove the gamble. And you *can*.

When you begin those treks down used-car row, your best friend is patience. So often people rush into a used-car deal as if there's no tomorrow. Salesmen capitalize on buyer impatience. "Better hurry and decide now," the salesman may tell you, "because there's another customer itching to buy this car." Never let that sort of talk stampede you. If it takes you two weeks to find just the right car—even two months—don't rush yourself.

1. While you're settling down, think long and hard about what sort of car you really need. Everyone's talking small cars these days. But if you've got five kids, two dogs, a 15-foot house trailer, and you're a rockhound, it's not likely you'll be totally happy with a used Volkswagen as your family car.

Common sense tells you to balance such factors as passenger and carrying capacity, fuel economy, number of doors and so forth against the size of your family (present and future), how long you plan to keep the car, plus cost and availability of repairs.

Make and year of car aren't as important as condition and the candidate's ability to fill your needs. Say you've settled on a particular Dart as your ideal year, size and type of car. Don't look just at that Dart, though. Look too at same-age

Novas, Mavericks, Valiants, Hornets, Comets, Apollos, Omegas, Venturas, Volvos and Peugeots. That way you open up a lot more prospects for finding a good, clean low-mileage used compact.

2. Eyeball the car. Check for exterior ripples and defects by sighting down all sheet-metal surfaces: fenders, hood, decklid, doors, roof. Ripples mean bodywork, possibly because of an accident or rust holes. Fresh paint and/or paint

over-spray might mean the same thing. Remember that light colors tend to hide ripples and blemishes. Always inspect a used car in sunlight, never at dusk (after working hours) or under artificial lamps of any type.

3. Also look for interior abuse. The odometer reading should match pedal and carpet wear and seat sag. Be on the lookout for a punctured headliner, ripped seats, scorched fabric, a scuffed package tray, re-dyed carpets or vinyl, new rugs and new pedal pads.

Most used cars have been "detailed," which means the dealer, or a shop that works for him, has tried to cover signs of wear and tear with dye jobs, a new package tray, new trunk mat, respraying the dashboard padding, spraying carpets or replacing worn ones, installing new armrests, even reglazing bull's-eyes in windshields. Be alert for "detail" jobs and try to look beyond them.

4. Detailing extends to the used car's mechanicals. Detailers usually steam-clean and then spray-paint the engine, radiator, air-cleaner and the like, and sometimes they replace underhood decals. The purpose again is to make the car look as new as possible, and that's fine, but it masks evidence of the car's previous use and maintenance. A gummy, grease-encrusted engine at least tells you something about the car's history. A detailed engine tells you nothing. Again, you have to look beyond the fresh paint and new decals. Search for areas that have eluded the detailer. Check, for example, the condition of the battery box, fan belts, air-cleaner element, cracked ignition wires, rusty sparkplugs and so forth.

Smoke from the oil filler or breather, especially if it's heavy, can tell you that the running engine is burning or pumping oil. Rusty water spots on the firewall give clues to previous radiator boilovers.

5. Make sure everything works. Prospective buyers always try a car's radio (and dealers therefore make sure it's playing), but also note whether gauges are functioning. Roll all windows up and down. Test lights, locks, air-conditioner, heater, all accessories, seat adjustment.

6. The biggest gamble remover, the best warranty, the greatest lemon protection you can give yourself when you're shopping for a used car is this step: Take every car you're seriously considering buying to a professional mechanic or an auto diagnostic clinic for a thorough check. Such an inspection usually costs $10 to $12. Make an appointment with the shop or person who'll do the inspecting, and then drive the candidate car to that place of business. Tell the used-car dealer that you'll be doing this, and if he won't let you (he'll say his insurance doesn't cover such events, but that's not so), forget that car.

Professional inspections usually take about 40 minutes and should always include an engine compression check—all cylinders should show amply high and fairly equal readings.

7. Brakes and front-end alignment. The mechanic should pull one front wheel or drum to inspect the disc or lining. At the same time he should test the front end for play in the ball joints, steering, links, and suspension components. Front-end maladies can be particularly expensive, and most used-car buyers never test for them before they make their purchase.

8. While the car is still on the lift, have the mechanic look for frame damage or bent underpinnings that might indicate past collisions. Also poke around for rust holes, not just in the rockers and floor pan but also in the exhaust system-muffler, pipes, catalytic converter, and so forth. Note condition of all four tires plus springs and especially shocks. And look for telltale leaks from brake cylinders and lines, engine, transmission, rear axle, radiator and gas tank. Any abnormal leaks (a *little* lube leakage is normal) could spell bills soon.

9. After the diagnostician gets the car back on the ground, let him take it for a short test drive. Ask him to check transmission operation, noting smoothness of shifting, delay in going into gear, and play in universal joints and rear axle. At some point he should also remove the transmission dipstick and sniff the fluid for the odor of scorching. That simple test can often tell volumes about an automatic transmission's condition.

In cars with manual gearboxes, clutch action should be smooth and positive. Shifts shouldn't demand struggle or guesswork. If the stick ever pops out of gear during acceleration or deceleration, or if you hear growling or rapping sounds from the transmission, be wary.

10. During a test drive, even if it's only to the shop making your professional inspection, listen for odd noises, rattles and hums. Mention these to the mechanic. Also check brakes for veer, steering for play, suspension for bounciness or looseness. Accelerate and decelerate sharply to conduct your own test for sloppy U-joints and rear axle.

11. Try to avoid cars with four-barrel carburetors. Four barrels almost always take premium fuel. Engines with two-barrel and single-barrel carbs get by on regular gas. It's not the four-barrel carb that makes a car burn premium—it's the higher compression ratio and advanced ignition timing that go along with four-barrels.

big-car bargains

12. Keep in mind that the used-car market has done a complete flipflop since the energy crisis. It used to be that the full-sized American cars—particularly Fords, Chevys and Plymouths—were hot sellers before the oil embargo.

Today, though, big Detroit sedans and wagons can go begging on used-car lots. You can often pick up a late-model, low-mileage, full-sized Detroiter for a good deal less than a minicar or compact of the same year and mileage.

The popular (thus expensive) used cars nowadays fall into seven specific categories: 1. economy imports like VW, Datsun, Toyota, Opel, Colt and Capri, but also to a lesser extent Mazda, Renault, Peugeot and Subaru; 2. used domestic economy cars, particularly Pinto; 3. used American ponycars, the hottest being Camaro, Mustang and Firebird; 4. used sports cars—Corvette, MG, TR-6, 240-Z and 260-Z, and the big Austin-Healeys; 5. luxury "heavies" such as Cadillacs and Mark IVs; 6. some intermediate-sized U.S. cars like Chevelle and Skylark; and 7. all four-wheel-drive vehicles—Jeep, Blazer, Scout and the like.

13. When you buy a used car, try to avoid financing if you possibly can. Pay cash instead. You nearly always up the cost of a used car by a third or so through financing and mandatory insurance.

shop for best terms

14. If you must finance, shop for terms as you shop for the car. Life insurance and credit union loans are least expensive; dealer and finance-company loans are most expensive, with banks in the middle. Pay off a loan as quickly as possible.

And set a ceiling on what you plan to pay for a car.

15. You've probably asked yourself whether you should buy from a private party, a used-car dealer, or a new-car dealer who carries used cars. All three have good and bad points, but experts pretty much agree that you get the best cars from small, clean, neat, independent used-car lots. These dealers often buy the creampuffs of new-car trade-ins. Try to deal with the lot owner directly, not one of his commissioned salesmen.

Buying from a private party can lead to heartaches, especially if something goes grossly wrong with the car or deal. Buying from a new-car dealer usually means paying more than at an independent lot, because the new-car dealer has greater overhead —but you'll usually get some type of warranty on the car, usually 60 to 90 days. These, though, are generalities and don't apply in every situation. You probably ought to shop all three before you decide.

16. Don't be afraid to dicker, but never get huffy or nasty during price negotiations. Again, be patient—use time to your advantage. Never panic when the salesman urges you to buy today. Prices don't change or cars vanish that quickly.

don't trade old car in

17. Avoid trading in your present car if possible. Sell you old car privately before you buy a newer one. Be shopping, though, while you're selling your present car. If you can sell it privately, you'll be more likely to get "retail" for it. As a trade-in, though, you'll never get more than "wholesale." Also, the cash from a private sale will give you a price and financing advantage.

18. Where do you find out what used cars are worth? Banks and finance companies can and will lend you used-car price guides—so-called "blue books." These are much more accurate than the ones you can buy on newsstands. Ask one of the bank loan officers to lend you a blue book. Figures shown will let you check asking prices of cars for sale and will also let you put a realistic value on your present car when selling or trading it.

19. Put no faith in used-car warranties of any sort. They might or might not prove worth the

paper they're written on. Never let a warranty sway you toward a purchase. A used-car dealer's reputation counts for a lot more than any warranty. Remember that you never get any sort of warranty from a private seller; also that your best warranty is the used-car inspection I mentioned in No. 6.

20. Sign nothing—no sale contract, no power of attorney, no credit application—until you've read it completely and understood every word. Now that's easy to say and hard to do. If you have questions, let the salesman explain. And if his explanations don't make sense, take a copy of the document to your attorney for interpretation.

All blanks in a contract should be filled in before you sign it. Leave no deposits while test driving a car or having it inspected. Do not let the dealer "park" or drive your car for you if you're not planning to trade it in. Your car might end up being a "hostage" while the dealer wears your patience and resistance by keeping you waiting.

the best years to look for

The best used cars are usually from two to four years old, with between 10,000 and 15,000 miles a year on the odometer. The average American car, properly treated and maintained, will give 100,000 miles of service before a major mechanical breakdown. Body longevity varies with locality and depends largely on salt corrosion.

If you keep these 20 points in mind, your chances of finding a good, reliable, trouble-free used car are around 80 percent. Which means there's still a risk. But then there's a risk in buying a new car, too, and considering how much less used cars cost than new ones, their risk factor at 80 percent still makes them more attractive.

New gear that conquers the cold

BY BILL McKEOWN

New clothing and gadgets, some of which were designed for the Apollo space program, let you plug in, switch on or bounce back body heat. They are made from a variety of materials that insulate you in the coldest weather

■ THE HOTTEST NEWS in cool-weather wear is an assortment of aids that could keep you comfortable under a snowdrift. Or on a snowmobile or cross-country skis; in a wintry stadium, an ice-fishing shelter, duck blind; or almost anywhere any time of year when you feel like an icicle in the making. Downhill ski clothes are fine for an active sport, but extras are needed when exercise can't control a chill.

Fingers, feet and face are the first to feel like ice cubes as blood circulation to them slows to go instead to your central core. Thin metallic sheeting like that used in spacesuits can reflect back body heat that would be lost. Thermos All-Weather Blankets and the Handwarmer gauntlet

gloves from Comfort Products, Box 9200, Aspen, CO., use this type of material. In addition, the Handwarmers (approximately $100), designed by engineers of the Apollo space program, have a heating element and rechargeable power unit in each glove that are regulated by flipping individual switches. Much less expensive is air—acting as insulation between several layers of gloves. Nylon or silk gloves topped with wool knit gloves or mittens under leather mitts are available from camping and climbing gear shops. These triple layers, like face masks and frostbite prevention creams, do not create heat but help retard loss of it from the body.

Hand and pocket warmers like the catalytic liquid fuel Optimus and Jon-E models, the Stag Hotstik solid fuel burner, the Scotty reusable-chemical hand and back belt warmers from Scotty Manufacturing and the battery-heated Lectra-Mits and Lectra-Pad body belt by Timely Products all worked well in our field tests, although exact heat control was sometimes difficult.

Warmth from the inside out combines snowmobile clothes insulated with synthetics plus electricity to hands and feet. One and two-piece snowmo suits by MidWest Outerwear are lined with PolarGuard. Frostline booties are filled with down, and Lectra-Sox heat by battery. Handwarmer gloves recharge; insulated Royal Red Ball boots and Thermos All-Weather blankets hold the heat

Frigid feet can be prevented with socks and insulated boots. New Royal Red Ball waterproof has Thermo-Ply lining, zipper closure. Leather-top Red Ball can add felt liner. Field-boot Lectra-Sox use D cells

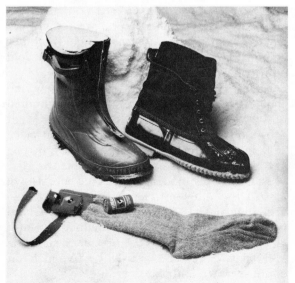

Slip-in soles, from Comfort Products, can heat boots, shoes, waders through wires from a belt pack that recharges, delivers up to eight hours of heat (about $50). Ski Footwarmer, Power unit, sole are about $85

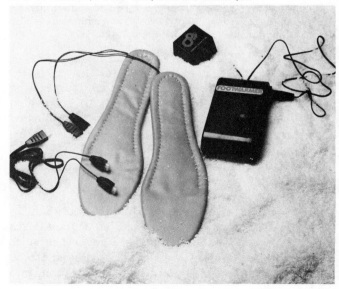

Hand warmers, created by Comfort Products engineers who helped design astronaut clothes, charge overnight, warm up after switches are flicked on.

Multilayer gloves and solid and liquid hand warmers cure cold hands. Wool gloves fit in leather mittens. Stag Hotstik hand warmer holds solid fuel

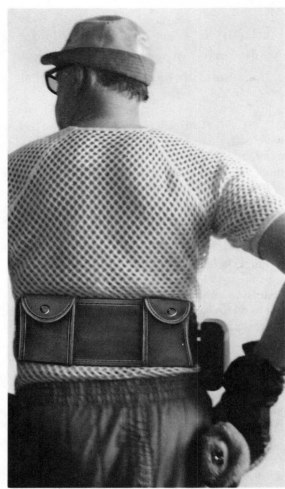

Chemical heat is supplied from packets in Body Warmer belt by Scotty Mfg. Also shown are fishnet shirt, quilted under pants, battery pack, electric gloves

Unlike hands, it's harder to tuck your feet into your pockets or under armpits to keep them warm. Like hands, feet should be well shielded from the cold with protective layers. One or two pairs of socks and well-fitting quality boots—leather, fabric, rubber or a mix according to expected wetness—are a good beginning. Battery-heated Lectra-Sox from Timely Products, Fairfield, CT, are about $12. Hot Foot, San Diego, CA., has electric insert soles at around $25 a pair, and Comfort Products' Footwarmer soles with rechargeable belt pack are around $49.50 for regular models and around $85 for fitting into ski boots. These foot heaters, we found, can make a tremendous difference in cold-weather comfort, but expect them to be too hot or cold until you get used to adjustments.

Layering for body warmth is not new and should start with regular, net, thermal or quilted underwear according to conditions. Most snowmobile companies make one and two-piece suits in colors to match their machines, or you can choose PolarGuard lined suits like the Mid-West Outerwear models we selected here. Down is still the most efficient—and expensive—insulating material, but Fiberfill and PolarGuard rival it, and are superior in wet climates. But if you plan to climb Everest or winter-camp on McKinley, expedition wear with a five-inch loft of goose down is the answer.

Illuminating options for any outing: At top left, miní kerosene lamp and tent light can sit or hang; scout candle uses wax and cardboard wick in tuna can; flashlight, Eveready Swivel Lite and two spotlights use batteries. At bottom, Lowrance spot-and-flood can be recharged; wick lamp uses lighter fluid; hanging candle lantern shields flame; emergency extension light uses lighter socket. Larger table lamps, Ashflash and utility headlamps are behind long-burn candles and palm flash. Spotlight mounts on 6-volt battery, burns underwater

Bright light for camping

Latest lantern from Coleman's long line, twin-mantle Model 275 gasoline burner, has semi-defused globe, new styling. Primus Explorer Minilantern regulates from dim up to equivalent of 75-watt bulb, can hang from chain, weighs just over a pound with an eight-hour cartridge can

■ CAMP LIGHT used to mean a flashlight and a Coleman lantern. Improved models of these nighttime standbys are still first choices after dark, but there are now a number of other bright options. Coleman's latest, more than 76 years and 28 million lanterns since the first one, is called the 275 and has frosted globe stripes for softer light. Accessories include a tree bracket that will hold the lantern out so it won't singe the bark. Reflectors for some models keep glare away from neighboring campsites.

But the real trend is to LP-gas lanterns small enough to backpack, battery lights of assorted sizes, headband lamps that leave both hands free for cave climbing or pitching a tent at midnight.

Backpackers, who add up every ounce, may choose a palm-size flashlight and small camp light like the Primus Explorer Minilantern with cartridge can of propane gas that can be switched to an infrared heater head or a tripod pack stove. Some hikers are changing from alkaline to MSR lithium batteries. Though one D-cell costs much more, the dependable double life is reported to be worth it.

Car campers and RV owners are in luck. Old-fashioned kerosene lamps, cigaret-lighter extension-cord lights, dual-purpose battery/110-volt fluorescent and standard lamps are all suitable. For all campers, long-life 45-percent stearic acid candles are always in style.

ATTACHED HOOD

AIR-RELEASE VALVE FOR BUOYANCY ADJUSTMENT

5000-P.S.I. TANK PRESSURE GAUGE

TANK BELT

CYCOLAC-PLASTIC AIR INTAKE VALVE

FULL FACE MASK WITH CYKLON 300 REGULATOR

WEIGHT BELT

THREE-FINGER DRY GLOVES

INDEPENDENT SUIT-INFLATION-SYSTEM BOTTLE

ATTACHED RUBBER BOOTS

New gear for scuba divers

BY STUART JAMES

■ THINGS ARE LOOKING UP down under. A sudden boom in technology has hit scuba diving, and new gear—from inflatable dry suits to electronic digital depth/ascent indicators—looks like props for a new run of *Star Trek*.

"The inflatables will set the trend for future diving," claims Dave Townsend, a Florida Keys diving instructor. "They're expensive, but slowly coming on for the serious diver."

"You're going to see more innovative developments for scuba gear," says Gary Heller, a representative of Farallon Industries, a California company that engineers scuba equipment. "We're making it easier and safer to dive in comfort."

The wet suit, when it arrived in the '50s, was a godsend. Before that, scuba divers went dry—struggling into a one-piece suit with a single opening. It was like cutting a 12-inch hole in an inner tube and trying to crawl inside. It took several friends to get a diver suited. Then came the wet suit with its zippers, two pieces, snug fit and a nice layer of warm water between suit and skin.

And now, 25 years later, the dry suit is back in refined form, made of tough neoprene instead of latex. About 10 brands are now on the market and all can be partially inflated with air to prevent squeeze and give a layer of warm insulation.

zipper wizardry

It was a simple thing like an improved zipper that signaled the breakthrough in diving comfort. Originally designed for NASA, the new slide fastener (made by Talon and Dynat) is gas, water and pressure-proof. Parkway was the first to adapt this zipper to diving when it introduced the Unisuit about 10 years ago. Acceptance was enthusiastic, but sales were minimal.

When the U.S. Navy got interested, however, the diving industry and public began to pay attention. The Navy tested the Unisuit in a pressure chamber with refrigerated water at 40° F. and dropped two divers to a simulated depth of 70 feet. After 35 minutes, one diver in a custom-fitted wet suit was on the verge of tissue damage from the cold, while the other diver in a Unisuit was still warm and comfortable. The results

Treasure hunting while diving is the claim for the Amphibian TR-8 Goldmaster from White's Electronics. The instrument (about $270) has an eight-inch underwater loop with a land probe option available. Settings are for metals and minerals

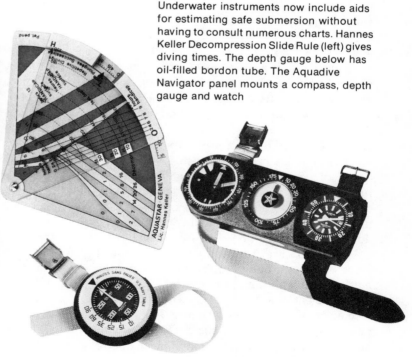

Underwater instruments now include aids for estimating safe submersion without having to consult numerous charts. Hannes Keller Decompression Slide Rule (left) gives diving times. The depth gauge below has an oil-filled bordon tube. The Aquadive Navigator panel mounts a compass, depth gauge and watch

were convincing, and commercial divers began switching to dry suits.

inflatable suits

Now made by Poseidon Systems U.S.A., a division of Parkway Fabricators, the Unisuit has improved over the years and is one of the more popular dry inflatables. Like the other models, it has an air-intake valve that attaches to your air tank. To inflate the suit, you simply press a button and air flows from the tank. A purge button releases air from the suit.

Most suits can be equipped with a small compressed air bottle just for inflation, and many have oral inflator hoses. Suit prices range from about $250 to more than $600, with an average sport model about $325—versus a good wet suit at about $100.

The big difference between dry suits is the position of the entry zipper. The White Stag Thermal Suit, for example, has a 50-inch zipper that makes it one of the easiest to put on. The U.S. Divers model has no zipper, and entry through the neck is more difficult. Seatec's suit zipper runs across the back and down to the waist. Sub-Aquatic Systems has a zipper across the back and a buddy is needed to help the diver in. Sea Suits has a chest zipper, as does the Bayley Aquastatic; O'Neil Supersuit and Imperial Bubblesuit run it across the shoulders in back. The Unisuit zipper runs from the back of the neck down under the crotch and up to the waist in front.

new developments

While dry suits are big news, just about every piece of equipment has undergone development. A diver's needs are basically the same as when Jacques Cousteau invented the Aqua-Lung; the difference is in what new gear can do. Fins haven't changed much, for example, but Farallon has added a brace and piston system that transfers leg power directly to the fin, allows a fin surface at least 30 percent larger, and is claimed to almost double propulsion power. This increased frogpower costs about $60, more than double an ordinary fin set at around $22.

Face masks are shallower and more comfortable. Most companies offer the low-volume mask that fits closer to the face and takes less effort to clear of water. Scubapro now markets a face mask of nonallergenic rubber. Farallon has new snorkels that can be custom-fitted to your mouth by first softening the mouthpiece in boiling water. To correct dry-mouth discomfort

from breathing compressed air, its moisturizer unit can be mounted between regulator and mouthpiece.

Standard instruments have been improved, and new ones added for serious divers. Console units running off the air tank now house all the instruments that used to be strapped to a diver's wrists. A typical panel has a depth gauge, tank-pressure gauge, compass, dive timer—and runs about $200. Farallon's lighted "Navigator Console" is about $196.

Scubapro has an automatic decompression computer that continuously memorizes repetitive and multiple-depth dives, noting time and depth for decompression when it is required. The size of a large wristwatch, the instrument (approximately $80) estimates the rate at which nitrogen goes into and out of solution in the blood stream.

Farallon's similar instrument, the Multi-tissue Decomputer (about $75), uses a color display to tell when you should surface after multiple dives to avoid decompression stops. It also has a new Digital Depth/Ascent Rate Indicator for around $225 that flashes when you are surfacing too rapidly.

controlled lifevests

The old lifevest has undergone changes to become a buoyancy compensating vest and controls a diver's float level—for about $85 to $150. Lung-shaped buoyancy-control system bags attached to the tank harness are $200 to $300.

Beginning divers in particular worry about sharks, but so do professionals. Cousteau's divers carry a "shark billy," a length of wood with a wrist strap at one end and a bottle cap nailed to the other. Poking the shark with it is claimed to be effective. The bang-stick, a long pole with a firing device on the end, pumps a shotgun shell into a shark on contact, but is a bloody business that can attract more sharks.

The Naval Undersea Center, however, has developed the Shark Dart, a hand-held device that looks like a dagger and fires a CO_2 cartridge when stabbed into a shark. The expanding gas ruptures internal organs and kills the shark without spreading blood. Farallon markets it in knife and arm-length models, plus a repeater that is attached to a compressed-air bottle. Prices range from around $40 to $175. The invention is regarded as effective, but the maker warns: "Sharks should be regarded as extremely dangerous. Being armed with a Shark Dart does not make a diver the shark's equal."

Kayak surfing

Hanging in the curl like a bobsledder, Danny Broadhurst reaches speeds up to 30 MPH

BY PETER BARMONDE

Surfing designs like Extra Sport's Ripper (left) and Surf Ski (right) are a long advance over standard kayaks and surfboards. The Surf Ski, without a deck, allows action without the need to learn the difficult Eskimo roll

■ TAKE ALMOST ANY stretch of open wave-splashed beach. It's all you need to launch you and your surf kayak on a new water adventure.

These new craft, specially designed to handle the combers, are flat-bottomed, snub-nosed surfers that deliver more thrills per dollar than almost any other boat afloat. Speeds over 30 mph in the curl are not uncommon. Acceleration is phenomenal, any wave over three feet tall looms above your head, and the hull doesn't burn any gas to get going.

First advantage of this kayak over a regular surfboard is that it can be paddled swiftly into position. Riding sitting down is a second plus and, third, you can slide along on surf that would be impossible on a board. Size and design of some surf kayaks let a skilled rider do 360° spins while shooting down the face of a wave.

"It's like riding a floating bobsled!" reports Danny Broadhurst, former designer of kayaks in Great Britain and now with Extra Sport USA, surf kayak importer at 90 Washington Dr., Centerport, NY. Kayak surfing has been around since the first Eskimo took to water, but regular kayaks are difficult to turn in surf and tend to loop or plow in headfirst. Special boats like the California Surf Shoe appeared about 1970, Broadhurst notes, and became a hit in England which now has over 500 surfers.

The sport is not difficult or dangerous, but you must be able to swim, always wear a life jacket and helmet, and never surf alone. It is important to learn the Eskimo roll—bailing out can be dangerous. Wipe-outs, though spectacular, rarely cause injury and collision is the greatest risk. If it appears imminent, capsize at once, the experts advise; your body will act as a drogue to slow you down.

About $500 can get you started. Extra Sport USA offers five models (average $325) including the Surf Ski without deck for beginners. Old Town Canoe's Surfer, from Old Town, ME, is about $385. Add a paddle, life jacket, spray deck, helmet and, if necessary, a wet suit and you're all set for watery action.

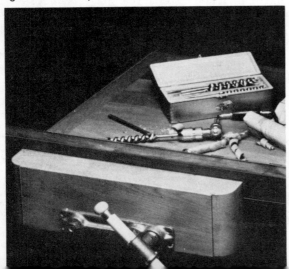

A front vise such as the one below has a 22-inch bearing against the clamp which is useful for long work

A nylon shoulder clamp fits into the slotted bar (at any height) that is clamped into the tail vise

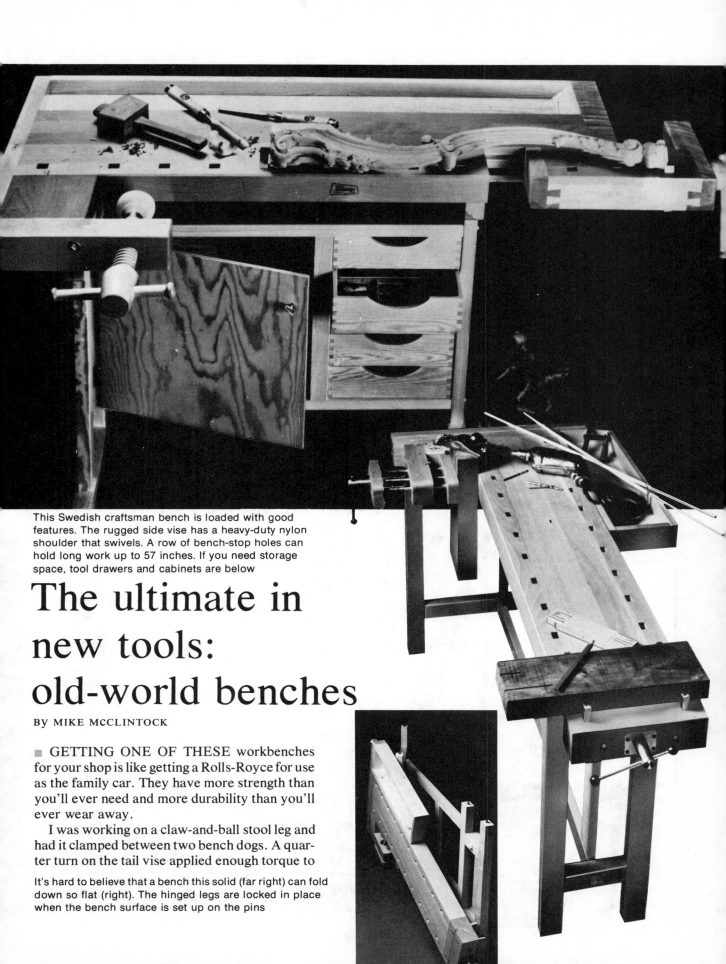

This Swedish craftsman bench is loaded with good features. The rugged side vise has a heavy-duty nylon shoulder that swivels. A row of bench-stop holes can hold long work up to 57 inches. If you need storage space, tool drawers and cabinets are below

The ultimate in new tools: old-world benches

BY MIKE McCLINTOCK

■ GETTING ONE OF THESE workbenches for your shop is like getting a Rolls-Royce for use as the family car. They have more strength than you'll ever need and more durability than you'll ever wear away.

I was working on a claw-and-ball stool leg and had it clamped between two bench dogs. A quarter turn on the tail vise applied enough torque to

It's hard to believe that a bench this solid (far right) can fold down so flat (right). The hinged legs are locked in place when the bench surface is set up on the pins

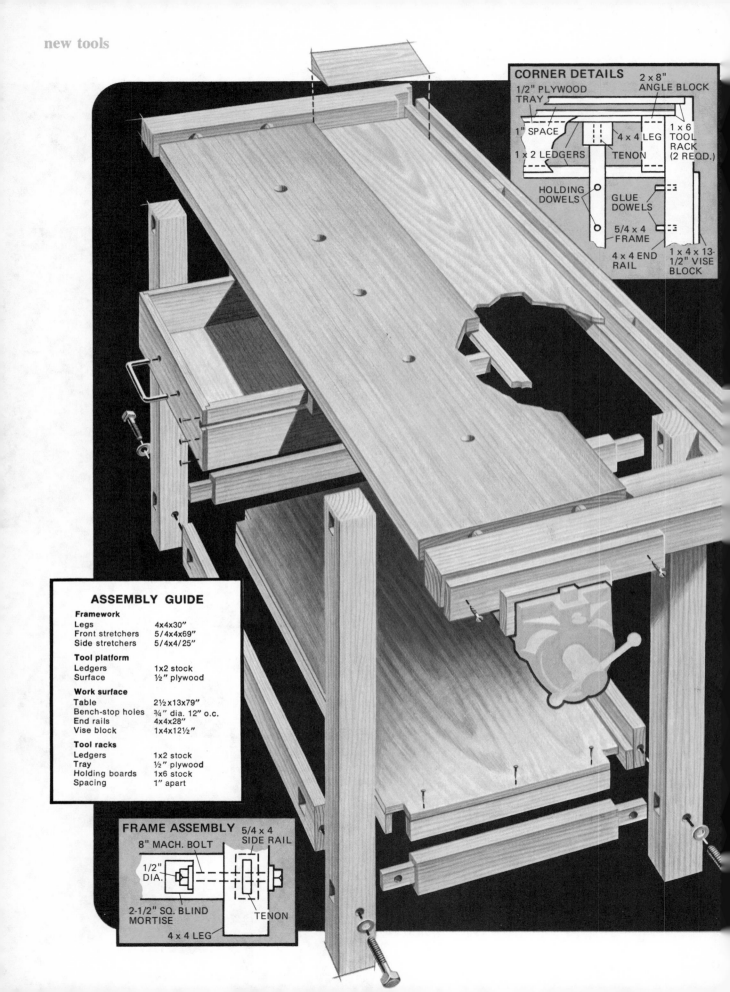

CORNER DETAILS

1/2" PLYWOOD TRAY

2 x 8" ANGLE BLOCK

1" SPACE

4 x 4 LEG

TENON

1 x 6 TOOL RACK (2 REQD.)

1 x 2 LEDGERS

HOLDING DOWELS

GLUE DOWELS

5/4 x 4 FRAME

4 x 4 END RAIL

1 x 4 x 13-1/2" VISE BLOCK

ASSEMBLY GUIDE

Framework

Legs	4x4x30"
Front stretchers	5/4x4x69"
Side stretchers	5/4x4/25"

Tool platform

Ledgers	1x2 stock
Surface	½" plywood

Work surface

Table	2½x13x79"
Bench-stop holes	¾" dia. 12" o.c.
End rails	4x4x28"
Vise block	1x4x12½"

Tool racks

Ledgers	1x2 stock
Tray	½" plywood
Holding boards	1x6 stock
Spacing	1" apart

FRAME ASSEMBLY

8" MACH. BOLT

5/4 x 4 SIDE RAIL

1/2" DIA.

2-1/2" SQ. BLIND MORTISE

TENON

4 x 4 LEG

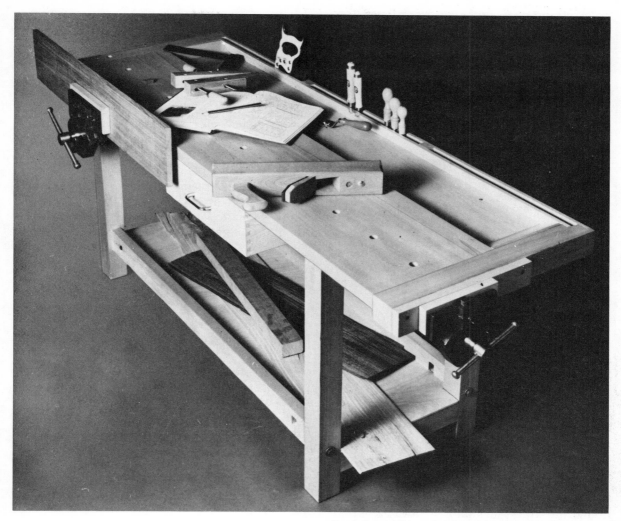

English model bench (above) features Sheffield-made steel vises. There's a unique quick-release lever that lets the vise (below) slide in or out without turning the handle. A full-length slot for hand tools and a recessed tray keep the surface clear

lock it in place. The vise has so much strength that I was able to raise the whole end of the bench off the ground by lifting the clamped leg. Any piece of wood, even one requiring heavy mallet and chisel work, will stay locked in place. It will break in half before it slips out.

The bench dogs can be fitted into holes along the full length of the table, including the tail vise. The bench shown on page 30 can hold work up to 81 in. long. The combination of vises including the shoulder vise accessory (inset on page 30) lets you set the work securely in the best and most comfortable position.

This kind of strength and versatility comes from a long heritage of European cabinetmaking. My Steiner bench is made of European red beech, a heavy, dense wood that is impregnated with linseed oil. It weighs 240 pounds and is so stable that you don't have to bolt it down.

Steiner classic bench

Material	European red beech
Length	87 in.
Width	33 in.
Weight	240 lbs.
Work surface	9½ sq. ft.
Clamping capacity	8 ft.
Approximate price	$450

Swedish craftsman bench

Material	Swedish silver birch
Length	62¼ in.
Width	29½ in.
Weight	102 lbs.
Work surface	6½ sq. ft.
Clamping capacity	57 in.
Approximate price	$300

Danish folding bench

Material	Danish beech
Length	54 in.
Width	29½ in.
Weight	83 lbs.
Work surface	3¾ sq. ft.
Clamping capacity	50½ in.
Approximate price	$300

English model bench

Material	Beech, steel vises
Length	79 in.
Width	34½ in.
Weight	235 lbs.
Work surface	6¾ sq. ft.
Clamping capacity	78¼ in.
Approximate price	$400

George Ott Inc., another West German firm, makes similar benches that are exported to firms around the world, including Steinway & Sons, the piano manufacturer. Ulmia benches are available through Woodcraft Supply Corp., 313 Montvale Ave., Woburn, MA. Leichtung Co. at 5187 Mayfield Rd., Cleveland, OH, offers a line of Danish benches. But I found the most complete selection, including all benches on these pages, at a relatively new company, Garrett Wade, based at 302 Fifth Ave., NY. The firm has done a thorough scouting job to come up with such variety and also offer a beautiful and extensive line of imported hand tools.

Can a great piece of equipment make you a better craftsman? Absolutely. You can work faster and more accurately with these benches. It's easy to stay organized during a complicated project; clamp a glue joint in the tail vise, cut precision dovetails on a board in the front vise, and plane a shelf edge clamped between the bench dogs. The amount of storage built into the Swedish craftsman bench will go a long way toward keeping tools clean, neat and within reach.

If you're really cramped for space the folding bench is a perfect solution. But once it's up you may never want to take advantage of unique folding feature and put it away.

We used the English bench as a model for the assembly guide (page 32). Even though it has steel vises instead of elaborate wooden ones, it is still a complicated project and a challenge to any woodworker. Before attempting a bench like this you should be aware that hardwood assembly requires incredibly sharp tools with experienced hands behind them. There is little margin for error, and joints, to seat properly, must be absolutely square.

Laminating a flat bench surface of this size might be a stumbling block unless you have a full array of pipe clamps and can fall back on a thickness planer for finishing. You can overcome this by getting a maple (or other hardwood) countertop and cutting it to fit your bench. You should adjust the dimensions given to suit your shop space and your size.

Include in your plans the features from other benches that will give you the most service.

The same construction can be applied to a scaled-down version for a child's bench about 48 in. long. If you haven't attempted complicated cabinetwork before, you could try making this smaller bench out of kiln-dried fir which is easy to work with. If you stick to the layout for mortise and tenon joints with bolted stretchers you'll wind up with an extremely strong bench.

dry-assemble all joints first

Don't rely on white glue. Each wood surface to be glued should be scored with a rough file and you should coat all surfaces and edges in the joint. Use an epoxy resin or liquid-hide glue. These are long-setting and will give you time to complete a series of joints for the end frame and get them completely clamped. Check instructions on the glue bottle for clamping times and don't glue below the temperature limit listed. If you get a good bond in an epoxy resin joint, you'll have to break the wood to get it apart. So dry-assemble all joints first to check your measurements.

To be honest, these benches are the best available and will require a sizeable investment of money (over $400 for the large Steiner bench) or time for construction. But using a great bench makes woodworking tremendously satisfying and the improved quality it can bring to your projects will encourage you to undertake more and more complex cabinetwork in the future.

Here's a 4-in-1 workhorse

BY WAYNE C. LECKEY

■ THE MANUFACTURER of this unique molder-planer calls it a tool that's second only to a table saw. After having put it to the test, I can see why—I found it to be a real workhorse and as versatile as a one-man band.

Not only is it a molder and a thickness planer, it's a jointer and edger as well. And with the tool's open-side design, the 7⅛-in. cutter head can surface a board up to 14 in. wide. Just reverse the board and pass it through a second time.

The machine comes in both handfeed (approximately $248) and power-feed (approximately $390) models, and has an output capacity of 15 ft. per minute. It's a veritable planing mill in that it can be used to convert waste and rough-sawn material into dressed lumber free of wave and chatter marks. It's made by Williams & Hussey Machine Corp., Milford, NH 03055.

Wood blocks (above, left) should be clamped to machine's fixed table. They are used to guide the work straight under the feed rollers and cutter head when jointing or molding top edge. Alignment strips (right) clamped to the base keep the stock passing straight under twin molding knives. The cutter head turns at 7000 rpm. The machine requires a 1-hp motor and a 5-in. pulley to operate

Crank arm (left photo below) moves both the cutter head and infeed and outfeed rollers up and down to suit the work's thickness or width. Husky capscrews (center photo) can be turned with a wrench to lock two high-speed steel knives securely in the milled shoulders of 1½-in.-sq. arbor. By loosening the capscrews (right photo) the slotted knives can easily be removed in a matter of minutes for sharpening or switching to molding knives. 41 different sets of knives for this machine are available from the manufacturer

MACHINE
MEASURES
11-1/8"
FRONT
TO BACK,
STANDS
ABOUT
18-1/2" HIGH

WHEEL-LOCKING
KNOB

SHATTERPROOF
ABRASIVE WHEEL

110-V. MOTOR,
27 HP,

ON-OFF
SWITCH

See-through grinder for your shop

BY WALTER E. BURTON

You can watch the metal vanish
from the surface of a tool as you work it
into shape with this unique new grinder.
The light shines right through the wheel

Horizontally rotating abrasive wheel carries sparks and grit safely away from the operator

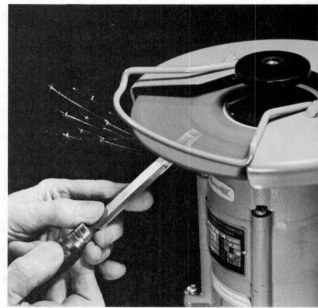

■ A NEW IMPORT on the American market is a bench grinder that's truly unique. It's called the Stephan invisible-wheel grinder and you can actually look through the spinning wheel to see exactly what is happening to the edge you are grinding; no need to constantly remove the tool to inspect the bevel.

Here's how this see-through grinder works: The horizontally mounted grinding wheel has six slots in it. Rotating at 3200 rpm, the wheel becomes "invisible" in the same way as a spinning airplane propeller. A lamp, mounted directly over the wheel, beams light through the slots onto the workpiece. You work against the underside of the wheel.

The same slots that allow light to pass through the spinning wheel also let you observe the surface being ground. Short notches in the rim of the wheel enable you to watch the grinding and polishing of grooves which require the use of the edge of the wheel. Sparks and wheel particles are thrown downward away from the operator.

The 8½-in.-dia. grinding wheel has abrasive material on both sides, resin-bonded to a steel disc. The one that comes with the machine is for alloyed tool steel and is about ³/₁₆ in. thick. Six-in. felt and cotton polishing wheels are also available. Slots in the wheel air-cool it, which helps to minimize "burning" and drawing temper of the tool steels.

I found the grinder easy to use, requiring very light pressure to grind a perfect bevel.

Installing a wheel is somewhat like placing a record on a phonograph. After fiddling with the plastic hand knob that locks the wheel on its shaft, I discovered that it has a left-hand thread. When I first turned on the motor, I expected the lamp to light—but it didn't. I eventually found that it is controlled by a pushbutton switch hiding under a rubber diaphragm at the top of the lampshade.

The grinder I tested ran smoothly. I had little difficulty manipulating a tool or other object precisely against the grinding surface. It was fascinating to watch the metal vanish from a surface, corner or edge as a piece of steel was shaped. The clarity with which a workpiece can

be observed is affected by the light-reflecting ability of the piece and the position in which it is held.

The instructions suggest that an hour's practice will make the user an "expert grinder." Even less practice gave me the courage to tackle the sharpening of a wood-lathe gouge successfully. And I encountered no difficulty in surface-grinding a steel block: It showed no tendency to snag on the wheel slots.

The slotted wheel seemed to cut more coolly than a conventional type. The manufacturer says the slots produce a cooling action, and visual control makes it easier to maintain a light, even pressure.

versatile slotted wheels

Four types of slotted wheels, each available in a range of grit sizes, can handle structural steel, alloyed tool steels, cast steel, malleable and gray cast iron, aluminum and other nonferrous metals, as well as a variety of nonmetallic materials.

I did not test for wheel life because each wheel has two abrasive surfaces, and since grinding action can take place over a band nearly 2¾ in. wide, reasonably long grinding life would seem likely. As with any grinder, however, wheel life is influenced by the operator's habits and the material being ground.

One of the labels cautions that a wheel should be used only when the protective hood (guard) is in place. When using any grinder, the operator should wear either protective goggles or a face shield; a dust mask might also be desirable. I found that the wheel-locking knob can loosen if it has not been tightened sufficiently.

The grinder base measures 5¾ x 6¼ in. and is anchored by four bolts or screws. The motor has factory-lubricated ball bearings. Most parts of the machine are finished in gray enamel.

The lamp is an essential part of the grinder because it makes the see-through features possible.

available by mail

The grinder, a West German product, is distributed in the United States by Leichtung, Inc., 5187 Mayfield Rd., Cleveland, OH 44124 and is priced at about $250 ready to run. Most abrasive wheels are approximately $18 each; the one for hardened steels and milling cutters is approximately $28. Polishing wheels range from around $15 (for a 6-in., hard-felt, general-purpose type) to around $19.50. All wheels are somewhat less costly in lots of three or more.

The machine comes with a No. 60 grit (medium) EF wheel. Fine and very fine wheels are also available

what's new in photography

Bend the light path and you shrink the optics. It's done with mirrors in Vivitar's new 600-mm "solid cat" lens (1); conventional telephoto of a mere 400-mm towers over it. Roof-prism design shrinks Honeywell Pentax monocular (3) which doubles as a 22X microscope (2), and Minolta Pocket binoculars (4) which fold compactly (5)

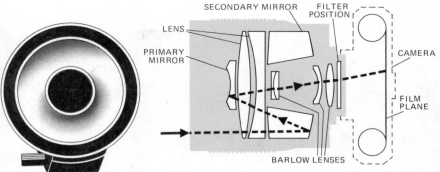

Vivitar "solid cat" (above) reflects the light twice to lengthen the path while shortening the lens; light enters in a ring around the primary mirror at the lens's front. Barlow lenses at rear of the lens act as teleconverters to magnify the image and increase the power. To keep the filters small and economical, they fit at the rear of the lens. Camera mounts are interchangeable

Big performance from small optics

■ HOW DO YOU SHRINK a pair of binoculars? Or a camera lens? You fold it—not by bending the glass, but by using prisms and mirror surfaces to bend the light rays that pass through the optical system.

That's the secret behind a raft of new optical devices which have been made incredibly compact without serious losses in performance.

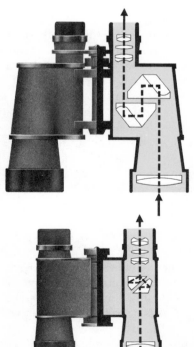

Compact binoculars below are (clockwise from upper left corner); Bushnell, Minolta/Celtic Compact 6x20, Minolta Celtic Compact 8x20 and Minolta/Celtic Pocket 6x20. The binocular in the center is a full-size 7x35 Scope model shown for size comparison. Straight tubes of the Pocket model are due to roof-prism design (lower left diagram), that folds light back on itself. Compare this to the conventional design above it

Magnification of 600-mm telephoto lens is 12 times that of a normal 50-mm lens. Compare the lower shot taken with 600-mm "solid cat" to upper shot taken with a normal lens. Note how bright spots in the out-of-focus foliage behind the child in the 600-mm shot register as circles. These blurry doughnuts are one of the drawbacks of using all catadioptric mirror lenses

Most dramatic of this new breed is Vivitar's "solid cat" 600-mm telephoto lens. Just 3¾ inches long, it has a focal length of 600-mm (23.6 inches). That's 12 times the focal length and magnification of a normal 50-mm lens, in a housing only about twice as long as a 50, though considerably wider.

Mirror lenses are not new. What distinguishes the Vivitar from other such "catadioptric" designs, however, is that it's practically solid, with little airspace between its elements—hence the nickname "solid cat."

Solid construction saves space. The Vivitar 600 is about half the length of many conventional, airspaced 500-mm mirror lenses and an inch shorter than the shortest 500. Solid construction also makes the lens more rugged and more stable in changing temperatures. And it concentrates the lens's weight close to the camera, making it easier, though still chancy, to take shots with the camera supported only by hand.

Mirror lenses have their drawbacks, though. They have only one f-stop, nearly always f/8. Neutral-density filters must be fitted if you want the exposure you'd get from smaller apertures. (To keep filters small and economical, they fit behind the lens.) Out-of-focus light spots register as blurry doughnuts instead of fuzzy dots. Contrast is often so low that focusing can be difficult. To these drawbacks add the disadvantages of weight (at 3 pounds, 5½ ounces, the "solid cat" is about a pound heavier than most mirror 500s) and high price (approximately $800).

Still to come are 800 and 1200-mm "solid cats" where compactness should really pay off in those super-telephoto focal lengths and help offset the disadvantages of using such unique telephoto lenses.

prisms for binoculars too

Binoculars also use light-folding techniques —the bulge in their shape and the offset that puts the objective lenses farther apart than the eye-pieces are both due to the use of prism systems. What's new here is the extensive trend to "roof prism" designs that turn the light path around enough extra corners to equal the path length of a standard binocular while keeping the tube straight and free of offsets and bulges. Roof prisms have been around a while, too, but in recent years binocular makers such as Konica, Redfield and Asanuma have taken advantage of this design's compact, tubular shape to make folding models. Minolta has now taken this a step farther, with binoculars that fold but still have the convenience of center-wheel focusing. Still another approach to compact designs is taken by Minolta, Bushnell and others who reverse the binocular offset, so that the objectives are closer together than the eyepieces.

And for the ultimate in compactness, try a monocular. Again, they're not new, but the latest wrinkle in them is the use of closeup attachments, such as the one that makes the Pentax monocular a 22X microscope with stand.

Make giant prints at home

■ MAKING PHOTOMURALS in a home dark-room isn't easy. But it is possible—and the re-sults are quite impressive. Kodak enlarging pa-pers are available in large rolls (Porter's in Cedar Rapids, IA, sells them by mail), and most enlarg-ers can be tilted to project big images on the wall or the floor.

For developing the big prints, there's lots of equipment available. Perhaps the least expen-sive are the Maxwell Photomural tanks that hold paper up to 30 by 40 inches (other sizes hold up to 48 by 96), develop them in just one quart of chemicals, and cost approximately $25 up.

A more elaborate approach is the Big Dipper for around $120, which holds the paper under moderate tension while you raise one side and lower the other to pass the paper through the chemicals in the troughs below. It processes paper up to 30 by 50 inches, using only 32 ounces of chemicals, and gives you a view of the print's surface while it's developing. Four trays are in-cluded, one for each chemical plus a washing tray with hose attachments. There's also a Little Dipper for about $30; the difference is that the overhead hoist is eliminated, leaving you to pass the paper up and down by hand.

For professional labs, CPI's Mural 2000 (about $865 without pump and motor drive) han-dles paper up to 5 by 35 feet! But the 5-foot trays are available separately for approximately $78 each.

You'll find it handy to have help when you're making murals—not just for handling the big sheets of paper (they get very floppy when wet, and wrinkles can crack the emulsion), but also for focusing: One of you can stand by the paper checking while the other focuses.

Prints this size and bigger demand care in processing. New darkroom hardware makes it easier. A couple of examples are the Maxwell tank (below, left) which is relatively inexpensive and saves chemicals. The Big Dipper (right) is expensive, but its crank system makes it easy to roll paper through chemicals evenly

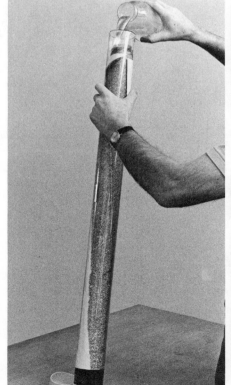

Two new film tanks

■ TIRED OF SITTING in the darkroom, agitating your developing tank? Unicolor's new Film Drum system will do it—and quite a bit besides.

Designed for color, where chemicals are expensive, the Film Drum has two unique chemical-saving features: Its piston bottom adjusts the tank's volume to the number of reels inside, from one 110-size reel to six 35-mm or four 120 reels. And you needn't fill even that volume with chemicals: Since the tank lies on its side and rotates, it need only be half full.

You could roll the tank by hand, but a far better way is to use Unicolor's motorized Uniroller, which rolls the tank around one way, then rolls it back again, to avoid the streaks of one-way agitation. Since agitation is continuous, developing time is cut about 15 percent. A color print drum (shown) also uses the Uniroller.

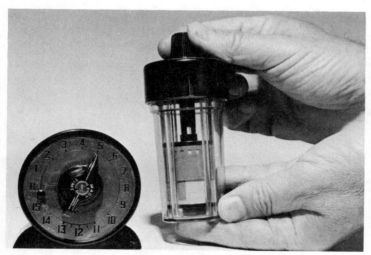 

■ "PROCESS A ROLL of 35-mm black-and-white film in its own cassette." When I read this blurb for the Brooks/Sigell developing tank I thought it was a put-on. It's not.

The process is limited to 20-exposure rolls because it depends on the loose spooling of the film to admit the developing solutions; the much longer 36-frame rolls are too tight. One important preliminary precaution must be observed: When the exposed film in the camera is being rewound, its tapered tongue must be left free so you can turn it back around the cassette.

The tank proper is a small plastic cylinder. When the cassette is attached to the one-piece cap/twirler and pushed into the tank, the lip wedges against the inner surface and prevents the film container from turning when the twirler is twirled. The film expands and contracts as the knob is twisted back and forth, thus keeping the solution circulating.

The Brooks/Sigell tank is about $5 from Porter's Camera Store, Cedar Rapids, IA 50613.

Light kits that freeze action

RAPID-FIRE, repeating ''strobe'' lights are fantastic for visually freezing the action of rotating or reciprocating parts and for reducing other actions into overlapping slices to be seen and photographed. Now you can buy such lights in kit form at a modest cost—about $30 for Radio Shack's ArcherKit No. 28-3210, about $20 for Graymark's 523-R. You can build either in an hour or less.

It's a good thing the kits are simple, though, for the instructions aren't quite as clear as they should be, especially Graymark's—often where they can't be seen when you're working on steps relating to them.

Perhaps the most practical use for a repeating strobe is freezing action: Adjust the flashing rate so the moving part you're looking at (a fan blade, for instance) is always passing through the same position at the instant the light flashes. The part will seem to be standing still. We found the ArcherKit better for this since it can be adjusted to flash at any rate from about 1 to 15 times per second; the Graymark's maximum speed is only about 5 flashes per second.

For photography, the advantage is reversed. We measured the Graymark's flash guide number at 12.5 and the Archer's at 8 for ASA 400 film. That means you can use it only for fairly close action with very fast film.

Some tricks to keep in mind when photographing with these repeating strobes: Use exposure time long enough to keep the shutter open the whole length of the action you're shooting—enough to catch several flashes. (The golf shot above, made with a professional repeating strobe unit, caught 25 flashes on the frame.)

Since the background of the shot will be exposed to every flash in the sequence, it must be as black as possible, or it will be overexposed and wash out any objects in front. Studio photographers use black velvet; you can get the same effect by shooting outdoors at night, keeping well away from any background object.

Some cautions to observe when using these lights: Never look directly at the light when it's flashing; turn the light off at once if you feel dizzy or ill at ease, and never use it in the presence of an epileptic.

Rapid-fire repeating strobe lights in kit form include (top, left to right): Graymark 523-R and Radio Shack ArcherKit 28-3210. Inside views show simple construction

New for photographers

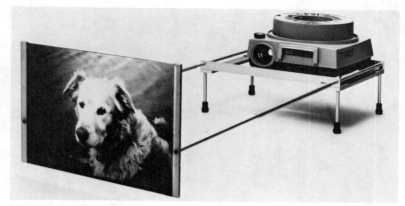

PORTABLE SLIDE THEATER has its own rigid screen attached, always ready for a show. Screen size is 11 by 17 inches. Disassembled unit fits inside a briefcase, can be used in normal room light. It's available from Visual Horizons, 208 Westfall Road, Rochester NY 14620

HERE'S A FINE SOLUTION to the irritating problem of disappearing lens caps. CapKeeper has a pressure-sensitive tab that attaches to the lens cap, connected by cord to the camera. Available from Sima Products Corp.,7574 N. Lincoln Ave., Skokie IL 60076

PROTECT YOUR LENSES in a cushion of air. AirShield is a plastic pouch with built-in air bags. You pack your lenses, then inflate the bags with a few puffs of air. Available in three sizes from Sima Products Corp., 7574 N. Lincoln Ave., Skokie IL 60076

FLASH DIFFUSER kit has a soft diffuser for direct lighting, and a super-white diffuser for bounce-light effect. Available from Sima Products Corp., 7574 N. Lincoln Ave., Skokie IL 60076

SPECTRA METERS with silicon blue cells offer an amazing range—from 0.004 to 100,000 foot-candles. Instant f-stop readings. Ehrenreich Photo-Optical Industries, 101 Crossways Park West, Woodbury NY 11797

BACKDROP KIT takes four rolls of seamless paper. Brackets can be mounted anywhere in the wall standards. Thin-wall conduit (not provided) holds rolls. Rangine Corp., 51 Harvard Ave., West Medford, MA 02155

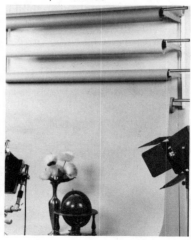

85-210-mm zoom Tamron (above, left) and Sun (above, center) are hardly bigger than nonzoom 200-mm Vivitar tele (above, right). Sun's lens hood is detachable; others' slide back. Special features (right) include interchangeable camera adapter and "EE" diaphragm setting for camera with electric eye (Tamron), and a handy tab for quicker zooming on Sun Telephoto

Zoom telephotos are getting compact, sharp and less expensive. Here is a report on a couple of them you may want to consider

The shrinking of the zoom

BY IVAN BERGER

■ ZOOM LENSES are getting almost as light, compact, sharp and inexpensive as fixed-focal-length ones, to judge from the 85-210-mm Spiratone/Sun and Tamron zooms that I've just tested.

Zooms have always had two advantages over fixed lenses: You have only one lens to buy and carry to match the coverage of two or more conventional lenses. It's quicker to adjust a zoom lens than to remove a lens and mount another one. And zooms give you not only the standard focal lengths like 85, 105, 135 and 200-mm, but all the nonstandard ones in between. So if you need a 167½-mm lens to frame your picture precisely as you want it, then only a zoom will do.

But zooms are larger, heavier and more expensive than any one of the lenses they replace. And they're never quite as sharp as lenses of fixed focal length.

When comparing the Spiratone/Sun and Tamron to a modern 200-mm lens, though, the zooms stand up quite well. In size, the Tamron is just under 6 inches long, the thinner Sun lens 6¾ inches—an inch or two longer than our reference 200 mm, but shorter than some others and a bit slimmer. In weight, both the 26-ounce Tamron and 22-ounce Sun are heavier than our 18-ounce reference, but again lighter than some older 200-mm designs.

The big question is performance—and these zooms do perform. Our reference telephoto did have slightly better contrast and sharpness than the zooms, but not to any great degree. You'd be more apt to feel hampered by the one-stop difference between the f/4.5 zooms and an f/3.5 tele. Price of the sleekly styled Tamron lens is about $310; the Spiratone/Sun is approximately $110-$125, depending on the mount that is selected.

CITIZENS' BAND RADIOS have become the hottest items in "hot" merchandise. They're small, but valuable. They're in demand, and—left alone so often in unattended cars—they're all too easy to steal.

Think about the CB in your car for a moment. You probably have a big, distinctive antenna advertising the fact that you have a radio worth stealing (some thieves find the antennas worth stealing, too). And the average curb-side thief can usually spot that radio's location with a quick glance through your car's side window, then pry it out and run off with the CB in about as little time as it takes him to break into your car.

And a break-in can cost you not only your CB but whatever else of value there is in your car—plus the cost of fixing any damage.

But make it a little harder for a thief to find and steal your set, and you'll keep it a lot longer.

And, responding to the rise in CB thefts (State Farm Mutual Insurance estimates nearly one-fourth of its 1975 auto accessory theft payments went for CB radios), manufacturers are flooding the market with gadgets designed to avert thefts.

A CB antenna on your car is very "in" these days. You can even buy a dummy to "give your car that 'CB' look." But keeping that antenna in the car, where it won't betray the presence of a CB, is better. An intelligent thief (and the really dumb ones don't last long) would rather make a beeline for the car with the 108-inch whip than

How to end the CB ripoff

BY IVAN BERGER

Rugged lock-mounts, like this Shur-Lok, can protect your set—if anchored well enough to your car's frame

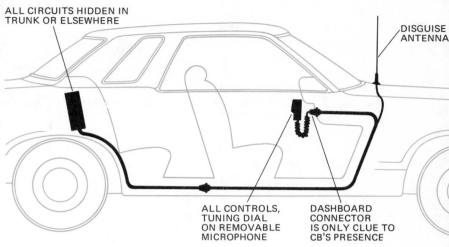

ALL CIRCUITS HIDDEN IN
TRUNK OR ELSEWHERE

DISGUISE
ANTENNA

ALL CONTROLS,
TUNING DIAL
ON REMOVABLE
MICROPHONE

DASHBOARD
CONNECTOR
IS ONLY CLUE TO
CB'S PRESENCE

Hide the fact you have a set: Hy-Gain 9 (above) has all its controls, plus a digital channel readout, on its microphone, with the rest of its works in a featureless, and easily hidden black box. With optional extension cables, you can even hide the box in your trunk—yet still have all controls near the driver (right)

walk up and down the aisles of a parking lot looking through car windows to spot a car with a CB inside. The beeline approach is less likely to attract suspicion—and it's less work.

The simplest way to foil a thief is to remove your antenna whenever you leave your car. That still leaves a telltale socket, but it's not visible from as far away as the antenna was. Antenna Specialists and Radio Shack make quick-disconnects that let you remove your antenna with a simple push and twist. (But so can a thief, so be sure to take it off when you park.) You can also just unscrew the mast, but that takes longer; if you do, it's wise to keep rain and dirt off the now-exposed contacts with one of the little plastic caps made by Antenna, Inc., Antenna Specialists and Radio Shack; buy extras—they're easy to lose.

An easier approach, if a bit more expensive, is to buy one of the many brackets that let you fold your antenna down into your trunk when you park. Most of these attach to the lip surrounding

the trunk opening, and let you open the lid and fold the antenna down inside. The one shown here, from Holly Enterprises, attaches to the trunk lid instead; it could be a bit handier when you're loading or unloading. Such brackets average about $15 each; one—the SouthCom Foiler—is $5.

You can use an antenna with these brackets, as long as it's shorter than the width of your trunk opening (allow a bit for the bracket's height, too). But since you have to mount the assembly at the side of the opening, your antenna's radiation pattern will be asymmetrical, pointing diagonally across the car from its mounting point (see *How to Add Ears to Your Wheels*, p. 166).

If you don't want to stop each time you park to open and relock your trunk, you can get an electrically retracted antenna, like the Tenna model shown, or similar ones from Royal, Sound, Kraco, Antenna Specialists, CPD, Metro Sound and Valor.

Swing the antenna into the trunk with this mount from Holly Enterprises. You don't have to break connections to do it. Similar mounts are available from many sources. Most mount on the edge of the trunk opening, not the lid as this model does

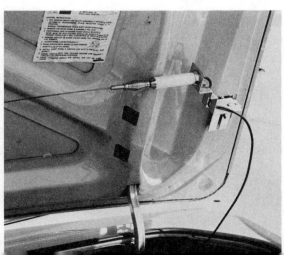

Since these must be mounted at the side of the car, they also radiate asymmetrically—and they don't radiate as well as regular antennas, either. Antenna makers estimate a loss of about 3-6 dB in signal strength, which they claim will not cause a significant reduction in range. And retractables cost about $40 to $70.

Antenna Specialists' "disguise" antenna is a slightly less expensive ($30) solution. It looks like a normal AM-FM antenna, and doubles as one, too. But like the retractables, it must be mounted asymmetrically, and is also about 3 dB less efficient than conventional antennas. The makers say there's no significant loss of AM or FM reception, though. And the disguise antenna, unlike the folddown or retractable types, must be unscrewed when you're going through a car wash.

Removable antennas are another answer. Magnetic mounts can be placed in the center of the roof for the most even radiation, and will stick on well beyond legal speeds on all cars but those with vinyl roof covers or convertible or plastic tops. For side mounting (and asymmetrical radiation again) there are many mounts that clip on a car's rain gutter. A new one from Channel Master clips to the edge of the side-window glass. Then there's the removable trunk-lip mount from Antenna Specialists.

Even without "advertising," sooner or later someone will look in your car window and be tempted by your CB's shiny chrome. Or maybe they'll be looking for—but not finding—your set.

Out of sight, out of mind is what counts. So some CB owners install their sets in such spots as the glove compartment, under the driver's

Mounted in your dashboard's radio slot, a CB is harder to steal—and looks so much like a regular car radio that many thieves may not even notice it. But lock up the microphone—it can be stolen readily

seat, or beneath the dash but way back near the firewall. The set's now out of sight, all right, but so are its controls.

That's one reason you'll find more and more sets with most or all of their controls on the microphone. Radio Shack's One-Hander puts them all there; similar sets from Royce and Midland leave a few on a small control box, which can be easily tucked into the glovebox.

But the set ideally adapted to this approach is the Hy-Gain 9. Unplug its microphone control head, and the only sign of the set's existence is the round black jack—easily concealed—that the mike plugs into. The rest of the circuits are in a featureless black box, which can be mounted almost anywhere in the car, especially if you use the optional extension cables.

Retract your antenna and it won't attract thieves—or vandals, either. This model, from Tenna, is center-loaded. Many makes of retractable antennas are available, some of them doubling as antennas for ordinary AM and FM car radios

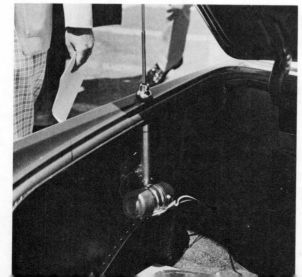

Cross a Kriket with a camel, and you get a Kamel that sits on your car's hump, holds a Kar Kriket speaker for clearer sound and takes your CB. When you park, it transfers readily to your trunk. The unit is manufactured by AFS and sells for around $30

Performance of this set is excellent, though its controls take a bit of getting used to (they seem to work backward). Its digital channel readout in the mike is easy to read. The only drawback inherent in this approach is that the microphone must double as a speaker. At moderate volumes this works well, but at high volume, distortion is a problem. There is a connection on the black box for an external speaker, but that's another component to conceal.

(By contrast, the microphone in Radio Shack's One-Hander was not nearly as good a speaker as the Hy-Gain's—but the big speaker in the One-Hander's main box was a far better one.)

If you already own a set, you can hide it another way, with a slide-in mount that makes and breaks the set's connections for power, for the external speaker (if you're using one), and sometimes for the antenna as well.

This has an added advantage: If the bracket's visible and empty, it shows the set has been removed, which might discourage a would-be thief from hunting for it. If you've already stolen the set, he can't.

But there are also disadvantages: If you forget to take it out, you make a thief's job all the easier. And some insurance policies pay off only on thefts of sets which are rigidly mounted as "part of the car."

Once you've slid your set out, what then? You can tuck it under the seat (probably the first place a thief would look, though), hide it in the glove compartment (if it fits), or lock it in the trunk (best done out of sight of the area where you'll be parking your car). Or you can take the set away with you: Platt Luggage even makes a molded carry case just for that purpose.

Other mounts, such as the Shur-Lok, take the opposite approach. Instead of making the set easy to remove, they make it hard to take—hard enough, you hope, to discourage a thief's attempt. But unless the mount is anchored with great care, it can be ripped out and the set removed.

Mounting the set in your dashboard is a neater way to make it hard to steal. Combinations of CB, tape and AM/FM to fit your dashboard's radio slot are available from JIL, Royce, Boman/Astrosonix, Automatic Radio and Audiovox.

Combinations give you fewer controls to fiddle with, and place them all where they'll be handy. But they make you pay a lot—and all in one lump. If any part needs fixing, the whole system will have to be out for repair (and it's reasonable to suspect that cramming all that into one box increases the chance of something going wrong). And the set's high value might tempt a thief into ripping up your dashboard.

All these tactics are designed to convince a thief it's not worth his while to break into your car. But what if he does anyway?

Then your last resort—short of an armed guard in the car—is to rig your car with an alarm in hopes of scaring him off again before he has stolen anything worthwhile.

There are car alarms designed to ring, scream or blow your car's horn if the car is jostled or opened, or if your set or antenna is removed. But don't count on anyone's responding unless you're within earshot yourself. And alarms work best only if your CB is so well secured that a thief must spend a long time getting it. So consider an alarm as a supplement to other measures, not a substitute.

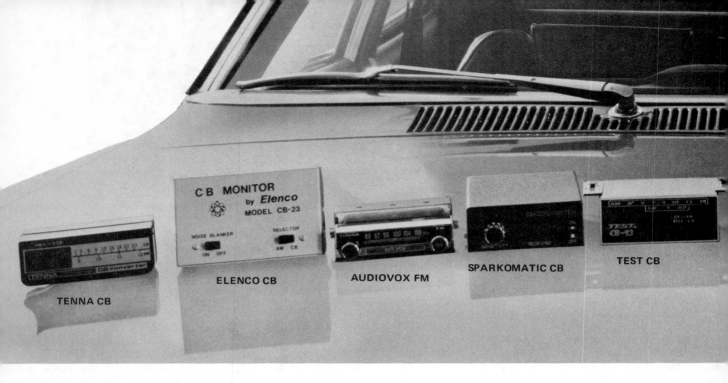

CB MONITOR by *Elenco* MODEL CB-23 — NOISE BLANKER ON OFF — SELECTOR AM CB

TENNA CB

ELENCO CB

AUDIOVOX FM

SPARKOMATIC CB

TEST CB

Convert your car radio to FM

■ THE AIR IS FULL of fascinating things to listen to, but your car radio can't hear them all. Though more and more car radios pick up both AM and FM, surprisingly many still do without FM's clearer sound and greater freedom from fading under bridges. And even AM-FM sets miss CB chatter, government weather broadcasts and TV sound tracks.

But you needn't replace that radio now in the dash to get them. Just add a converter.

Converters plug in between your car's radio and antenna. That and attaching a power lead to a 12-volt source are all you do to install them.

Switched off, they have no effect on the signals reaching your radio. Switched on, they either shift the frequency of amplitude—modulated signals like CB onto the AM band, or tune in and demodulate a frequency-modulated signal from FM broadcasts, TV sound, government weather service forecasts or fire and police calls. That signal is then amplitude-modulated on a new frequency your AM radio can pick up.

Most frequency-shifting converters shift all frequencies equally on the band they pick up. You tune in the individual stations with your car radio's regular tuning knob. Most FM-type converters have their own tuning knobs, so that all the stations they pick up will come in at the same point on your car radio's dial; you can set one pushbutton to that point.

■ FM converters tend to work well, possibly because of FM's inherent resistance to interference problems. There are dozens on the market. We tried Audiovox's FMC-1C (about $40. All prices are approximate). In the city, it brings in as many stations as the FM band of a good car radio, though with less high-frequency response, and not in stereo. In the country, where sensitivity is more important, it gets fewer stations than a top-notch FM car radio, but still more than many radios do.

The FM band of Audiovox's FMC-TV ($85) worked just as well, but it also picked up TV and weather signals. Theoretically, you just click from channel to channel as you do on a TV set; in practice, some channels require adjustment of the fine-tuning ring surrounding the channel-selector knob.

■ Other weather-service attachments can sometimes be unorthodox. Audiovox's WB-70 (not shown) takes only about as much dash space as two commemorative stamps, uses a simple frequency converter to adapt FM weather broadcasts to FM car radios, and costs $23.

Instalert EM-1W ($124) from Electrosonics not only lets you listen to forecasts, but shrieks an alarm in response to weather-service severe storm warnings when you're not listening. Since converters are switched off when you're not lis-

AUDIOVOX CB

INSTALERT WEATHER

BEAR BUSTER CB

Two radios? No. Hanging under the Philco-Ford car radio (right) is a converter—Audiovox's $85 FMC-TV that adds the sound from VHF TV channels and government weather forecasts, plus FM (if your radio doesn't have that already). Converters are easy to install between a car's radio and antenna. Shown on the hood of the car are (left to right): Tenna CBC-23 ($30), Elenco CB-23 ($35), Audiovox FMC-1C ($40), Sparkomatic CB-10 ($20), Test CB-23 ($29), Audiovox CBC-100 ($74), Electrosonics Instalert EM-1W ($124) and Bear Buster CBM-19S ($45). All prices are approximate

tening to them, Instalert isn't a converter, but a radio you wire in along with your broadcast set.

■ CB converters are booming, but they suffer frequently from static. Most worked fairly well when our test car's ignition was turned off, but picked up lots of static with the motor running. The Tenna CBC-23 ($30) suffered most from this, followed by the Test CB-23; both would be okay, though, on cars with more static-free electrical systems. Both sets had scales to help you locate CB channels on your radio's dial.

The squelch control on Electronic Circuits and Devices' Bear Buster CBM-19S ($45) helped reduce static as well as cut noise between CB signals. The Bear Buster also had a cigaret-lighter plug for easy power connection, a pilot light to let you know it was on, and an oscillator that broadcast a distinctive tone to help you find the spot on your radio's dial where Channel 19, the highway traffic channel, would come in.

Sparkomatic's CB-10 ($20) also had a pilot light, plus a sensitivity control which acted somewhat like a squelch in controlling noise, and could also cure overloading from strong local signals. Elenco's CB-23 ($35) had a noise-blanker switch, which reduced ignition noise greatly; the CB-23's broad, flat shape though, makes it more suitable for sticking to the dash, rather than hanging under it.

All these CB converters were fairly well matched in convenience and performance. But the Audiovox CBC-100 ($74) was in a class of its own. It looks like a regular CB transceiver and has most of the features of one—except the ability to transmit, of course. Tuning is by a 23-click, illuminated dial; there's an illuminated "S" meter that's bigger and easier to read than those on most transceivers; there's a squelch control; and the CBC-100's sensitivity and noise rejection seem better than those of any of the other CB converters we tried.

TOSHIBA

SANSUI

PHILIPS

We test some low-cost turntables

BY HANS FANTEL

We tested 11 under-$130 single-play turntables.
We found some great values, and some that were not so great. Here's how
we tested them and what we discovered

■TURNTABLE PRICES have been climbing faster than a scared squirrel, but you can still get good—and not-so-good—component turntables for less than $130 each, including arm, base and dust cover. Of 11 I've just tested, several are unqualifiedly excellent—only two did not measure up to acceptable standards.

None of the 11 models tested was a changer. All were single-play designs, a type that's fast gaining popularity.

Few albums now require stacking on a changer—with most you play one side, then flip the record over (even a changer can't do this for you). Besides, in the low and moderate price ranges, single-play turntables offer higher quality per dollar.

But though they aren't changers, most of our single-play turntables do offer some automation.

KENWOOD

ROTEL

PIONEER

GARRARD

AR

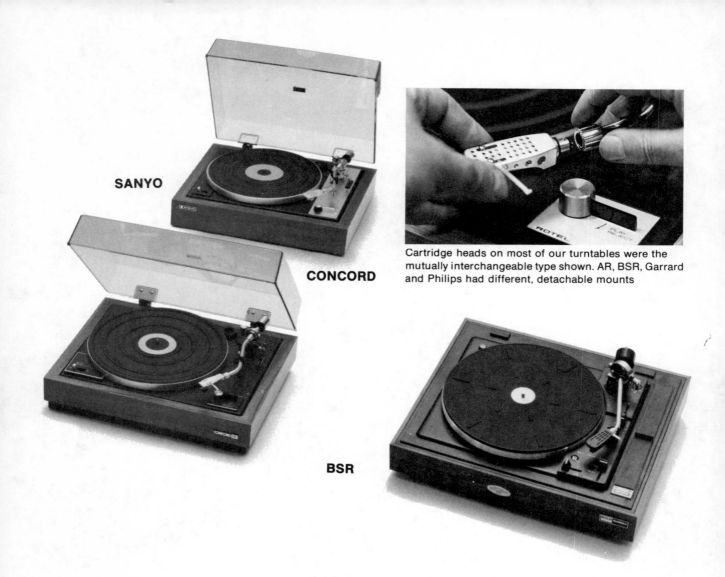

SANYO

CONCORD

BSR

Cartridge heads on most of our turntables were the mutually interchangeable type shown. AR, BSR, Garrard and Philips had different, detachable mounts

All but two lift the tone arm when the record ends, and return the arm to its rest position; two models tested will also set the arm down for you in the record's starting groove.

Auto-return is the bigger boon. Without it, you have to jump up at the end of the record. To help you set the arm down safely, all the tested models except the Acoustic Research AR-XA have cue controls that let you place the arm over any part of the disc without touching the needle to the grooves, then lower the arm gently.

All that turntables have to do is turn a record in a circle while an arm swings freely over the disc surface. But in a glance, you can often see craftsmanship that's a clue to the precision inside and the overall quality of the machine.

For example, the turntable platter not only has to rotate, but to rotate with almost no vibration; otherwise, the phono cartridge picks up this vi-

bration along with the music, causing "rumble." Especially if your speakers have good bass response, rumble will sound like thunder in the distance, fogging over the soft passages of music. A turntable with lots of rumble can so overload the amplifier with these low-frequency noises that it constantly distorts the music. Rumble filters on some amplifiers help, but they also cut out some low notes with the rumble.

Keeping vibration at a minimum means machining parts to fine tolerances and carefully fitting them in strong supporting frames and precision bearings—all of which adds to the cost.

All the turntables in this report also link their motors and platters with elastic drive belts, which filter residual vibration still more.

Constant speed is another requirement. Fast speed variations (known as "flutter") and slow ones (known as "wow") are annoying, espe-

The stylus force gauge on the Philips turntable was a scale whose platform also served the purpose of the tone-arm rest, as shown above

The stylus position gauge on the Pioneer was this pop-up post. Others used detachable gauges where gauges were supplied on the units

LOW-COST SINGLE-PLAY TURNTABLES

Make and Model	Arm Position	Arm Return	Minimum Tracking Force (grams)	Feedback and Shock Resistance	Rumble Level	Dimensions With Lid Closed (inches)	Price
Acoustic Research AR-XA	Manual	Manual	0.75	Excellent	Excellent	16½ x 12½ x 5¾	$115
BSR 20 BPX*	Auto	Auto	1.5	Fair	Fair	17 x 14½ x 7½	100
Concord BA 300	Manual	Auto	0.75	Fair	Good	17¾ x 14 x 6½	130
Garrard 125SB	Auto	Auto	2.00	Excellent	Poor	15½ x 14 x 8¼	110
Kenwood KD-2033	Manual	Auto	0.75	Good	Excellent	18¾ x 13¾ x 6¾	130
Philips GA-427	Manual	Auto	0.75	Excellent	Excellent	15 x 12½ x 5	100
Pioneer PL-12D-II	Manual	Manual	0.75	Good	Excellent	16¼ x 12¾ x 6¾	100
Rotel RP-1000	Manual	Auto	0.75	Good	Excellent	18½ x 13¾ x 7¾	130
Sansui SR-212	Manual	Auto	0.75	Good	Excellent	17½ x 14 x 6½	130
Sanyo TP600A	Manual	Auto	0.75	Fair	Good	17 x 14 x 6½	100
Toshiba	Manual	Auto	0.75	Poor	Excellent	17 x 14 x 6½	130

* The BSR comes equipped with a factory-mounted ADC K6E cartridge and was tested with it.

cially on long-held organ or piano notes. Speed constancy depends partly on the quality of the drive motor, but also on the drive system and on the mass and balance of the turntable platter, which acts as a flywheel to smooth the motion.

Finally, the turntable must be isolated from outside vibrations, which could make the tone arm jump or skip. Footsteps on a shaky floor are one source of such vibration, but even trickier are airborne or floorborne vibrations from the speaker. If these vibrations shake the record, arm or table, you have ''acoustic feedback''—a rumbling sound or, in extreme cases, a moaning howl when the volume is turned up.

As for the tone arm, it may seem to be just a stick on a swivel. But to let the phono cartridge it holds track across the record properly, it must hold the cartridge at a precise angle, move with exceptionally low bearing friction and have just

Antiskating adjustments were mostly either string-and-weight type (near side of the tone arm, top) or the weight-and-lever type (the rods visible behind the tone arm in the bottom photo). I found no difference—even with the AR, which had no antiskating controls. Results of the tests are shown in the table above

the proper resonance and balance. The single best measure of a tone arm's quality is the minimum tracking force it needs to let a high-compliance cartridge track a loud recorded passage cleanly.

how turntables were tested

Numerical specifications are useful ways to compare turntable performance, but what matters to most users are two basic questions: "Can I hear it?" and "Will it bother me?"

That's why I set up strictly user-oriented tests for these turntables. To check rumble, I played silent grooves on the Stereo Review SR-12 test record, through Yamaha's excellent CA-800 amplifier and two Dynaco 40XL speakers which have plenty of bass response. What I heard shows up in the table.

This test record also has an ingenious flutter test: The same piano recording is repeated several times, with differing, measured amounts of flutter. When you can no longer hear a difference between one band and the next, you've reached the point where your turntable's flutter is equal to that on the record band.

To check feedback isolation, I put the speakers next to the turntable, turned up volume and measured it at the point where feedback began to become audible. To check isolation from mechanical shock, I dropped a dictionary from a one-foot height next to the turntable, to see if it would make the arm jump.

To test tone arm tracking, I mounted a Pickering XV-15/400E cartridge in each arm (except the BSR's, which comes with an ADC cartridge already mounted), and determined the minimum tracking force at which this cartridge would cleanly track a massively orchestrated musical passage. The lower the tracking force, the better the arm.

I picked the Pickering for several reasons: List-priced at about $55 but usually sold for less, it's the type of cartridge most likely to be used with this type of turntable. Its sound is excellent. Also, its neat plastic mounting shims make the cartridges easiest to mount—and I had to mount 10 of them.

The two models with the most automation turned out to be the worst performers: The Garrard's arm requires twice as much tracking force as the others, and its flimsy platter rumbles like the New York subway. You can't reach the cue control without jolting the arm, the cartridge shell has no finger lift and the unhinged lid is a bulky nuisance. The BSR is advertised as "the

silent performer." It isn't. Rumble cuts right through the music when you crank up the gain. The controls are so clunky that everything shakes when you push the start switch. And if you use the cue control to lift the arm, the arm flies up sideways like a frisbee. Also, BSR and Garrard were the only models in the group with perceptible flutter.

Pioneer is a best buy

Pick of the lot, dollarwise, is Pioneer's PL-12D/II. In all performance factors it ranks with the best. And because Pioneer just introduced an improved version (the PL-112D, with improved suspension), the PL-12D/II will now be widely discounted to around $70. The Pioneer is more compact than most, neatly styled in a no-nonsense way, and has two control features I admired: the single-lever operating control for start, stop and cue; and the stylus-alignment gauge. Its only drawback is that it has no automatic arm return.

The Acoustic Research AR-XA also lacks automatic arm return, has no cue control and no antiskate adjustment. Instead of the cue control (available on the slightly more expensive AR-XB), the arm has a viscous, slow-drop feature. The design is Spartan, but the performance is excellent, and an ingenious spring suspension resists feedback and mechanical shock superbly.

The same fancy suspension, a floating sub-frame for both platter and arm, is also used by the Philips 427, with the result that it remained rock-steady when blasted point blank by the speaker or my dictionary test. If you like to dance and have shaky floorboards, that's something to consider. Consider also its design of simple elegance, the most compact of the group by far, and that it works well in other respects, with an exceptionally precise cue control.

The Toshiba was a standout in every way but two—feedback and shock resistance—which was a pity. But the controls are velvet-smooth, and if floor shake is not a problem for you, you might find it well worth your while.

The remaining units tested were basically similar, all good performers, with only minor differences between them. I particularly liked Sansui's very precise cue control, which puts the arm back in the original groove after you lift and lower it—most of the others swung the arm back a groove or two. I also liked Rotel's single-lever control, and Kenwood's variable arm-return speed. The Sanyo, though, was just a trifle below par in shock and feedback isolation.

SECTION 2

GREAT PROJECTS OF THE YEAR

On the following pages you'll find the finest of the famous Popular Mechanics *projects:*

Projects to improve your home
Projects to challenge your craftsmanship
Photo projects
Electronics know-how
Projects just for fun

You'll also find how-to information in related fields:

Shop know-how
Tool techniques
How-to tips for the great outdoors

Turn the page to find the first article on home improvement—and go on from there!

One big skylight turned this enclosed porch into a solarium that is bright on the dreariest days. At night you can stay warm while you count the stars

Let the sun shine in

BY MIKE MCCLINTOCK

■ AS A BUILDER I've installed many different skylights in many different locations. I'm still amazed at the difference one can make in a room. The enclosed porch in these pictures was added onto the house, and although there are windows all along the outside wall, little light was transmitted across the porch into the adjacent living room. And dark wood on walls and ceilings made the porch seem smaller than it really was.

A dormer might have worked here, or a raised roof. But of all possibilities, the easiest and least expensive was also the best. A neighbor and I opened the ceiling with the largest skylight available, a 46-inch-square unit from Ventarama Corp., 40 Haven Ave., Port Washington, NY. I think they're the best units going and have never had a callback on a job where I've used them. They're fully assembled and framed, use integral copper flashing and have a screen and an operator mechanism to lift the bubble for summer venting. I recommend this type instead of a fixed unit because it is less susceptible to condensation caused by hot, humid air collecting near the ceiling. For a vaulted ceiling or crawlspace over a flat ceiling, the roof installation is the same. A dropped ceiling needs more framing to close off the crawlspace.

To start, we located the skylight area inside and made corresponding measurements to get the exact location on the roof. On a vaulted ceiling, after cutting away the Sheetrock, drive a

home improvement

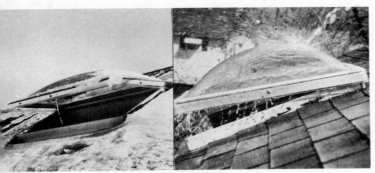

Rain, ice and snow don't bother the Ventarama unit shown above. You can leave it open for ventilation and not run home to close it if it starts to rain. A curved flange at the base keeps water from dripping into the opening. The hardware is strong enough to break through a crust of ice after a storm (left). Check your job with a hose test (right)

10d nail up through the roof at each corner of the opening to mark the cutout. With the area outlined, we pulled off shingles and felt paper and cut through the roof deck with a sabre saw (drawing 1). Then we cut away the center rafter. Be sure to cut an extra 3 inches at each end to allow for double headers that frame the opening and carry the load from the interrupted rafter (draw-

TOOLS OF THE TRADE

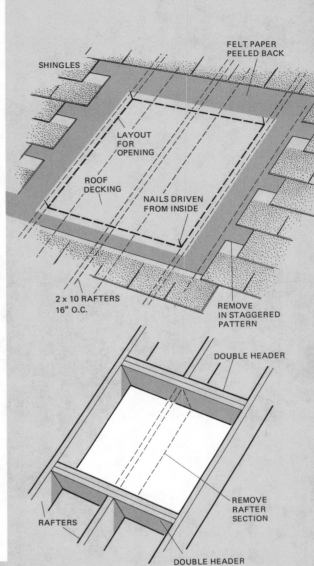

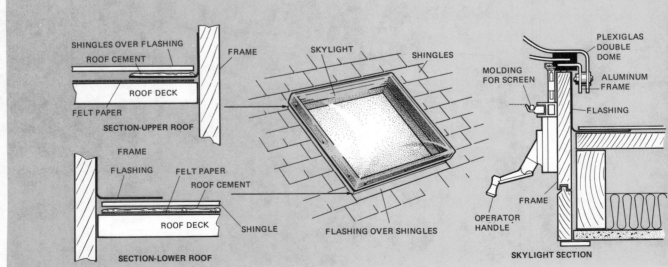

The roof window shown above is made in Denmark. It's from Velux-American, 80 Cummings Park, Woburn, MA

ing 2). We repeated this cut in the wooden ceiling below but increased the depth of the opening to let in more light. We then nailed 2x4 uprights along edges of the two openings to frame the short tunnel between outer and inner roofs.

For a more waterproof condition, we set flashing around the unit in a bed of roof cement and secured the bubble with nails through the frame into the adjacent rafters (drawing 3). The final step outside is to lace the shingles (use the ones you removed) back into the roofing pattern and cut them to fit the flashing. Above the unit we set the shingles in a second bed of cement over the copper flange to prevent water from backing up underneath. Along sides, shingles should run 2 to 3 in. past the lip of the flashing that is secured to the roof with copper clips. On the lower edge, the flashing sits in a bed of roof cement spread on

top of the shingles so all water will run onto the roof surface. While the frame is open, check the installation for leaks by simulating a downpour with a garden hose.

We used ¼-inch A-C plywood over the tunnel frame and painted it white to reflect as much light as possible. Molding strips along edges of the ceiling cutout gave a final finishing touch. You can treat the interior many ways (even with mirrors) but you must make the exterior waterproof. Follow the maker's instructions and the steps outlined. Pinpointing the source of a leak later on is, at best, a guessing game; you may have to redo all the flashing. On our job we angled the back wall of the tunnel to let the sun's rays stream directly through double glass doors into the living room. The porch is now so bright that we converted it into a solarium with plants.

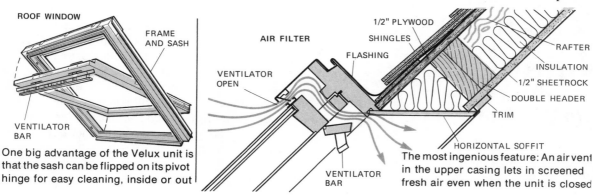

One big advantage of the Velux unit is that the sash can be flipped on its pivot hinge for easy cleaning, inside or out

The most ingenious feature: An air vent in the upper casing lets in screened fresh air even when the unit is closed

Vacation all summer in a low-cost pool

■ INVEST A FEW DAYS this summer and bring a piece of the ocean into your back yard. Above-ground pools are dotting lawns all across the country, and with good reason. Most are small enough to bring home in a station wagon, and big enough to keep your family and friends wet, happy and cool all summer long. Pool designs are pretty much the same, either round or oval, although different manufacturers offer a variety of finishes and assembly hardware. After you've shopped around, you should base your choice on two factors—quality and safety. Here are some guidelines:

Pools are great for keeping your family cool and calm on blistering summer weekends. You can take a quick dip before dinner or spend all afternoon splashing with the kids. Young children will learn to swim here faster than at the beach, and you'll be able to supervise them properly. The most common complaint about above-ground pools is the stark appearance of the side walls. Good landscaping (above) is the answer. Picture yourself (lower right) catching up on your daydreams, floating lazily under the summer sun

Select from reputable makers. They will offer guarantees on filter tanks and warranties on pool liners. Stay away from pools with electro-galvanized steel walls. They look all right, but they're not durable. For a good-quality, economical pool, look for roll-formed aluminum or hot-dipped, galvanized steel walls. Extruded aluminum or steel walls with a copper additive are excellent quality but more expensive. Finishing should include a two or three-coat paint process with a final bonderizer application. A simple guide to quality is that aluminum pools should be embossed for strength and painted to resist cor-

rosion. Steel pools should have corrugated walls, not flat sheeting. If you can't get this kind of information from a salesman, watch out.

The major responsibility for running a safe pool rests with the owner who must supervise who goes in and how they act. But there are areas you can't control and here's where a good manufacturer should step in to help. Most pool ladders can be easily climbed by children who can't swim once they get to the other side. When you're not around, this is a danger. To prevent it, safety ladders were developed. The outside steps and frame are hinge-mounted so they can

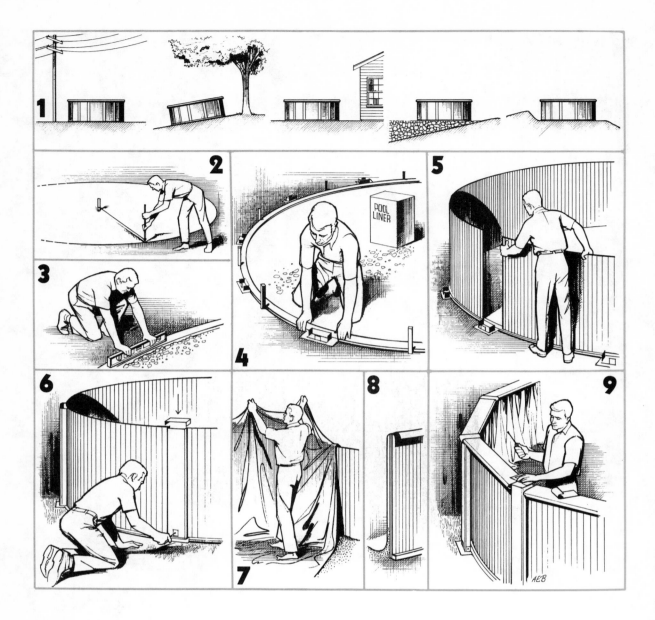

Putting in your pool

1. Pick the right site. Stay away from overhead obstructions, especially electrical lines. A level site with good drainage is best

2. Drive a stake in at the center of your site. Use string to scribe a circle two feet larger than your pool size. Note: avoid areas where chemical weed killers have been used

3. Check for level thoroughly. Use a level on top of a straight 2x4 to increase accuracy. Water in the pool will be level no matter what you do. But if the rim turns out to be uneven, you'll be wasting space at one end of the pool that could have been filled

4. Use temporary stakes between the support pads to keep the bottom rim in line as you work. Follow the manufacturer's instructions carefully—you're building the foundation for a large and heavy amount of water

5. Take my advice and get some help for this step. The one-piece steel wall can be as wriggly as an eel. Use 1x2 stakes to keep the wall steady while you're fitting the rim

6. Get a good, tight assembly on your uprights. They're the backbone that keeps the wall rigid

7. Take off your shoes—they'll wreck the liner. Try for no wrinkles (you'll get a few anyway) and leave an overlap (check the specs for how much) at the top edge of the pool wall

8. Make sure you've built up a round cove of earth at the inside bottom edge of the pool wall. If you don't, the tremendous water pressure may force the liner under the wall and tear it

9. Installing the rim locks up a job well done

The sun dome above uses aluminum frames to support vinyl that keeps in heat and extends your swimming season. The dome is from Fabrico, 1300 West Exchange, Chicago, IL 60609. Such covers can actually raise the water temperature 10 to 15 degrees

The whirlpool spa (top) from American Leisure, 718 N.W. First St., Fort Lauderdale, FL, is a unique above-ground fiberglass pool with jet-action circulators. Safety ladders (bottom) from Coleco, 945 Asylum, Hartford, CT 06105, have fold-up steps

be swung up off the ground out of reach. This is good protection against a child's wandering over to take a dip when no adults are around.

Safety ladders will also help prevent accidents as swimmers get in and out of the pool because they are anchored, usually by two chains, to the edge of the pool wall. Most of them bear a sign saying NO DIVING, a caution that goes for the rim of the pool, too. A ladder without chains is likely to tip with the weight of a swimmer pulling himself onto the step.

When electricity and water come together, accidents happen. You must decide how to run the electric cord to the pool (don't run the lawnmower over it), but the manufacturer should provide built-in protection against shock hazards. You can help by using a GFCI on the cir-cuit. Another safeguard is to look for a UL-approved label. This means that Underwriters Laboratories has inspected the electrical system. Some dealers may show you a UL tag on the wire, but that's not enough. Make sure the filter pump is tagged as well.

Most makers provide clear and complete installation instructions. A typical job is shown here to let you know what's involved. Twelve or 15-foot pools can be set up in a day. For larger ones you'll need a few friends and a weekend. Select a site that's as flat as possible. Dig down to create a level surface if you have to. Freshly built-up earth will compress and settle, causing part of the rim to sink with it. Enlist as much help as possible when you're fitting the steel wall into the bottom rim. It's like trying to hold five slip-

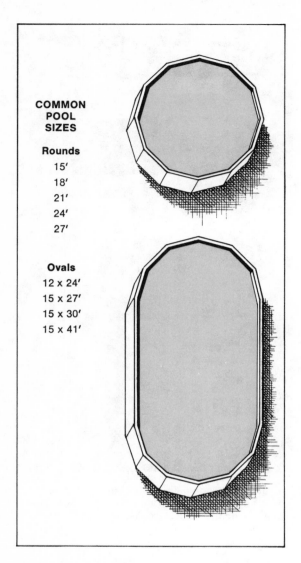

**COMMON
POOL
SIZES**

Rounds

15'
18'
21'
24'
27'

Ovals
12 x 24'
15 x 27'
15 x 30'
15 x 41'

Tools of the trade

Tamper	Packing down fresh earth
Shovel	Removing the sod
Wrench	Bolting the frame
Hammer	Driving rim stakes
Screwdriver	Assembling the uprights
Level	Checking the grade
Tape measure	Laying out the site
Rake	Clearing the dirt floor
Masking tape	Protecting the liner rim
String	Scribing the circle
Clothespins	Holding liner as you go

A new product worth noting is the solar pool cover panel, available through Wards (about $30 for a package of 4). The polyethylene bubble pads can raise the water temperature 10 to 15 degrees when floated on the surface and roll up for easy storage.

Choose the right pool and invest in quality equipment. It will pay off in years of summer fun for your family.

pery eels by the tail—as you grab one, another slides away. Try a few 1x2 temporary stakes to brace one section while you're fitting the opposite side.

smooth as silk

Before you fit the liner, go over all of the ground with a fine-tooth rake. A small pebble or sharp twig can work its way through the liner and cause a leak. Any hard edge will be extremely uncomfortable underfoot. Fit the liner carefully and be sure to provide enough fill to create a soft corner where the liner meets the bottom edge of the pool wall. Bare feet are mandatory during this operation. Get the liner as wrinkle-free as possible and leave a healthy overlap on the rim. A 16-gauge material, standard on most pools, doesn't have much of a tolerance for stretching. Twenty-gauge liners are available and will adjust to a stress without ripping.

Pool safety guidelines

Structure:
  Check local codes for fence regulations.
  Eliminate any sharp metal edges.
  Stay away from overhead wires.

Equipment:
  Use UL-approved filter and wire.
  Provide life-saving equipment.
  Maintain filter for clean water.

Use:
  Permit absolutely no diving.
  Always supervise children.
  Install a fold-up safety ladder.

Water treatment guidelines

How to figure total gallons:
  Rounds = diameter × diameter × average depth × 5.9
  Ovals = length × width × average depth × 5.9.

How to add chlorine:
  Weekly: 1 oz. per 1000 gal.
  Every other day: 1½ oz. per 5000 gal.
  Shock treatment: 10 oz. per 5000 gal.

Add a handsome low-cost fireplace

■ MOST PEOPLE NOWADAYS are warmed by fires they never see. All across the country, blue-tipped flames burn away symmetrically inside furnaces and water heaters. It's pretty hard to get romantic about that. But when you put a match to logs in a fireplace, you can curl up in

An indoor fireplace is both functional and beautiful. It can warm you on those cold winter nights and also add a romantic glow to your home

PREWAY FIREPLACES

front of it with a friend and stare into the flames for hours. It's not hard to add a good-looking fireplace to your home. In fact, you can do it in a weekend. Freestanding and built-in prefabricated units come in a wide variety of colors, shapes and sizes, with fittings you can adapt to any installation. When the energy crunch hit a few years ago, there was a stampede to get Franklin stoves, old log-burners, pot-bellied stoves—anything that would provide an extra (and inexpensive) heat source. Even now, fuel prices being what they are, an efficient fireplace is starting to be more of a necessity than a luxury. The Franklin stove on page 67 is in a 16x24-

MAJESTIC FIREPLACES

Clean, straight-line styling makes this double-wall steel hearth one of the best looking and most flexible. The Manchester-Pierce is like a modern Franklin stove with black matte finish and either top or back venting. The unit is 21x34 in. with a 16x28-in. screened opening. It sells for about $300 from Majestic Co., Huntington, IN 46750

The Large Freestander (left) is 28x42 in. Its octagonal design is available in black, red or green. A built-in damper, ash guard and stainless-steel baffles keep down surface temperature. Preway Fireplaces, Wisconsin Rapids, WI 54494, also makes built-ins such as the open-end unit shown in the photo above. Shown below is a typical prefab chimney layout

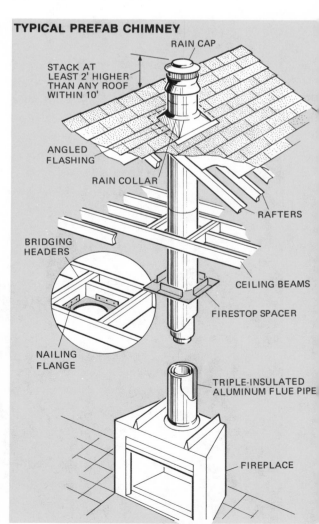

TYPICAL PREFAB CHIMNEY

RAIN CAP

STACK AT LEAST 2' HIGHER THAN ANY ROOF WITHIN 10'

ANGLED FLASHING

RAIN COLLAR

RAFTERS

BRIDGING HEADERS

CEILING BEAMS

FIRESTOP SPACER

NAILING FLANGE

TRIPLE-INSULATED ALUMINUM FLUE PIPE

FIREPLACE

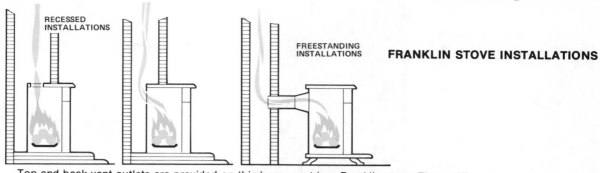

RECESSED INSTALLATIONS

FREESTANDING INSTALLATIONS

FRANKLIN STOVE INSTALLATIONS

Top and back vent outlets are provided on this heavy cast-iron Franklin stove. Three different sizes are available from Atlanta Stove Works, Box 5254, Atlanta, GA 30307. Shown above are alternatives to the installation made below

Here are some tips on building a masonry flue:
1. Assemble the stovepipes to measure the wall cut
2. A ring connector isolates the pipe from the wall
3. The thimble must fall in the center of the block
4. Provide a slab or footing for your chimney
5. Metal clips anchor every third block to the house
6. Holes help break the block to fit around the pipe

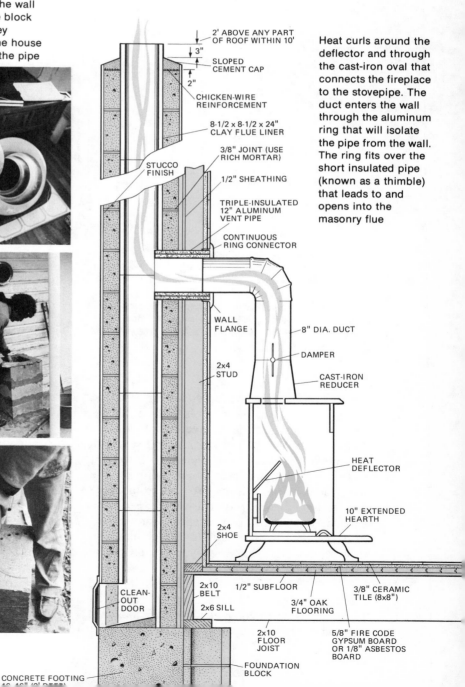

2' ABOVE ANY PART OF ROOF WITHIN 10'

3"

SLOPED CEMENT CAP

2"

CHICKEN-WIRE REINFORCEMENT

8-1/2 x 8-1/2 x 24" CLAY FLUE LINER

3/8" JOINT (USE RICH MORTAR)

1/2" SHEATHING

STUCCO FINISH

TRIPLE-INSULATED 12" ALUMINUM VENT PIPE

CONTINUOUS RING CONNECTOR

WALL FLANGE

8" DIA. DUCT

DAMPER

CAST-IRON REDUCER

2x4 STUD

HEAT DEFLECTOR

10" EXTENDED HEARTH

2x4 SHOE

CLEAN-OUT DOOR

2x10 BELT

2x6 SILL

1/2" SUBFLOOR

3/4" OAK FLOORING

3/8" CERAMIC TILE (8x8")

2x10 FLOOR JOIST

5/8" FIRE CODE GYPSUM BOARD OR 1/8" ASBESTOS BOARD

FOUNDATION BLOCK

CONCRETE FOOTING

Heat curls around the deflector and through the cast-iron oval that connects the fireplace to the stovepipe. The duct enters the wall through the aluminum ring that will isolate the pipe from the wall. The ring fits over the short insulated pipe (known as a thimble) that leads to and opens into the masonry flue

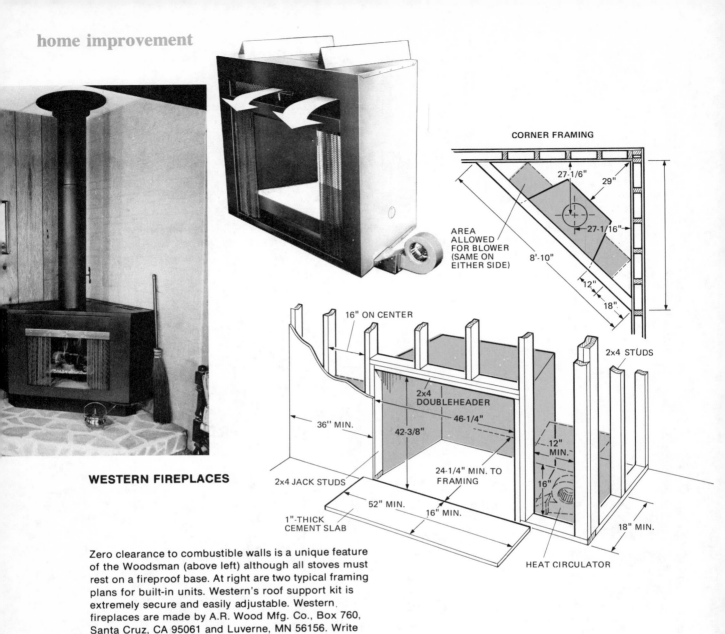

WESTERN FIREPLACES

Zero clearance to combustible walls is a unique feature of the Woodsman (above left) although all stoves must rest on a fireproof base. At right are two typical framing plans for built-in units. Western's roof support kit is extremely secure and easily adjustable. Western, fireplaces are made by A.R. Wood Mfg. Co., Box 760, Santa Cruz, CA 95061 and Luverne, MN 56156. Write them for details

ft. living room heated by forced hot air. With the stove in operation, the home's fuel-oil bill decreased about one third. Conventional masonry fireplaces are nice to look at, but can't save you that much fuel. Most of their heat goes straight up the chimney. But freestanding units act like giant radiators and throw off heat from every side, including the exposed stovepipe leading to the flue. Many built-in units capture some of this chimney heat with circulator chambers and blower fans. But whichever type you pick, you have to install it carefully.

You should build the flue so that even if it filled with flames, fire could not escape into the walls. Think of this when you pick a fireplace location. Venting directly through an outside wall is easier than running a stack up through two stories and an attic.

If you have an existing flue, most of your work is already done. But it pays to check it carefully for cracked masonry (you can point it up with cement and a trowel) and for soot deposits. A heavy cloth bag, filled with sand and tied to a rope, can be hauled up and down the flue from the roof to break loose many deposits that could ignite from a large spark. The weakest link in most flues is the point where the stovepipe passes through wall or ceiling. You must protect this area from fire and heat by using a masonry thimble or a short section of insulated aluminum pipe. One end fits over the thin stovepipe; the other opens into the flue.

Prefabricated chimneys are expensive—each section is made from triple-wall, insulated aluminum—but they're easy to install and safe. Ends of the sections are threaded and the seams covered by overlapping flanges. If your location means venting up through the center of the house, this is the way to go. Be sure your vent kit is complete, including a fire-stop spacer, angled flashing pan for the roof, storm collar and rain cap. A common accessory is a fake brick chimney cap that hides the aluminum pipe exposed above the roof.

building your own flue

A masonry flue is good for an outside wall. You'll need a few bags of concrete (it comes premixed), four or five bags of mortar mix (also premixed) for joining the block, cement flue block and clay flue liners. Most lumberyards stock these. Just build one block on top of another with about a ⅜-in.-thick layer of mortar mix in between. Flue liners fit inside the block and are also joined with mortar. Make sure the seams of the stacks are staggered and check each block with a level. String a plumb line from ground to roof; use it to lay the block neatly and evenly.

In all prefab units your first five or six fires should be small. It's hard to resist the temptation to fire them to the limit, but you should give the metal a little time to temper. Don't be surprised if you get some metallic odors at first. They will stop as your fireplace is broken in. Then you'll be ready for a winter of warm, cozy evenings, around the new heart of your home, the fireplace.

Classic cast-iron designs include this ornate Atlantic wood-burning cooker and the incredibly efficient pot-bellied stove. This company makes its stoves from original manufacturing patterns. The cook stove at the left below is 24x38 in., has four 8-in.-diameter cooktop covers, an array of dampers and even a removable, copper hot-water reservoir. The pot-bellies range from 12 to 20-in. diameters, with the largest being 51 in. high and weighing 426 lbs. From the Portland Stove Foundry Co., 57 Kennebec St., Portland, ME 04104. Stoves built on authentic designs serve two functions. They not only give off a good deal of heat to reduce your heating bills, but they fit in well with antique furniture

PORTLAND STOVES

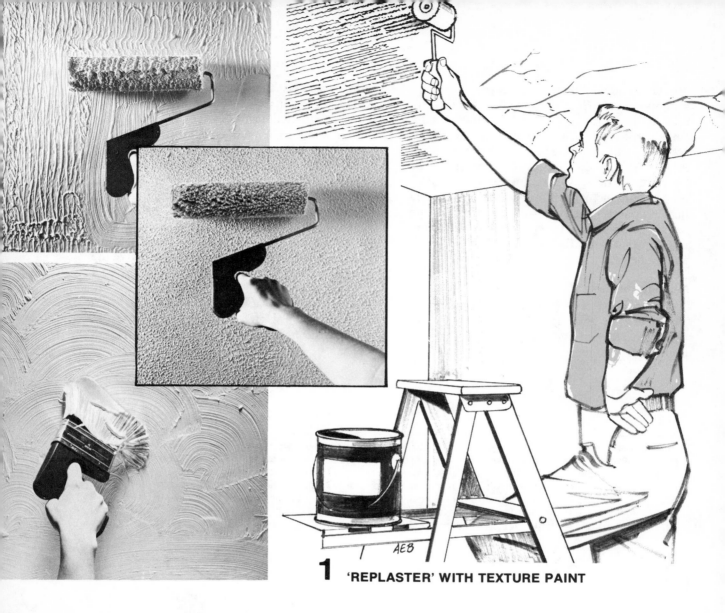

1 'REPLASTER' WITH TEXTURE PAINT

Three ways to handle problem ceilings

BY WAYNE C. LECKEY

■ IF YOUR HOME is old (40 years or more) and has plastered walls and ceilings, consider yourself lucky if the plaster hasn't cracked during the years due to structural settling. Most homes don't fare so well. Cracked ceilings are common in older homes and cause homeowners a continual headache.

Of the three ways to tackle a cracked ceiling, painting with texture paint requires the least work and is the least expensive. You put it on directly from the can with brush or roller, then while it's still wet you give it a stucco-like tex-

ture by pouncing, stippling or swirling with a stiff-bristle brush, sponge or crumpled paper to achieve the pattern you prefer. The resulting sculptured finish makes an attractive ceiling as you see above, and it does cover cracks. Its one drawback is that you're stuck with it—its not easy to remove should you want to go back to a smooth untextured surface. Some brands I hear can be steamed off like wallpaper although I haven't tried it.

Basically, all texture paints are thick, heavy-bodied coatings which come in a choice of finishes: smooth texture, stucco texture and sand finish. If it's a sand finish you like, you'd pick sand-finish paint, apply it with brush or roller and leave the effect without touching it further. If you want a more sculptured look, you'd use stucco finish, apply it thick and give it an additional texture by twirling the brush or by sweeping the roller in overlapping semicircles. The paint is applied a few square feet at a time, then worked over to gain the effect you want.

As with any paint job, there's surface preparation to be done. All scaling paint must be scraped off. Holes where the plaster is missing must be filled level with spackling compound. It's best to pull off wallpaper.

I've always opened windows as recommended for proper ventilation and drying. Coverage per gallon varies from 60 to 120 sq. ft. depending on the thickness of the texture pattern. Texture paint from Arvon Products (which I've used) runs about $8.00 a gallon. It can be tinted if you don't want flat white. You can buy special deep-contour rollers 4 in. wide which are made to dip into a gallon can, also brushes with a pistol-grip handle which I've found easy on the wrist in working overhead. Sometimes a small trowel is used for smoothing the high spots in the textured surface as the wetness disappears.

2   COVER WITH PLASTERBOARD

■ WHEN A PLASTERED ceiling is too far gone and so badly cracked you could not hope to take care of it with texture paint, you have two options—cover it with sheets of plasterboard or hide the cracks with ceiling tile. If you prefer plasterboard over tile and the smooth paintable surface it provides, it will take some muscle.

Fine someone to assist with the heavy 4x8 sheets of gypsum board and hike them up against the ceiling. Support tees make this part of the job less difficult than you might think, and fortunately you'll only have to struggle with a minimum of full sheets since cross joints must be staggered. You'll be working with less than full sheets once the big ones are up.

Pick a starting corner where the ceiling joists run crosswise to the sheet, and position the sheet so its end falls midway on a joist to provide nailing for the abutting sheet. Your support tees should be about 1 in. longer than the floor-to-ceiling height so they will force the plasterboard tight against the ceiling when wedged under it.

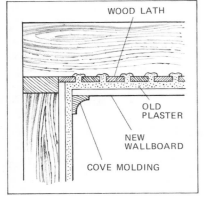

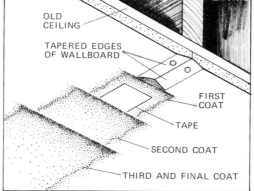

Support tees (above) are used to raise and wedge plasterboard against ceiling for nailing. Plank across sawhorses lets you reach it. Cutaway (far left) shows how the new wallboard fits over the old plaster. Careful jointwork (near left) will give smooth job.

WOOD LATH
OLD PLASTER
NEW WALLBOARD
COVE MOLDING

OLD CEILING
TAPERED EDGES OF WALLBOARD
FIRST COAT
TAPE
SECOND COAT
THIRD AND FINAL COAT

Drive nails in rows 7 in. apart, then strike each nail one more time to "dimple" (set) the head, taking care not to break the face paper. Continue filling in and nailing the smaller pieces until the whole ceiling is covered wall to wall.

The hard part is done although taping and filling the joints and dimpled nailheads with joint compound can be a tedious job. Use premixed joint compound and, with a 4-in.-wide joint-finishing knife, apply compound in the valley created by the two adjoining tapered edges. Next take your joint tape, center it firmly in the wet bedding compound with a knife at a 45° angle. The pressure should squeeze out some of the compound, but enough must remain for a good firm bond.

When it's thoroughly dry (at least 24 hours), apply a fill coat extending a few inches beyond the edge of the tape and feather the edges of the compound. When the first finishing coat is thoroughly dry, use a 10-in. joint-finishing knife and apply a second coat and feather the edges about 1½ in. beyond the first coat. When this coat is dry, sand lightly, wipe off the dust and apply the third and final coat. The feathered width of the joint should now be 12 to 14 in.

Use basically the same steps with the butted end joints. But since there is no valley to fill, feather the compound well out on each side so there is no ridge buildup to cast a shadow. No tape is used in covering nailheads—just the same three-coat treatment. The thing to avoid with nailheads is bowing the knife with excess pressure as this tends to scoop compound from the dimpled area.

Stock ceiling cove molding is used to conceal the joint around the perimeter. The ceiling is now ready for paint.

3 TILE IT WITH A SECOND CEILING

■ CEILING TILE is a dependable problem solver—even if the problem is more than a cracked ceiling. It can be a ceiling that's simply too high or has exposed pipes, ductwork or other low-hanging obstructions.

There are four ways to treat a cracked ceiling with tile: 1. You can cement it directly to the old ceiling. 2. You can staple it to wood furring strips nailed to the ceiling. 3. You can support it by a metal channel system screwed to the ceiling. 4. You can suspend it below the old ceiling by a hanging concealed grid.

tile can go directly onto plaster

When the existing ceiling is sound and level but has many hairline cracks, tile can be cemented directly to the old plaster after removing any flaking paint or loose wallpaper.

When a ceiling is not level or has humps, you must use furring, wood or metal, to make it so. There are self-leveling metal furring channels that you attach directly to the existing ceiling and into which cross tees lock to hold 12x12 or 12x48-in. tile. Being rigid, the channels can't bend to assume the unevenness of a ceiling. Wood furring will bend, so the strips must be shimmed where needed with shingle points to make them level in both directions.

When your problem ceiling involves more than cracks, a suspended-ceiling system such as Armstrong Cork's Integrid is best. Here you hang metal supporting runners by wires which you attach to the ceiling with screw eyes. Then you install tile and cross tees to the main runners. A unique tongue-into-flange edge has a slotted kerf that receives the cross tee and conceals it.

When cementing tile directly to the ceiling, you have to work outward in four directions from centerlines that divide the area in four quarters and place the tile edges along the lines. To find the center of the ceiling, stretch lines diagonally from the four corners and make a mark where they cross. By starting from centerlines, border tiles at the ends and sides of the ceiling will be the same width, not narrow ones along one side.

Another thing to remember when applying wood or metal furring to a ceiling: The furring must be placed crosswise to the ceiling joists so you can nail or screw it to solid structural members.

Use of furring, metal or wood, as illustrated, is one of three ways to hide a cracked ceiling with tile. When ceiling has hairline cracks but is sound, tile can be glued directly to it with dabs of brush-on cement. When the ceiling is in bad repair, a suspended ceiling in which the tile is supported by a grid system may be the best answer

1. When you install suspended ceiling, chalk new ceiling height around the perimeter of the room. Next, nail a metal molding to the studs along the line

2. Turn the screw eyes in rows into your ceiling joists. Then insert hanger wires through the eyes and attach firmly by twisting them around themselves

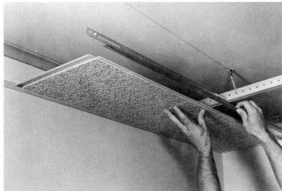

3. Main runner sections are supported by wires threaded through holes and then twisted. Suspend the runners perpendicular to the joists above them

4. First 1x4-ft. tile (or four 12x12-in. tiles) rest on wall molding. The cross tee snaps on the runner and slides into the slotted edge of tile

Built-in versatility

The Homosote panel can be hung with eye
hooks on the side wall (above) or over the
storage area (right). One side is a decorative
dart target the other side a movie screen.
Note the foldaway shop benches

Double use
for your
garage

BY RAY GILL

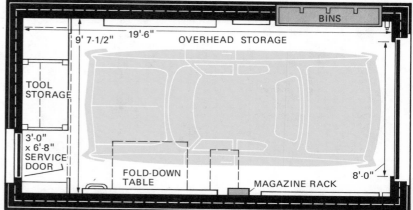

9' 7-1/2"   19'-6"   OVERHEAD STORAGE

BINS

TOOL
STORAGE

3'-0"
x 6'-8"
SERVICE
DOOR

FOLD-DOWN
TABLE

MAGAZINE RACK

8'-0"

PLAN VIEW

■ EVEN THE SMALLEST one-car garage can
add an unbelievable amount of living and working space to your home. Some people may shy
away from a project such as this from fear of
what it might cost, but this can be done on a
surprisingly low budget without moving walls or
building extensions. It all takes some time in
careful planning and organization. The trick is to
build in well-organized and flexible units that can
be of service when you need them, and be out of
the way when you don't. That way you can still
get the car in. The garage I worked with is fairly

typical. It is attached, with a utility room, to a
small Cape Cod-style house and has measurements of 9 ft. 7½ in. x 19½ ft. Though this
may not seem like much to work in, I developed
this area into three separate uses:
• a versatile shop,
• a gardening center and
• a flexible storage facility.
  As you can see in the picture, I am still able to
get the car in.
  Since no neglected garage is ever in very good
shape, I found it necessary to start by repairing

76

Gardening center

The trestle table is demountable. The 4x8 plywood top is stored in "dead" space above the garage door tracks, and sawhorse brackets are removable. Space-saving shelves were cut into the wall. Bins underneath will hold bags of fertilizer and grass seed. A section of the rear wall has dowel pegs to hold tools and the grass bag for the mower

Storage area

Storage units are 25 in. deep, a dimension I got by pulling the car into the garage and measuring the room I needed for passage. This wall holds gardening equipment, a radial-arm saw (on casters), power tools and every kind of leftover from closets in the house

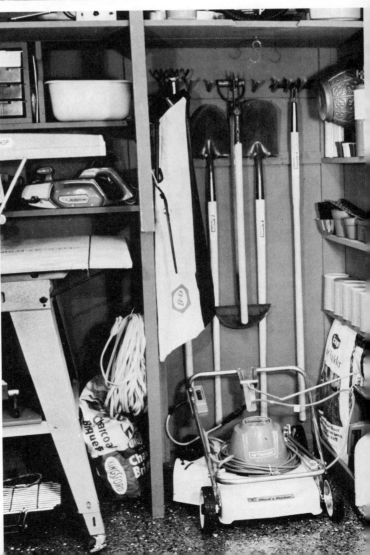

Workshop wall

Activity here is centered around two worktables and a 4x8 pegboard sheet for tool storage. We mounted the ¼-in. board on heavy-duty spacers with screws into each stud. The main workbench is secured with four 3½-in. butt hinges to a 2x4 ledger. The legs are also on hinges. A smaller surface to the left is built for heavy-duty use with a 2x6 ledger and 4x6-in. T-hinges

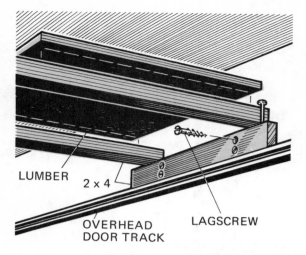

OVERHEAD RACK

LUMBER 2 x 4 OVERHEAD DOOR TRACK LAGSCREW

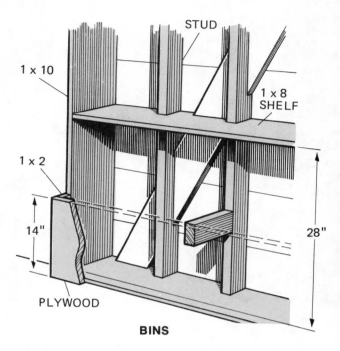

STUD
1 x 10
1 x 8 SHELF
1 x 2
14"
28"
PLYWOOD

BINS

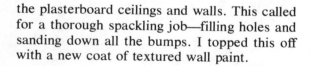

A simple rack placed over the garage door uses "dead" space effectively for storing large and long objects

the plasterboard ceilings and walls. This called for a thorough spackling job—filling holes and sanding down all the bumps. I topped this off with a new coat of textured wall paint.

a liquid vinyl floor

The floor needed quite a bit of work, as will most garage floors before a project like this can begin. After a good cleaning I flash-patched the bad spots and then laid down a liquid vinyl floor. To do this I spread a thick water-based epoxy, sprinkled on multi-colored vinyl chips and finished with three coats of clear sealer. This turned out to be the best solution to the problem for three reasons: the installation was fairly easy, I was surprised at how low the maintenance is and it proved to be extremely durable.

Shelves are recessed into wall studs for neat and efficient storage inside plastic containers

MAGAZINE RACK

1 x 2

RED PLEXIGLAS
IN 1/4" GROOVES

A magazine rack is handy and adds
a touch of color to the room. It is
relatively shallow and takes little
space

After refinishing all interior surfaces the garage took on an improved appearance. Then I
started "building in" the variety of uses wanted.
First I built the rack above the garage-door
tracks to begin using some "dead" space more
effectively. A 2x4 lagscrewed to the wall on each
side, with two 2x4s on edge bridging the span can
support any number of objects such as plywood
tabletops, sawhorse legs, heavy metal pipe
clamps, loose lumber and moldings. Almost
every room has some "dead" space, but with a
little ingenuity you can design a simple structure
like this to take advantage of all available space.

more storage

In my garage (and most others) the main storage unit for outsized items will have to be on the
back wall. But I wanted to avoid as much clutter
as possible so that my family wouldn't trip trying
to get around it to the car. A room like this, that
can be used in so many ways, is bound to collect
the remnants of all kinds of projects. So I needed
another storage area that could hold odds and
ends, such as art supplies, ball and bat, and paint
cans. Following the same idea of reclaiming un-
used space. I built in a storage unit by recessing
the shelves into the wall. After removing the
plasterboard, I framed the opening with 1x10s.
By cutting 1x8 boards to fit around the studs, I
was able to gain 4½ in. of shelf space. Use of
colorful plastic containers to organize the
shelves gave a uniform and attractive appearance. Labeling each bin made it easy to identify
stored items.

useful and colorful

As functional as this room is, it is also attractive and pleasant. One of the simplest built-in
units was the magazine rack. The 1x2 frame was
routed to accept the edges of the red plexiglass
sheets, then toenailed to the studs and painted to
match the wall. It didn't get in the way like a
bookshelf and was very useful in storing instruction books and repair manuals.

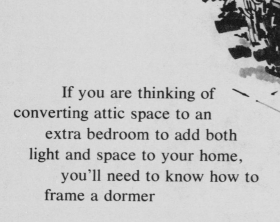

If you are thinking of converting attic space to an extra bedroom to add both light and space to your home, you'll need to know how to frame a dormer

How to add a dormer

■ WHEN A FAMILY starts outgrowing its house, moving to a larger one is not always the smart thing to do, especially if you have attic space that could be converted into the extra room you need.

Dormers play an important part in converting attic space into a bedroom or two. They provide not only added headroom that's often required but light and air as well. Dormers can also do a lot to perk up an uninteresting roof line.

Whether you can take on the job of framing a dormer yourself depends a lot on how handy you

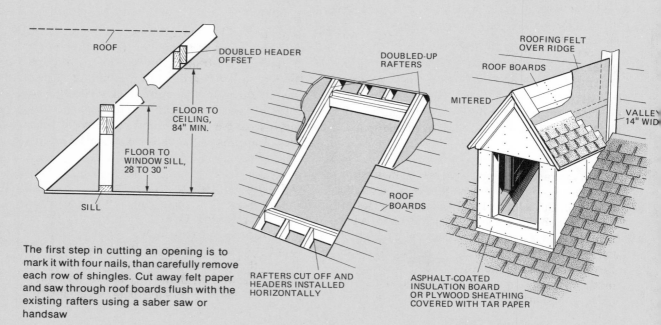

ROOF

DOUBLED HEADER OFFSET

FLOOR TO CEILING, 84" MIN.

FLOOR TO WINDOW SILL, 28 TO 30"

SILL

The first step in cutting an opening is to mark it with four nails, than carefully remove each row of shingles. Cut away felt paper and saw through roof boards flush with the existing rafters using a saber saw or handsaw

DOUBLED-UP RAFTERS

ROOF BOARDS

RAFTERS CUT OFF AND HEADERS INSTALLED HORIZONTALLY

ROOFING FELT OVER RIDGE

ROOF BOARDS

MITERED

VALLEY 14" WIDE

ASPHALT-COATED INSULATION BOARD OR PLYWOOD SHEATHING COVERED WITH TAR PAPER

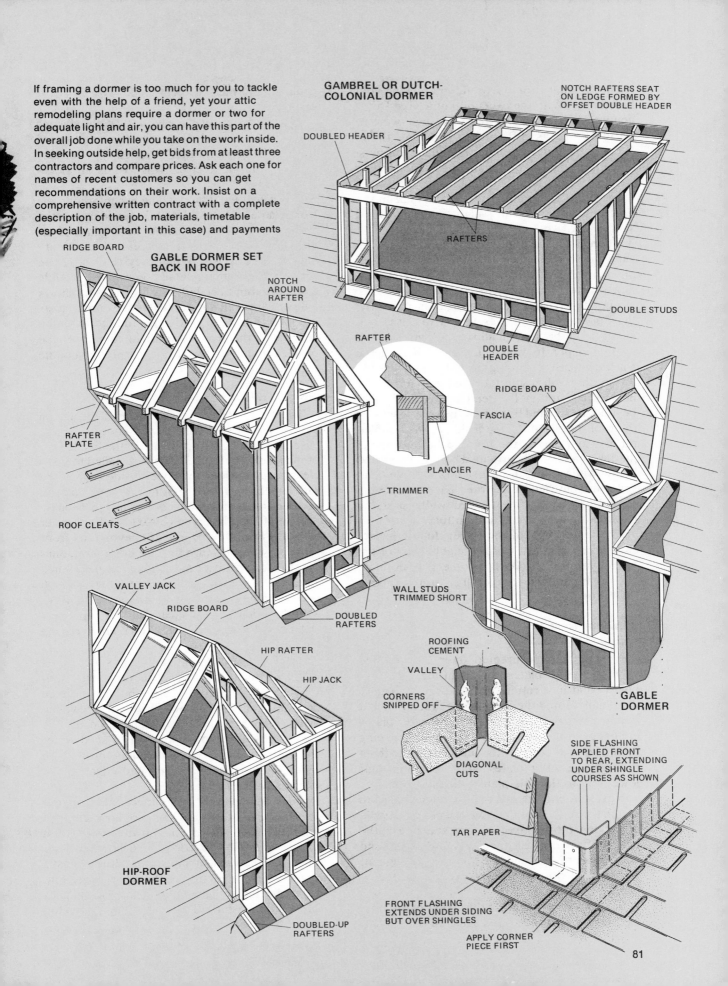

If framing a dormer is too much for you to tackle even with the help of a friend, yet your attic remodeling plans require a dormer or two for adequate light and air, you can have this part of the overall job done while you take on the work inside. In seeking outside help, get bids from at least three contractors and compare prices. Ask each one for names of recent customers so you can get recommendations on their work. Insist on a comprehensive written contract with a complete description of the job, materials, timetable (especially important in this case) and payments

GAMBREL OR DUTCH-COLONIAL DORMER

NOTCH RAFTERS SEAT ON LEDGE FORMED BY OFFSET DOUBLE HEADER

DOUBLED HEADER

RAFTERS

DOUBLE STUDS

GABLE DORMER SET BACK IN ROOF

NOTCH AROUND RAFTER

RAFTER

DOUBLE HEADER

RIDGE BOARD

RIDGE BOARD

FASCIA

PLANCIER

TRIMMER

RAFTER PLATE

ROOF CLEATS

VALLEY JACK

RIDGE BOARD

DOUBLED RAFTERS

WALL STUDS TRIMMED SHORT

GABLE DORMER

HIP RAFTER

HIP JACK

ROOFING CEMENT

VALLEY

CORNERS SNIPPED OFF

DIAGONAL CUTS

SIDE FLASHING APPLIED FRONT TO REAR, EXTENDING UNDER SHINGLE COURSES AS SHOWN

TAR PAPER

HIP-ROOF DORMER

DOUBLED-UP RAFTERS

FRONT FLASHING EXTENDS UNDER SIDING BUT OVER SHINGLES

APPLY CORNER PIECE FIRST

81

are with hammer and saw and in knowing your limitations. With the exception of a large Dutch colonial dormer, the framing of a single-window dormer isn't as difficult as you may think. Weather is a primary concern. Since you must cut an opening in the roof, you'll need clear weather for at least a couple of days. But be prepared for rain with a tarp you can tuck underneath the shingles and weight it down with a sandbag or two.

There are four basic types of dormers, as shown on page 81. Select the one that best complements the style of your house. Most important is to have it conform to local building codes.

First lay out the dormer location carefully, then pry up the shingles within the area and about a foot beyond on all sides. Trim back the roofing paper to within a few inches of the shingle line. Before doing any cutting, double the rafters that will frame the opening, cutting the new rafters so they'll extend at least 3 or 4 feet beyond the top and bottom of the hole Then saw the roof boards along the inside of the doubled rafters, and across the top and bottom of the marked opening. The trimmed boards above and below will support the cut rafters until you can spike double headers. Note that the opening should extend one roof-board width past the marked-out area at top and bottom.

The lower edge of the upper double header should be located at ceiling height. The bottom header members have their top edges set flush, at a height that will put the sill 28 to 30 in. above the floor.

frame the front first

Whenever possible, the side walls of the dormer should be erected over the doubled rafter—on sole plates nailed through the roof boards and into rafters below, using 20-penny (20d) nails. Build the front frame first and nail it in place, bracing it plumb until the rafter plates are in position. Then add the side studs, spacing them 16 in. o.c., driving 16d nails down into them through the rafter plates, and toenailing their lower end to the sole plate with 10d nails.

Next, cut out one end of a 1x6 ridge board to match the roof slope, leaving it overlong; level it by tacking it to a temporary prop standing on the header above the sash opening. Now, lay out and cut a master rafter and use this as a cutting pattern for all dormer rafters except the valley jacks.

Since spans are short in dormer construction, light framing stock is often selected. It isn't un-

usual for dormers to be framed with 2x4s (or even 2x3s).

Nail the rafters in place with 10d nails, starting from the outer end; then trim the ridge board flush with the outer rafters. A shed-type dormer, such as the gambrel shown, avoids all ridge-board fitting.

The rough window opening is centered in the front frame and should be 4¼ in. wider than the sash unit you select. Whether the trimmer studs are single or double depends on their proximity to the corner posts. When they're close, as in three of the framing details on page 81, double trimmers aren't needed. The fourth detail shows a flush-with-wall dormer where the corner posts are merely nailed to existing studs to extend a section of the wall upward; in this case, the rough framing of the window calls for double trimmers.

how a cornice turns corners

The front cornice construction depends on which type of side cornice you choose. In any case, the roof boards run only to the inside face of the front rafter, where they are nailed to a 2x2 cleat fastened along the upper inside edge of the rafter itself, to create the front overhang. In plain cornice construction, this overhang is braced by trim, but for the box type you extend the plancier (or soffit board) its own width beyond the front rafter so you can "turn the corner" with it, nailing the front plancier to a second cleat fastened along the lower front edge of the rafter. Though sketches show the roof boards beveled flush with the side fascia or sheathing, they may project an inch or so if you prefer an overhang effect.

Before shingling, lay a 14-in. sheet-metal valley where dormer and house roof meet, bending it until it lies flat against both roofs (see sketches, page 80.) Snap chalk lines up the valley to indicate where shingles must be trimmed. The top corners are also snipped off to shed water toward the valley. To avoid nailing through the valley, anchor the diagonally cut edges of the shingles with cement.

Where the dormer walls meet the roof, use step flashing, starting with a corner piece and working back each side, as shown in the bottom sketch, page 81. The side pieces should be 6 in. long, with the vertical flange extending at least 3 in. up under the siding and the other flange 4 in. out under the shingles. Don't nail the shingles through the flashing. The front strip rides on top of the shingles.

Screen house: Pilings are used to support this structure in a unique setting by the water. The design of a screen house beats mosquitoes in back yards, too

Garden gazebo: This back-yard house is so versatile that it can be elegant for entertaining, informal or used strictly by the gardener with the green thumb

Canopy gazebo: This simple canopy has lines which are perfectly elegant and simple. The construction blends in beautifully on a wooded site

Three gracious garden houses

BY MIKE MCCLINTOCK

These versatile buildings will make summer more fun around your house and may help you recall the "good old days" when families used to enjoy relaxing on a large porch

■ MANY HOUSES used to be built with a huge porch in front or off the side. On warm summer evenings you'd be likely to find a family sitting out there rather than inside a hot, stuffy house. Unfortunately, this is a thing of the past. There's another feature of the American homestead that's disappearing and that's the barn. As the car replaced the horse, garages and carports were built to shelter the new vehicles. Without a large porch or a barn, the modern American home has lost its outdoor living and working space. One of these garden houses, or a combination of some of their features could be the answer.

keep off the grass

All three have one thing in common—a wood floor. This gets you up off the ground, provides a dance floor, and means that you don't have to balance a drink between two dandelions. But in each case, the floor has been taken a crucial step further. The most common pitfall of outdoor structures is that they frequently look as if they were dropped out of a plane onto your back yard. They just don't look as though they belong there. All these gazebos have extended flooring, as deck platforms, a balcony, or a ramp, past the structural lines of the building. This softens the look of the structure and makes it more a part of the ground it's on.

SCREEN HOUSE

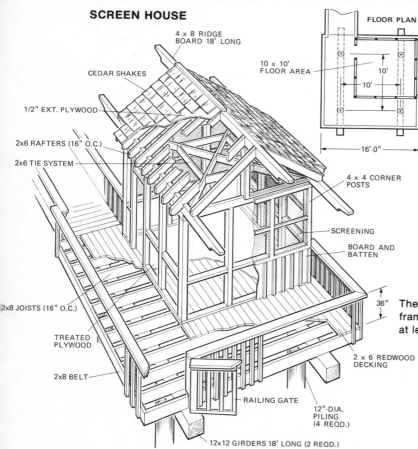

4 x 8 RIDGE BOARD 18' LONG

CEDAR SHAKES

1/2" EXT. PLYWOOD

2x6 RAFTERS (16" O.C.)

2x6 TIE SYSTEM

2x8 JOISTS (16" O.C.)

TREATED PLYWOOD

2x8 BELT

RAILING GATE

12x12 GIRDERS 18' LONG (2 REQD.)

12"-DIA. PILING (4 REQD.)

2 x 6 REDWOOD DECKING

BOARD AND BATTEN

SCREENING

4 x 4 CORNER POSTS

36"

FLOOR PLAN

10 x 10' FLOOR AREA

10'

10'

16'-0"

16'-0"

GARDEN GAZEBO

Working garden center is at the rear of the garden gazebo. Lattice doors on rubber wheels slide away to reveal a solid potting counter and plenty of storage space

The 10x10-ft. screen house is offset on the 16x16-ft. piling frame, thus creating pleasant deck space. The drawing at left gives good bird's-eye view of construction

You can even plant your garden around the gazebo. The 3x10-ft. deck units can be built to use as ramps or a walkway which leads through the garden

The trellis roof is made up of 2x2s in frames. This puts filtered light on the deck of the gazebo or you can use plywood for shade

turn the page

One section of deck was not completed so the lawnmower could be wheeled into the "closet." More storage area for pots is located under the bench

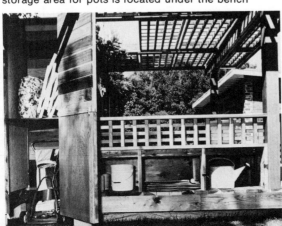

How about piling up some pillows and settling back on one of the benches for a sunbath? This corner deck is great to use for flowering plants too

CANOPY GAZEBO

Once you've sunk the four poles in the ground, construction can move quickly. Double girders, supported through the poles, are used to support conventional 2x8 joists. Single upper carriers support the roof. Construction techniques are simple but yield a strong and sturdy structure

Aside from the design considerations, another tool that will make a good-looking site is landscaping. This is most obvious in the location of the canopy gazebo. The roof line, which might have looked quite severe if it were out in an open area, is successfully nestled in a stand of trees. The simplicity of the construction, using treated poles, is totally harmonious with the surroundings. On a smaller scale, the lines of the deck on the garden gazebo can be muted with shrubs or planter boxes.

All the deck platforms outside the 4x4 posts on the garden gazebo are made up from 2x8 structural-grade redwood. The interior of each box is framed 16 inches on center with short lengths, and 2x4s are face-nailed to form the deck. The dimensions are all modular (4x8, 3x12

and so forth) so there is absolutely no material waste. These platforms are so dimensionally stable that they don't need footings. They can rest securely on level ground and you can arrange them in any way you prefer. A few well-placed toenails will hold one in place as a bridge that rests on two other decks to create different levels.

The roof of the garden gazebo is designed for a dry climate; 2x4-ft. panels are made up using 2x2s to form a lattice. This will cut the direct sun but still keep the light, airy feeling you want outside. Depending on the climate where you live, part of the roof could be solid. The lattice panels fit into the roof framing system and can be removed for a piece of plywood if you want more protection. Although the plans don't include wir-

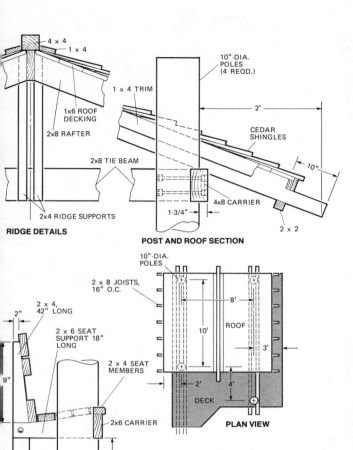

RIDGE DETAILS

4 x 4
1 x 4
1 x 6 ROOF DECKING
2x8 RAFTER
2x8 TIE BEAM
2x4 RIDGE SUPPORTS

POST AND ROOF SECTION

10"-DIA. POLES (4 REQD.)
1 x 4 TRIM
2'
CEDAR SHINGLES
10"
4x8 CARRIER
1-3/4"
2 x 2

POST AND SEAT SECTION

10"-DIA. POLES
2 x 8 JOISTS, 16" O.C.
8'
10'
ROOF
3'
2'
4'
DECK
PLAN VIEW

2 x 4, 42" LONG
2"
2 x 6 SEAT SUPPORT 18" LONG
2 x 4 SEAT MEMBERS
9"
2x6 CARRIER
10"

POST AND FLOOR SECTION

2 x 6 DECKING
2 x 8 FLOOR JOISTS
2x8 BELT
4 x 8 GIRDERS
12" BOLTS
1-3/4"

so you can easily bring out food and drink. It can't be far away from the garden or you'll spend too much time going back and forth with a wheelbarrow. It makes sense to try for a site in between. Check these guidelines.

sighting-in on a site

■ **Don't sink a pole** or pier over any underground piping or septic tank.
■ **Don't build in a natural grade depression** that collects ground water.
■ **Don't build too close** to your property line. Check local codes.
■ **Do look for a natural rise.** To get good drainage and minimum settling.
■ **Do plan ahead for access,** walkways, ramps and any electric lines.
■ **Do consult local building codes.** Make sure your site is legal.

good sense and good cents

If possible, try to keep construction time to a minimum. A smart move is to cover the surrounding lawn area with polyethylene for the few days needed, or build yourself a simple gangway into the construction area. On most jobs, the surrounding area takes such a beating that it needs major "renovating" after the building is done. The more foliage you can preserve during the job, the more natural the garden house will look on its site. Keeping the area reasonably clean can avoid reseeding or buying new sod.

keep a long-range point of view

■ **Don't** leave materials stacked on the lawn or you won't have one when you're done.
■ **Don't cut** through major roots of adjacent trees. Try a few test holes.
■ **Don't underbuild** the frame or leave it unsealed. It's outside all year round.
■ **Do protect trees and foliage** while building. They will be intact when you're done.
■ **Do use** preservative-treated timbers for all framing in contact with the ground.
■ **Do install** ground fault indicator fused circuits. It's national code for exteriors.

Don't be what I call a fair-weather carpenter. Make those toenails count. Use galvanized nails to avoid rust streaks on the wood. Try 10d nails on face-nailed decking instead of 8s. The extra bite will help minimize warping and cupping. In short, build your garden house to withstand the worst storm in 20 years. In the end, you'll save on maintenance and repairs and be able to see the results of your labors on a good-looking job.

ing diagrams, I urge you to run a code-approved line from your house out to the shelter. A few simple boxes with floodlights will make it look like a dream house at night and let the party keep going well after dark. I'd also install at least one duplex receptacle (grounded) for a radio, TV, warming tray or coffeemaker.

select your location

To get the most use from your garden house, it has to be located close enough to the main house

Remodel your bath for easy care

A LOT OF BATHROOMS are designed to look nice, but few are built for easy maintenance. In our remodeling project shown here, easy care is built into the design. It was obvious that the shiny new installation would look great in the beginning, but we wanted it to stay that way over the years with minimum cleaning. Here's how we went about eliminating those

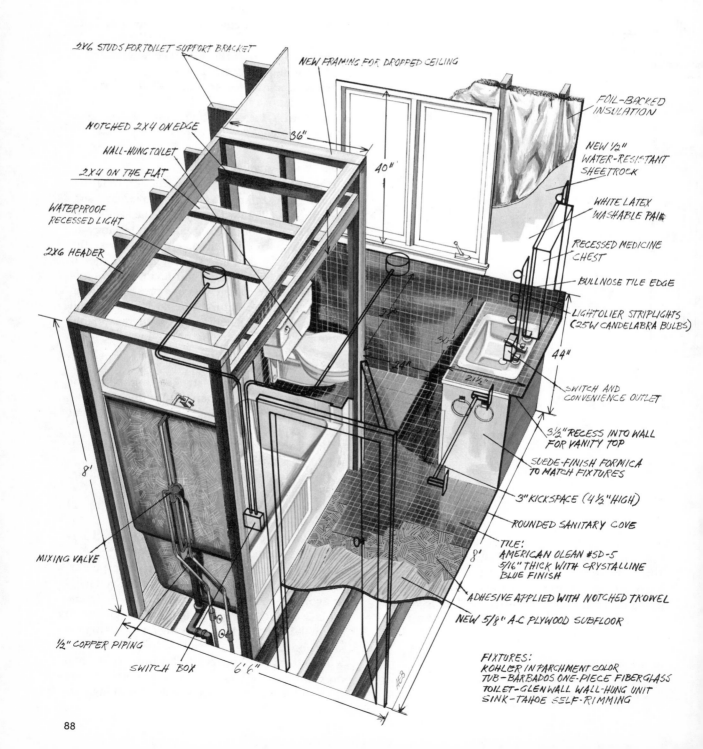

2X6 STUDS FOR TOILET SUPPORT BRACKET

NEW FRAMING FOR DROPPED CEILING

FOIL-BACKED INSULATION

NOTCHED 2X4 ON EDGE

36"

40"

NEW 1/2" WATER-RESISTANT SHEETROCK

WALL-HUNG TOILET

2X4 ON THE FLAT

WHITE LATEX WASHABLE PAINT

WATERPROOF RECESSED LIGHT

RECESSED MEDICINE CHEST

2X6 HEADER

BULLNOSE TILE EDGE

LIGHTOLIER STRIPLIGHTS (25W CANDELABRA BULBS)

44"

SWITCH AND CONVENIENCE OUTLET

21½"

3½" RECESS INTO WALL FOR VANITY TOP

SUEDE-FINISH FORMICA TO MATCH FIXTURES

8'

3" KICKSPACE (4½" HIGH)

ROUNDED SANITARY COVE

MIXING VALVE

8'

TILE: AMERICAN OLEAN #SD-5 5/16" THICK WITH CRYSTALLINE BLUE FINISH

ADHESIVE APPLIED WITH NOTCHED TROWEL

½" COPPER PIPING

NEW 5/8" A-C PLYWOOD SUBFLOOR

SWITCH BOX

6' 6"

FIXTURES:
KOHLER IN PARCHMENT COLOR
TUB-BARBADOS ONE-PIECE FIBERGLASS
TOILET-GLENWALL WALL-HUNG UNIT
SINK-TAHOE SELF-RIMMING

nooks and crannies that can trap dampness, germs and dirt that make a bathroom look old before its time.

The first job was a real pleasure—getting rid of the old fixtures, cracked vinyl tile and wallpaper.

Underneath this old skin were mildew, stains and soft spots from years of typical bathroom spills and splashes—not a good foundation for

Easy-cleaning tiles on the vanity are recessed in the wall. In a small bathroom you need all the floor space you can get. The white, dry-cure grout is sealed with liquid silicone. Combined with a crystalline finish on tiles, it forms a waterproof barrier

The one-piece tub and shower enclosure is made of fiberglass by Kohler. The smooth surface has many advantages; no hard corners, no seams or joints to crack, and the whole installation is a one-step operation. The off-white color is parchment

89

**CARPENTRY AND AN
EASY-CLEANING TUB**

A new ⅝-in. A-C exterior-grade plywood
subfloor provides a durable and solid
surface for the ceramic tile

The wall-hung toilet is supported by a steel
hanger that must be bolted through two
new 2x6 studs

A new dropped ceiling joins the partition
separating the tub and the toilet. The
one-piece unit fits inside

Moisture-resistant Sheetrock ½-in. thick is
a durable wall surface that's ideal for
ceramic-tile applications

the new fixtures and tile. So we went farther.
Old, moisture-ridden wallboard was easy to pull
off the studs and the water-logged plywood subfloor came up in pieces. We replaced insulation
batts that had settled in the outside wall with new
3½-in. foil-backed fiberglass insulation.

With the walls totally open, it was a simple
matter to run a new BX cable for the built-in light
over the new tub enclosure. Good access also
made it possible to solder a copper cap onto the
toilet waste drain below the floor and extend the
line to meet the in-the-wall drain of the new
wall-hung toilet. (This is a good time to snake
through your drains to avoid septic blockages
later.)

After we coated beams and sills with Woodlife
(a moisture-resistant sealer), we laid ⅝-in. A-C
exterior-grade plywood down to make a new

subfloor. Rough carpentry included adding two
2x6 studs at the corner of the room to give extra
support for the steel hanger that carries the
weight of the wall-hung toilet. We measured the
rough opening for the new tub and shower enclosure and framed a 3-ft.-wide 2x4 partition to
separate tub from toilet. Using 2x4s on the flat,
we framed a dropped ceiling over the enclosure.

For the new skin for the bath we re-covered all
walls with ½-in. moisture-resistant Sheetrock.
You can identify this special board at the lumberyard by its light green color. Its surface is
ideal for ceramic-tile installations. A three-coat
taping job completed the new surfaces.

We wanted a one-piece, fiberglass tub and
shower unit. The only problem was how to get it
into the room. The existing door was 32 in. wide;
the tub, 34 in. wide. Although it meant removing

Kohler's showerhead has a water-saving lever to cut down the flow. A rag will protect the finish from the wrench

The built-in "highhat" fixture has a rubber washer between glass bowl and the bulb to lock out moisture

Install the tub drain first. You can work the copper supply pipes around it to the single mixing valve (inset)

Four optional cover plates are provided for each faucet. The drain flange was sealed with silicone.

the door and jamb, getting the maintenance-free unit into the bathroom was definitely worthwhile. There are no hard corners on the smooth, glossy-surfaced enclosure; no seams to caulk, no tiles to fall off the walls and no nooks and crannies to collect dirt.

Our unit is made by Kohler in a new off-white color called parchment. We opted for this more subdued tone and added color with the tile, shower curtain and towels. It's easy to change if you tire of the color, but fixtures are there to stay.

The only other fixture to install was the vanity. We saved space here by recessing the vanity in the stud wall 3½ in. Front and side were covered with a suede-finish Formica colored like the fixtures. We used the paper template supplied to make the vanity-top cutout.

We chose a crystalline-finish, deep blue tile made by American Olean. Although you can find less expensive imported tiles, in general they are not as uniform in finish and size as American-made tiles. Even seams from one end of the bath to the other are essential for appearance.

First we established the tile height on the walls. For convenience, adjust height to accommodate the nearest full tile. We used a bullnose-edged tile to form the top border and a rounded cove tile at the base. We started work on the walls by spreading 3 or 4 square feet of adhesive with a notched trowel and placing the tiles next to each other with a firm press of the hand.

A durable finish is achieved with a two-step process. First, force the dry-cure grout into the seams with a rubber-coated trowel. Several

A GOOD-LOOKING VANITY

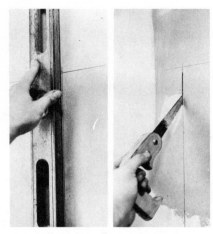

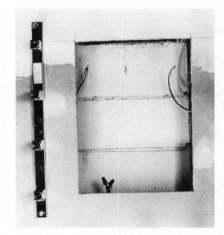

Pencil in the cut lines for the medicine chest with the aid of a level. Cut with a keyhole saw

Light strips flanking the chest are wired to a junction box above the opening. Use wire nuts on all splices

EASY-CARE TILE

Establish the wall height and lay out dry tiles to check it. We recessed the vanity 3½-in. into the wall

Spread three square feet of adhesive at a time with a trowel and press each tile into place firmly

Most local tile suppliers can rent you a cutter and chippers. After you score the surface, the tile snaps

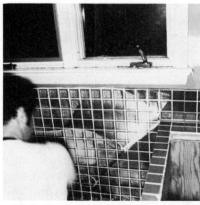

A coved base eliminates one more hard-to-clean crack. Make sure no nail-heads protrude from the plywood floor

Apply the grout liberally, forcing it into the seams by making continuous passes with a rubber-coated trowel

A window washer's squeegee is ideal for removing the excess grout. A rag removes the final film

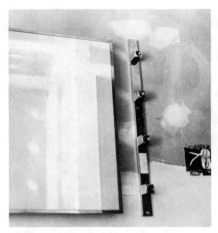

Soft light, 25-watt bulbs throw an even light on the vanity. Install a grounded receptacle next to the switch

We used a noncorroding PVC trap and copper tubing to connect the old pipes and new sink as shown above

AN EASY-MAINTENANCE, WALL-HUNG TOILET

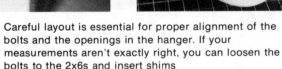

The wall-hung toilet is supported by a steel hanger. Drill holes for the bolts and remove enough tile for the waste drain connection. A plastic sleeve will protect the fixture as the threaded bolts pass through the wall.

Careful layout is essential for proper alignment of the bolts and the openings in the hanger. If your measurements aren't exactly right, you can loosen the bolts to the 2x6s and insert shims

passes over the same area will compact the grout. Don't worry about the excess. A window washer's squeegee will remove it. Follow this with a damp sponge; it will remove all but a fine film which can be "polished" away with a dry rag.

The following day we finished the tile job by brushing a liberal coating of liquid silicone on the grouted joints. This is tedious, but it will save you hours of maintenance.

Two coats of washable latex paint completed the resurfacing of our modern, efficient bath. The thorough installation will keep it looking good with a minimum of effort.

Careful preparation for a parquet floor

BASKET WEAVE PARALLEL

FOUR SQUARE FINGER

FOUR SQUARE DIAGONAL

DOUBLE HERRINGBONE

■ LAYING A PARQUET FLOOR used to be a job for a master craftman—but not any more. With industry innovations like prefinished surfaces and self-adhering backs, this job can now be tackled by homeowners. There is a wide variety of woods and patterns and a range in cost from raw wood, which must be set in paste, up to self-sticking tiles with stained, sealed and polished surfaces.

If you think it sounds too easy, you're right—there is a catch. You must start with a strong, clean, level surface. Putting your floor in shape might take only a layer of ¼-in. hardboard across old floorboards. We've outlined the most complete job you might have to do. Here's how.

1. prepare the surface

Whatever room and tile design you're working with, you must provide a smooth, strong and level surface to lay the tile on. It's also important to stagger the plywood end joints in order to

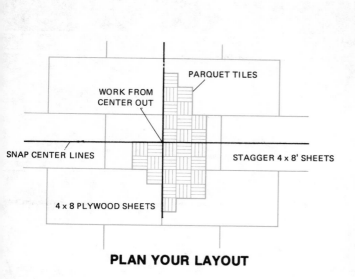

PLAN YOUR LAYOUT

WORK FROM CENTER OUT

PARQUET TILES

SNAP CENTER LINES

STAGGER 4 x 8' SHEETS

4 x 8 PLYWOOD SHEETS

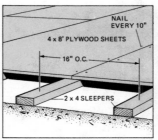

LAY 2X4 SLEEPERS

NAIL EVERY 10"

4 x 8' PLYWOOD SHEETS

16" O.C.

2 x 4 SLEEPERS

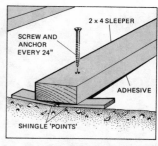

LEVEL UP WITH SHIMS

2 x 4 SLEEPER

SCREW AND ANCHOR EVERY 24"

ADHESIVE

SHINGLE 'POINTS'

GLUE AND NAIL PLYWOOD

4 x 8' PLYWOOD SHEET

NAIL EVERY 10"

DRIVE NAIL FLUSH

2 x 4 SLEEPER

ADHESIVE

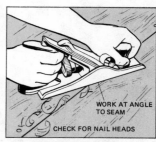

PLANE DOWN UNEVEN SEAMS

WORK AT ANGLE TO SEAM

CHECK FOR NAIL HEADS

distribute the load evenly across the floor. Any material, ranging from hardboard to 1x6 tongue-and-groove subflooring, should lap the end joints from one support to another.

In general, you should follow the same layout rules for tile floors as for tile ceilings: Snap center lines and work with the edges of the tiles along the lines, filling in from the middle of the room toward the walls. This way, if your room is not square, you stand a chance to make up the discrepancy behind furniture or under the baseboard where it won't be noticed.

2. most durable installation

Laying a new subfloor is the way to get the most complete and durable installation. It gives you a chance to level up bad spots, to provide a new, strong surface and to allow for a ventilated air space between the 2x4s that will keep the tiles warm and dry.

This will also make the floor more comfortable to walk on because a wood subfloor is more resilient than concrete.

3. bridge the low spots

The best way to handle low spots is to bridge them with 2x4 sleepers and then support the bridge with shingle points. You can drive one in from each side and let them overlap as much as needed to make the 2x4 level. You should check for level along the length of the board and across from one to another. Note that adhesive is used

along with screws and anchors to make sure this floor won't shift or squeak or start popping the tiles loose after it's in use.

4. combine nails and glue

A thin bead of construction adhesive between the sleepers and the concrete will give you the permanent and professional results you're looking for. Nails, on their own, may work loose and the joints may separate, but if you combine the force of the nails with that of the adhesive bond you will make this job true and tight.

5. check for flush surface

You're almost ready to lay the tiles—but give your floor one last check. Make sure the nailheads are driven down flush to the plywood. You don't want to discover protruding nails as you're spreading paste or laying tiles. If some of the plywood seams are uneven, now is the time to plane or sand them down and fill in any voids in the surface skin with water putty.

Any loose material on the plywood will prevent the tiles from adhering properly, so all good craftsmen will invest a little extra time in this last step to clean up the sawdust and double check their preparations.

Now you're ready for the easy part of the job—laying one tile next to another for a beautiful parquet floor.

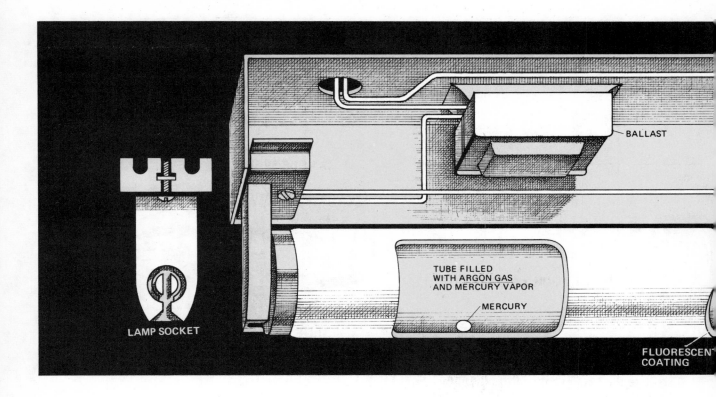

LAMP SOCKET

BALLAST

TUBE FILLED
WITH ARGON GAS
AND MERCURY VAPOR

MERCURY

FLUORESCENT
COATING

What you should know about fluorescent lamps

BY ED FRANZESE

■ THE FACT THAT IT saves energy—as well as money—makes fluorescence an increasingly popular alternative to incandescence in office and home. Energy-saving fluorescent lamps give two to four times as much light per watt of power as incandescent bulbs. They also have low surface brightness. Unlike incandescent lamps, which are bright in just a single spot, fluorescents have a lower brightness over a larger area, resulting in fewer shadows, less eyestrain and better distribution.

Tubular in form, fluorescent lamps are usually called tubes and come in straight and circular styles. Straight fluorescents vary in length from 4¼ to 96 in. and from 4 to 215 watts. Circular fluorescents are known as Circlarc or Circline lamps and are available in outside diameters of 8¼, 12 and 16 in. with popular powers of 22, 32 and 40 watts.

The ends of each tube contain a cap with two terminals as shown above. These terminals connect to an internal tungsten filament inside each end of the tube. Inside the tube is a small amount of argon gas and a drop of mercury; the inside surface is coated with a fluorescent chemical.

In addition to the tube, the circuit contains a switch, ballast (transformer) and starter. A pull-chain toggle or pushbutton switch turns the circuit on and off. The ballast provides the high voltage necessary to start the mercury-vapor arc inside the tube and stabilizes the circuit by keeping the operating current at a steady value, as shown in the two-lamp circuit diagram on page 99.

The starting switch closes the circuit between the two filaments when the lamp circuit is energized. It also opens the circuit between the two filaments after sufficient time has passed to heat

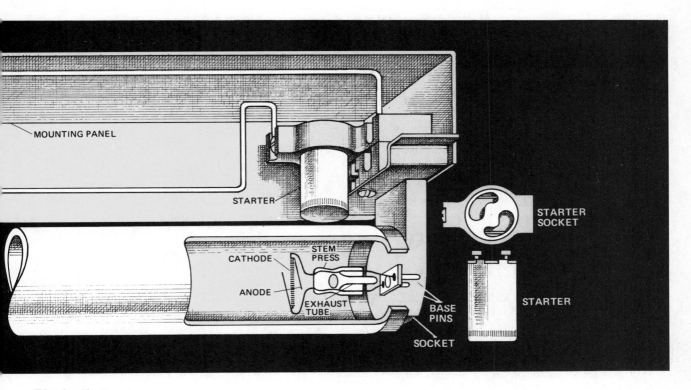

MOUNTING PANEL

STARTER

CATHODE

STEM PRESS

ANODE

EXHAUST TUBE

STARTER SOCKET

BASE PINS

STARTER

SOCKET

Blackening

POSSIBLE CAUSES	WHAT TO TRY
1. Mercury deposit inside of tube.	Normal.
2. Lamp failure.	Replace lamp.
3. Frequent starting.	Limit number of times lamp is turned on and off. Allow three to four hours of lamp operation.
4. Wrong-size ballast.	Check fluorescent specifications.
5. Low line voltage.	See "Lamp slow in starting," page 99.

Swirling and spiraling inside of lamp

POSSIBLE CAUSES	WHAT TO TRY
1. Lamp failure.	Replace lamp.
2. Improper or defective starter.	Check starter against fluorescent lamp circuit specifications. Replace defective starter.
3. Wrong-size ballast.	Check fluorescent specifications.
4. Low line voltage.	See "Lamp slow in starting," page 99.

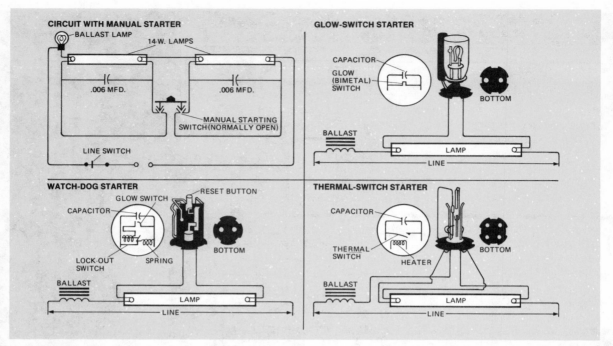

Four different starter circuits available for fluorescent lamps are shown. When you "turn on" a lamp by throwing a line switch, the circuit is closed, but the light does not appear immediately

The job of the starter element is to hold up the flow of electrical current until it has heated the two filaments in each lamp on the circuit to their proper temperature. The delay may take a second

LAMP WATT/LENGTH RATIO

Watts	Length (in.)
15	18
20	24
30	36
40	48
100	60

the filaments to the proper temperature. There are four different starter circuits available: manual, automatic glow-switch, automatic watchdog and automatic thermal-switch.

A circuit for a fluorescent tube is illustrated in the upper detail on page 99. Here a ballast is connected in series with the lamp. The automatic starter switch is in closed position when no current is flowing through the circuit, though the starter element is heating (diagram A, "Glow-switch operation," page 99). When the circuit is closed (diagram B), the two lamp filaments are connected in series through the starter to supply voltage. Since the automatic starter short-circuits the path, no current will flow in the lamp. Thus, the filaments are cold, and argon gas cannot conduct.

As the current begins to heat the lamp filaments to a certain temperature, the mercury in the lamp begins to vaporize. A few seconds later, the automatic starter opens (diagram C), breaks

the circuit and causes the ballast to produce high voltage between the filaments. This voltage strikes an arc through the argon gas and mercury vapor. The mercury-vapor arc then causes the fluorescent chemicals inside the tube to fluoresce, emitting a brilliant light which illuminates the lamp.

Fluorescent lamps are available in many colors and "whites." Colors are used for decorative purposes; whites for general lighting. These whites offer the most efficiency per dollar of cost, the best color-rendering per-dollar cost, the best color-rendering properties.

The life of fluorescent lamps is not only affected by voltage and current, but also by the number of times they are started. Homeowners can prolong this life by following these suggestions:

■ Operate lamps continuously for a three to four-hour period for maximum life. Turning the lamp on and off cuts its life considerably.

■ Room temperature should be at least 50° F. For colder rooms, special fluorescent lamps and starters can be used.

■ The right starter should be used with fluorescents. Check replacement starter numbers against numbers stamped on the original starter.

■ Be sure the ballast has the catalog or type number specified for the fluorescent lamp unit.

BASIC SINGLE-LAMP CIRCUIT

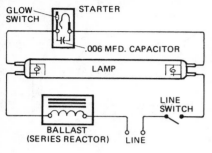

Ends of lamp remain lighted

POSSIBLE CAUSES	WHAT TO TRY
1. Shorted starter.	Replace starter.
2. Lamp failure.	Replace lamp.
3. Incorrect wiring.	Check wiring against manufacturer's schematic.

GLOW-SWITCH OPERATION

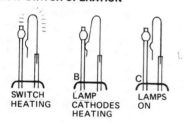

Lamp does not start

POSSIBLE CAUSES	WHAT TO TRY
1. Lamp not seated in sockets.	Reseat lamps firmly in sockets.
2. Defective starter.	Replace starter.
3. Defective lamp.	Replace lamp.
4. Defective switch.	Disconnect power. Place a continuity tester across switch. Turn switch on. A reading should exist. If not, replace switch.
5. Defective ballast.	If all of the above check good, then replace the ballast.

SINGLE-LAMP CIRCUIT WITH AUTOTRANSFORMER BALLAST

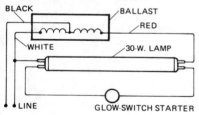

Lamp slow in starting

POSSIBLE CAUSES	WHAT TO TRY
1. Defective starter.	Replace starter.
2. Wrong-size ballast.	Check fluorescent specifications.
3. Low line voltage.	Check voltage. It must be ±10 percent of 120 v. If not, check with power company.

TWO-LAMP CIRCUIT

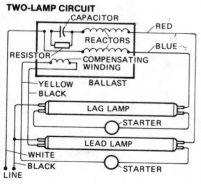

Lamp blinks on and off

POSSIBLE CAUSES	WHAT TO TRY
1. Lamp failure.	Replace lamp.
2. Defective starter.	Replace starter.
3. Cold drafts or low temperature	Block drafts or heat room up to above 50°F.
4. Wrong-size ballast.	Refer to previous section.
5. Low line voltage.	Refer to previous section.

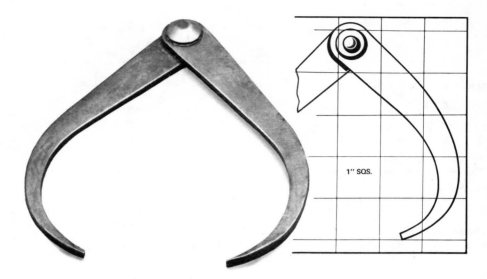

1" SQS.

Eight fine tools you can make

BY DAVID WARREN

By saving parts of
old tools, metal, and scraps of wood you
can make these handy tools

■ THERE ARE ANY NUMBER of hand tools and fixtures you can make for little or nothing. The eight shown here will prove extra handy at your drill press, lathe and bench. Among them is a fixture called a bench hook that hooks over a bench to hold small work for sawing, filing and the like. Shown in its simplest form, it can be made without much trouble and with a few boards you probably have around the shop.

Another simple item to make is a V-block which is used to cradle and hold dowels and other turnings when the job calls for drilling a hole through a piece dead-center. You will find it to be very valuable and there should be one near any drill press. Old worn-out bastard mill files make great scraping tools for woodturning when bevel-ground and fitted with a long handle. And you can't beat a pair of friction-type calipers for fast adjusting. It's a tool you can make from a couple of pieces of flat metal and a rivet. These are just some of the homemade tools suggested on these pages.

FRICTION-FIT CALIPERS ARE FAST-ADJUSTING

If you have a wood lathe and haven't bought a pair of calipers, don't. You can make a dandy 6-in. pair of friction calipers for far less than you can buy them. They're fast adjusting, for you simply pull them open or squeeze them shut. The legs are held with a roundhead rivet and spring washer. Make a pattern following the drawing above on blue ³/₃₂-in. Starret ground flat stock. Scribe the outline on it and cut out with a metal-cutting blade. Finish the sharp edges with a file. Be sure to use a spring washer under the rivet to provide the necessary friction fit

LATHE CHISELS FROM OLD FILES

You can make a scraping tool for your lathe from an old file. If the file is long, shorten it to about 10 in. Grind it smooth at the tip, then grind a 60° bevel. Hone the bevel but don't remove the wire edge—it helps the scraping action. Fit it with an 11-in. hardwood handle

TWO-FACED SANDER

With ¼-in. cork glued to one side and ³/₁₆-in. leather to the other, this sanding block keeps sandpaper from clogging and glazing. A 1 x 1½ x 5½-in. wood block fits the hand nicely and is the right size to take a quarter sheet of sandpaper. Use white glue to attach the leather and cork facings. Your hand holds the paper in place when you grip the block for sanding

HANDY BENCH HOOK

For hand work at the bench you can't beat a bench hook for holding work and protecting the bench's top. Generally it is used with a backsaw but you won't be using it just to saw—you'll be filing on it, chiseling and the like. It's nothing more than a flat board with cleats attached to opposite sides and ends so you can flip it over and use both sides. It's easy to replace

SAVE THAT BROKEN SLEDGE HANDLE

When you're swinging a sledge and wind up with a handle in your hand and no sledge, don't toss it away. The broken handle from a sledge, ax or ball bat provides the best kind of hardwood (hickory and ash) for turning new handles for files and beat-up chisels. The handle for a socket chisel is a simple tapered turning, and when fitting a handle to a chisel with a tang, you can size the collar for a drive-fit ferrule cut from thinwall conduit or brass tubing. For the final step, apply a 50/50 solution of shellac and linseed oil to the wood

SHOOTING BOARD PRODUCES SQUARE EDGES

A shooting board is a handy gadget for squaring the edge of a board when you don't have a jointer. The plane is used on its side and is pushed back and forth along a wood fence. The work is placed against a stop and on top of the fence. The plane removes the stock overhanging the fence. Tapered stop fits tapered dado and wedges in place. Lower edge chamfer forms dust groove

YOUR DRILL PRESS SHOULD HAVE A V-BLOCK

V-blocks are needed at the drill press to hold round stock securely and facilitate drilling through the exact center. To make one, cut a 1 x 2 x 6-in. hardwood block and run it through your table saw with the blade tilted 45°. Then run it a second time to form a V-groove. If you lack a table saw, you can mark the V and cut it by hand with a backsaw. Finish the shellac and bore a hole in it to hang by your drill press

SCRATCH STOCK FORMS BEAD BY SCRATCHING SURFACE

When you want to form a small bead along the edge of a table leg or apron, you can do it with a homemade tool called a scratch stock. It's made to fit over the edge of the work and cuts by scraping. All it consists of are two pieces of wood with a blade clamped between. The blade is made from a short piece of hacksaw blade ground to the shape you want. The photo shows the blade pulled out so you can see it. In use, only the tip is exposed in the very corner of the U-shaped block. It makes the neatest beading you ever saw

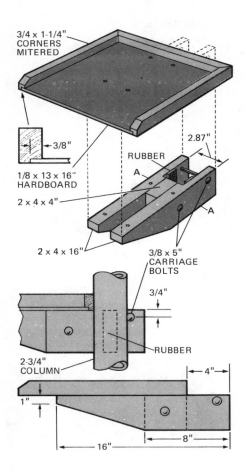

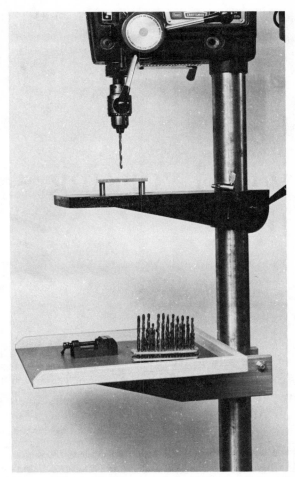

The worktable tray makes good use of the idle portion of the drill-press column

■ THOSE WHO HAVE a floor-model drill press will find this below-the-table tray useful for holding drill bits, chuck key, work in progress and the like. Made of wood and hardboard, it clamps to the column a foot or so below the normal position of the table. Rubber strips are cemented to the rabbeted faces of the 2x4 brackets to keep them from slipping down the column. The rubber strips should fit snugly against the column to reduce the clamping force needed to hold the tray in place. Also, the clamping bolt should just skim the column to hold the tray level.

Fasten the hardboard tray bottom in its rabbets and the tray to its brackets with flathead wood screws in countersunk holes. Paint or varnish the completed tray to keep oil from soaking into the wood. When an occasional drilling job requires the full use of the lower half of the column, it's simple enough to remove the tray from the column and later replace it. The tray can be of any size you wish—just don't make it so deep it interferes with standing in front of the machine.

A handy tray for your drill press

BY R. S. HEDIN

An expert's best woodworking tips

BY WAYNE C. LECKEY

You can bore a hole from one side of a board and wind up with a splintered mess, or you can bore from both sides and leave a hole as clean as a whistle. This is just one of the little tricks that is the mark of a good craftsman. One note of caution: Be sure to follow all safety procedures including using the blade guard on the table saw. To clearly illustrate some of the tips, we left it off in these photos

Angle in on screw pockets
Screw pockets for fastening tabletops are neatly formed in the table's aprons with a beveled 2x4 block clamped to the drill-press table. With the depth gauge set for the right depth, the work is clamped against the face of the slanting block. By cutting tangent to the surface, the bit forms a neat shouldered pocket for the screw. Using a much smaller drill, another hole is made in the bottom of the pocket for the screw

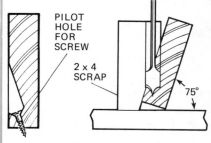

PILOT HOLE FOR SCREW

2 x 4 SCRAP

75°

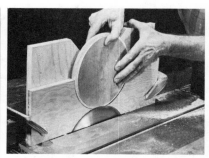

Rabbet wood discs on table saw
Rabbeting a disc is normally a job for a shaper, but when you don't own one, you can do it with a semicircular jig attached to the rip fence of your table saw. To start, gently lower the disc into the spinning blade, then rotate it slowly with your right hand while pressing inward with the left

Prevent creeping with sandpaper
Workpiece creeping is difficult to prevent when you make angle cuts greater than 45°. The expert will cement a sandpaper strip to the face of his miter gauge to add a nonslip surface

Guide your saw for a bevel

It takes a steady hand and a good eye to saw a uniform bevel the length of a board with a handsaw. However, there's nothing to it if you clamp a 2x4 scrap to the top of the work against which the saw blade can bear at an angle as you guide it along the pencil line. The 2x4 must be positioned to suit the angle that you are cutting; the greater the angle the farther the 2x4 must be from the line

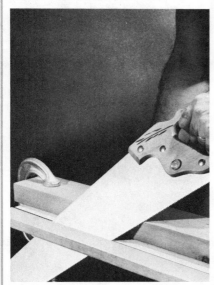

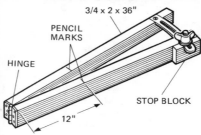

3/4 x 2 x 36"

PENCIL MARKS

HINGE

STOP BLOCK

12"

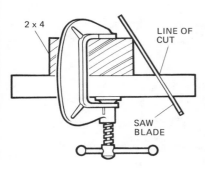

2 x 4

LINE OF CUT

SAW BLADE

Two ways to rip tapers

Taper ripping requires a jig to hold the work at the required angle as it goes through the saw. Details below show two jigs; one a two-leg hinged affair, the other a stepped block. The hinged jig is set by measuring across the legs at a point 12 in. from the end. By opening the legs 1 in. you set the angle for a 1-in.-per-ft. taper. The nonadjustable stepped jig is good for work tapered on four sides, such as table legs. The work rests in the first notch for the first pass, then in the second notch

FENCE

1ST STEP

TAPER

EQUAL STEPS

2ND STEP

Board for squaring odd pieces

A squaring board comes in handy for cutting a straight edge along irregularly shaped plywood leftovers from your jigsaw and bandsaw. It's nothing more than a sliding platform fitted with a runner that rides in the table groove. The squaring board is used to support and guide the work as it passes through the blade. The rip fence should never be used to make such cuts. A squaring board is especially good for small pieces. When you want to square-up the edge of a large piece, a strip is clamped to the underside and then it is guided along the edge of the saw table itself. Placement of the strip is dictated by the size of your saw table, plus what is required to true up the ragged edge. If your saw is small in size it may be difficult to guide the work along the table edge without a helper

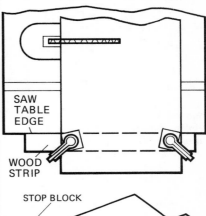

SAW TABLE EDGE

WOOD STRIP

STOP BLOCK

90°

TO FIT SAW-TABLE GROOVE

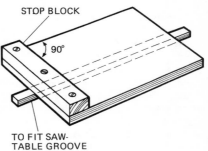

woodworking tips, continued

Miter molding faster with a jig
A miter jig is faster and more accurate than your saw's miter gauge for cutting right and left-hand miters. Runners are added to the underside of a plywood platform and the saw is used to make its own kerf. A plywood fence is positioned and screwed to the platform so it forms a perfect 90° angle at an exact 45° angle to the kerf. A strip of sandpaper glued to the face of each fence of the jig will help keep molding from shifting as it's being cut

Cut duplicates safely with block
Never use the fence itself as a stop when crosscutting duplicate pieces. The work will wedge between the fence and the blade and be thrown with force. Always butt the work against a stop block clamped to the table. This way there is no chance of the pieces getting caught and thrown by the saw

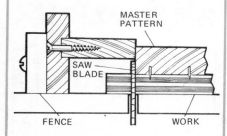

Mass-produce identical work
Pattern sawing is a fast way of duplicating straight-sided work. The setup requires an overhanging wood fence which is clamped or screwed to the saw's fence, and a master pattern of the part to be duplicated. The points of two brads in the master pattern embed in the wood. The wood fence is aligned flush with the outer face of the blade and the blade is raised just high enough to handle the thickness of the work. Clearance under the overhanging fence must suit the thickness of the work, and the pattern must be thick enough to ride the edge of the fence. The work must be cut up beforehand to the approximate (and slightly larger) size and shape

Crosscut wide boards
Place the miter gauge backwards in the table groove when crosscutting a wide board on a small saw. This utilizes all of the table in front of the blade and provides maximum support to the work. After you are halfway through turn off the saw and reverse the gauge in the groove to complete the cut

Duplicate identical dadoes
Extra-wide dadoes in duplicate work come out exactly the same length each time if you clamp a stepped block to the left corner of the saw table. Precut to suit the width of the dado blade and the length of the dado, the block determines each successive pass by resting work in the steps. The last step automatically sets the width. You can't miss since the block does the measuring

Forming cove molding

Making cove molding on your saw is possible by passing the workpiece repeatedly across the blade at an angle. The auxiliary fence is positioned to form the cove down the middle of the work, then clamped to the saw table. Stock is cut away by successive passes over the blade, cutting no more than 1/16 in. each pass. A combination blade works best and produces a smooth cut. Width of the cove establishes fence angle and is found with an adjustable parallel gauge as shown in the lower photo. Work is finally ripped down the center to produce two strips of cove molding

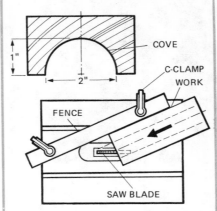

COVE
C-CLAMP
WORK
FENCE
SAW BLADE

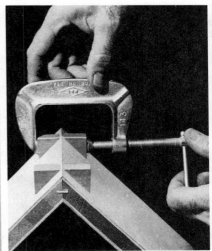

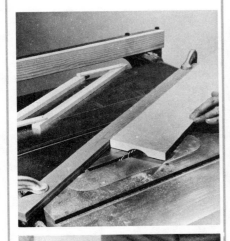

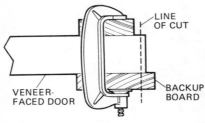

LINE OF CUT
VENEER-FACED DOOR
BACKUP BOARD

Trim bottom of door with backup

Sawing off a narrow strip from the bottom of a door with a handsaw presents two problems: guiding the saw so it won't run off and keeping it from splintering the opposite side. Both problems are solved by clamping a scrap board to the underside. With the board backing the cut, the saw can't chip or scar the veneer

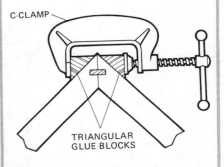

C-CLAMP
TRIANGULAR GLUE BLOCKS

Clamp mitered joints

While there are special "clothespin"-type clamps with swivel barbed jaws for holding mitered joints when gluing, you can make your regular C-clamps do by gluing several triangular clamping ears to each side of the joint. The ears are later chiseled off flush and the surface sanded

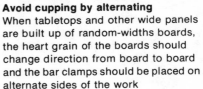

Avoid cupping by alternating

When tabletops and other wide panels are built up of random-widths boards, the heart grain of the boards should change direction from board to board and the bar clamps should be placed on alternate sides of the work

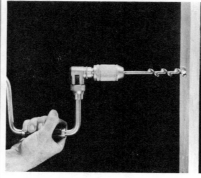

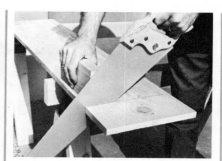

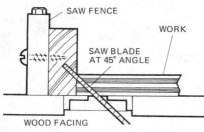

Miter wide boards

How do you rig your bench saw to cut a perfect miter along the edge of a wide board or plywood panel? First you add a wood facing to the rip fence, then with the blade tilted 45° and raised ¾ in., you ease the fence into the rotating blade enough to just bury the tip of the blade in the wood facing. Fence will support miter

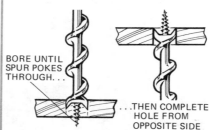

Bore clean-cut holes

Boring a hole from both sides is not always possible but when it is, remember this stunt for producing a clean-cut hole. Start boring from one side until the bit's spur pokes through the other side. Then back out, turn the work around and finish the hole by boring to meet the first. You'll have a clean hole and no splinters

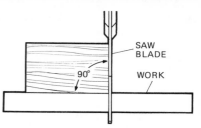

Block keeps handsaw vertical

With practice and a sharp handsaw it's no great feat to follow a line when sawing a wide board. The trick is holding the saw vertically the full length of the cut. When it's important that the cut be 90°, simply hold a square-cut scrap of 2x4 against the saw blade as you continue to saw

Contour legs with a sanding drum

For a perfect fit when doweling legs to a central turning such as the post of a lamp table, use a sanding drum. It works best when both the diameter of the drum and turning are equal. Notch a board to fit around the drum as shown and support it horizontally so its surface is at the very axis of the drum

Two ways to drill a disc

A V-notched board clamped to your drill-press table will uniformly space holes around the circumference of a disc. To bore them in the face, the table is kept horizontal. To bore them in the edge, the table is tilted 90°. The board must be positioned so the V-notch is in line with the bit

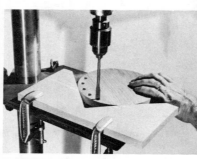

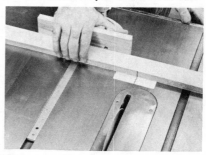

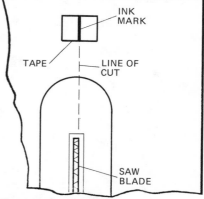

Saw precisely on line

Lining up the mark on the work with the saw blade is easy if you stick a piece of white tape to the saw table and make an ink mark on it directly in line with the inner face of the blade. You'll be right on target when you push the work across the table and into the blade

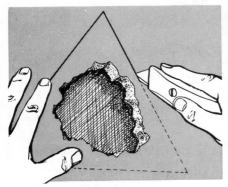

1. Cut the triangle

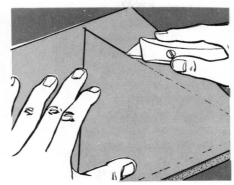

2. Cut the plug

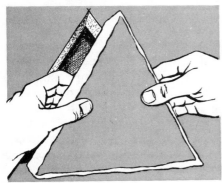

3. Butter the edges

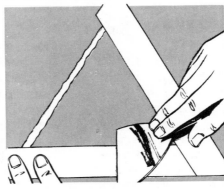

4. Tape to finish

A drywall patch you can't see

■ MOST PROBLEMS that can develop with drywall are literally skin deep. As your house goes through seasonal changes in temperature, wood framing members may shrink and shift. This can cause nailheads to pop and seams to ridge or separate. These situations can be solved by surface repair and spackling.

But what about larger holes? Like the time you were hanging a picture, missed the stud, and sank the nail and the hammer into the wall. Or you may have a nice round hole in a room where the doorknob has been driven through the drywall by a child crashing open the door on his way to dinner. You can't spackle these holes unless you intend to fill up the entire space between the studs—don't try it.

Some people follow this approach by cramming newspapers into the wall to fill the hole before spackling. This system doesn't provide much support for the spackle since the paper is not firm and will eventually fall. There is one good way to make a patch that is not only durable but unnoticeable.

■ **First:** Cut an equal-sided triangle around the hole. Make four or five passes with the knife; don't try to cut through with one stroke. As you cut, angle the blade edge 45° to the outside of the cut with the blade tip pointing toward the center of the triangle.

■ **Second:** Cut a duplicate triangle (also called a dutchman) holding the knife at the same angle. This will let the edges of the hole and the plug seat against each other and keep the plug flush with the wall surface.

■ **Third:** Check the plug in the hole for size. If the angles are a little off (they probably will be since you're cutting by eye) you can use a wood rasp to equal them off so the patch sits flush. When you have a good fit, butter the edges of the plug with joint compound and set it in place.

■ **Fourth:** Finally, proceed with conventional butt joint taping and feather out the last two coats for a smooth finish. If you have trouble cutting the angles, you can glue and clamp strips of drywall to the inside edges of the hole to make a good backstop for the plug.

Tape up your repair problems

BY PENELOPE ANGELL

Think you know tapes? Here are some with new or unexpected uses you'll find helpful around the house. Give them a try the next time you have a "sticky" problem. They are easy-to-use and require no messy cleanup

■ AS NEW TAPES ARE DEVELOPED and new applications for existing ones found, more and more homeowners are turning to tapes to solve their repair problems. And for good reasons: Tapes are handy, easy to apply, do a remarkable number of jobs, present no messy cleanup problems and are generally inexpensive.

There are the old reliable standbys—plastic electrical tape, medical adhesive tape and cellophane (Scotch) tape—that are probably used more around the house than any other types. But there are also a lot of less familiar, more specialized tapes that have many important household uses. Here's a rundown on some of the most versatile with suggestions for some useful applications you may not have thought of.

special drywall type

Flex Corner drywall tape helps make clean inside or outside corners. The tape has two ½-in. galvanized-steel reinforcing strips that are placed on either side of the corner to form and reinforce the angle. Flex Corner can be cut to length and applied with a standard three-coat, cement compound process (metal strips facing toward the wall), the same as with perforated tape. However, Flex Corner has the strength to prevent the seam from opening.

Drywall tape can also be used to reinforce joints, finish curved surfaces and arches, join drywall partitions to plastered walls and repair chipped or cracked plaster walls. Goldblatt Tool Co., 511 Osage, Kansas City, KS 66110.

aluminum-faced tape

Flashband, an aluminum-faced tape with a layer of self-adhesive asphalt, helps seal and waterproof your home. It is flexible enough to

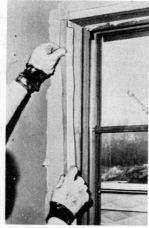

Cut the drywall tape or score with a knife and bend, fold it in half and press over the joint cement. Later, apply the finish coats and feather the edges

Flashband self-adhesive tape is a permanent sealer for this airconditioner

110

seal gutters, downspouts, irregular-shaped metal flashing, airconditioners, heating ducts and the like. Flashband is also available with a gray vinyl coating over the aluminum for situations where the aluminum might corrode (such as in a cabin at the seashore). Both types can be painted with water-base paint and can be purchased in 20-ft. rolls, ranging from 2 to 9-in. widths. The aluminum-faced type also comes in a patch pack.

Flashband was developed for use by professional roofers and has many roofing applications, but can also be used to repair swimming-pool covers, garden equipment, awnings and aluminum siding. Evode, Inc., 401 Kennedy Blvd., Somerdale, NJ 08083.

fiberglass repair patch

A fiberglass cloth patch that cures in the sunlight or when exposed to an ultraviolet lamp has many applications around the home. The

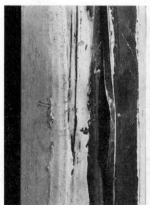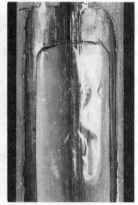

This downspout damaged by expanding ice was repaired with an "Auto-Pak" fiberglass patch which cures in the sun. It is invisible when painted

"Auto-Pak" lay-it-on body patch is made by 3M. A patch cut to cover the damaged area adheres on contact and hardens to make a permanent, waterproof repair when subjected to the proper light. The top covering is peeled away and the patch can be sanded and painted to match the color and finish of the surrounding surface. The patch repairs metal, wood or fiberglass surfaces.

As its name implies, the "Auto-Pak" patch was designed to be used on cars—to repair rust-outs. But it is also helpful in repairing cracked fiberglass shower stalls and laundry sinks, wood or metal gutters and downspouts, plus many other damaged wood, metal or fiberglass surfaces.

keep pipes from freezing

This "Heater Tape" from Smith-Gates is used to eliminate frozen water pipes. It is a heating wire wrapped around a glass-fiber core and encased in a vinyl jacket. The tape can be equipped with an automatic "Press-to-Test" thermostat as shown and a pilot lamp that lights when the tape is heating. The length of Heater Tape needed depends on the pipe size, length and lowest temperature expected. For example, according to the Heater Tape chart a 1-in.-diameter pipe 10 ft. long would need 15 feet of tape (wrapped three times per foot around the pipe) to keep it from freezing at 11° below zero. An additional fiberglass blanket with outer wrap for extra protection is available. A waterproof cover can also be purchased. Smith-Gates Corp., Farmington, CT 06032.

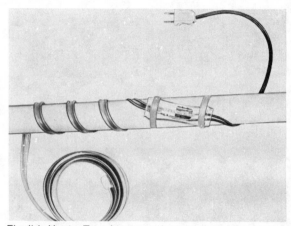

Flexible Heater Tape is wrapped around a pipe to prevent it from freezing in winter

seal threaded pipe joints

Wrap Chemplast Ready-Seal Thread Tape around threaded pipe to insure a leaktight joint. It is made of soft, pliable Teflon that conforms to any type or size of thread. It also seals hose fittings, sprinklers, nozzles and fire extinguishers. Chemplast, Inc., 150 Day Rd., Wayne, NJ 07470.

The Teflon tape is wrapped around male pipe threads to lubricate and seal the joint

experimental concrete patch

A wide range of concrete repairs will be possible for the homeowner with Rok-Rap, a tapelike material still in the experimental stages. Manufacturers propose that it can be used to patch concrete basement leaks, protect pipework and posts from corrosion both above and below the ground, repair spalled concrete, join and repair concrete pipes, face concrete structures and solve other problems. The tape is activated by wetting with a special activator or cold water. After drying out, the tape forms a dry, rugged rocklike, but resilient, protective covering. Evode, Inc., 401 Kennedy Blvd., Somerdale, NJ 08083.

Rok-Rap is used to patch a basement crack where water had been seeping in as shown above

tape 'staples' with many uses

Saw duplicate shapes in one operation. Join two pieces of wood together with Mystik masking tape. Then saw the pattern marked on the top piece through both pieces. Also use masking tape to cover trim while you're painting around it, and to wrap around plumbing fixtures to protect them from wrench marks.

With masking tape you can also keep small parts in order and in sight when assembling kits and complex units. Placed sticky side up on your worktable, the tape keeps easy-to-lose items from straying. Masking tape also helps to keep glued parts together until the glue has had a chance to set.

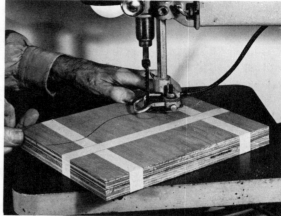

Masking tape is wrapped securely around boards at right angles to stop them from shifting while being cut.

Masking tape used sticky side up holds small parts in place until they are needed

protective sponge tape

With Mystik Sponge Tape you can protect fine wood and other delicate surfaces in your home from heavy or rough objects. Just cushion the bottom of such objects with strips of the tape. This tape can also be used as an insulator around windows and doors.

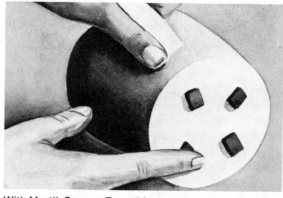

With Mystik Sponge Tape this pottery can now be safely placed on tables with no fear of damage

Install a snow-melting system

Stretch an electric cable out on your roof or embed a cable or hot
fluid system in your sidewalk and you will do away with the drudgery of snow removal,
prevent accidents and eliminate snow damage to your home

BY PENELOPE ANGELL

■ HOW MANY TIMES have you grumbled to yourself about there "being a better way" as you headed outdoors, shovel in hand, to clean the walks? There *is* a better way. Snowmelting systems can be installed to keep ice and snow from accumulating on your roof and to clear your driveways and sidewalks.

Three types of snow-melting systems are available for home use: 1. Electric heating cable can be installed on your roof to eliminate snow dams on the overhang. 2. An electric heating cable system can be embedded in driveways and sidewalks. 3. A hydronic pipe system in which a heated mixture of antifreeze solution or hot oil

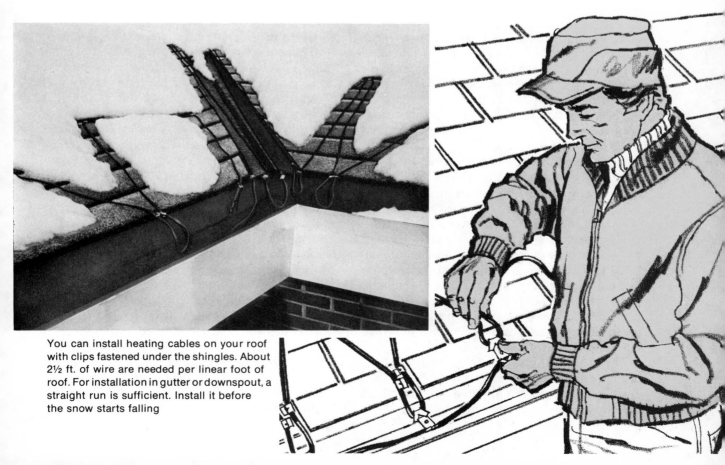

You can install heating cables on your roof with clips fastened under the shingles. About 2½ ft. of wire are needed per linear foot of roof. For installation in gutter or downspout, a straight run is sufficient. Install it before the snow starts falling

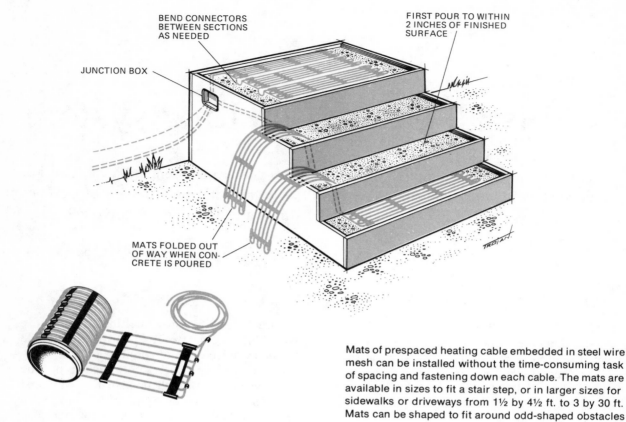

BEND CONNECTORS
BETWEEN SECTIONS
AS NEEDED

JUNCTION BOX

FIRST POUR TO WITHIN
2 INCHES OF FINISHED
SURFACE

MATS FOLDED OUT
OF WAY WHEN CON-
CRETE IS POURED

Mats of prespaced heating cable embedded in steel wire mesh can be installed without the time-consuming task of spacing and fastening down each cable. The mats are available in sizes to fit a stair step, or in larger sizes for sidewalks or driveways from 1½ by 4½ ft. to 3 by 30 ft. Mats can be shaped to fit around odd-shaped obstacles

circulates through the pipes to melt the snow can also be embedded in the pavement.

Heating cables can help prevent damage to the roof gutters and interior walls of your home. They melt the snow, eliminating heavy snow and ice accumulation on roof overhangs and stopping ice dams from forming in gutters and downspouts.

Ice and snow accumulations tend to develop particularly on homes with large roof overhangs that are not warmed by heat from the building interior. Snow dams are formed when sunshine and heat rising from the heated building partially melt ice and snow on the upper part of the roof. The slush runs down to the old gutter or unheated roof overhang where it again turns to ice and continues to collect. Beneath this buildup, water rises under the shingle tabs, spills over the back shingle edges and can drain through the layers of stapled felt paper, down the rafters, and onto interior ceilings and walls.

The cable that prevents these ice dams is an insulated wire that heats to melt the snow when electrical current flows through it. Available in varying lengths from 5 to over 160 feet, it can

cost from 50 cents per foot for the short lengths to 25 cents per foot for the long ones. The cable and kits that include clips for fastening it to the shingles are available at hardware stores and electrical supply houses. Each length of cable is equipped with a cold lead wire, several feet long. It plugs into a waterproof outlet box, usually located near the eave. The cable operates on normal house current of 120 volts and consumes electricity at a rate of 6 to 16 watts per foot.

You should install the cable in a zigzag pattern along the roof edge. In this pattern about 2½ feet of wire are needed per linear foot of roof. For installation in gutter and downspout a straight run of wire is used. Where eaves don't overhang the house, you may only need cable in the gutter and downspout to melt the snow. If heating cables are used on either roof overhang or gutter, the downspout must also be heated to carry away the water from the melted snow and ice. A heated length of wire is dropped inside the downspout to the bottom (even if it is underground), using weights if necessary. All gutters and downspouts should be grounded to a driven ground rod.

The best way to provide electric current to the cable is to locate waterproof outlets on the exterior walls of your home fed by a No. 12 gauge or other heavy wire. Cables can't be shortened or spliced. Each length must be plugged in separately.

To turn on the system easily, a switch should be located inside the house. A pilot light that shines when the system is on is recommended to remind you to turn off the system when it's not needed.

heating cables in pavement

Melting snow and ice on driveways and sidewalks is easily done by means of heating cables embedded in the cement or asphalt. These cables are available either already prespaced in mats, or in individual lengths which can be laid down at spaced intervals.

Mats can be cut to follow contours or to curve around objects. However, care must be taken that the heater wire is not damaged in the process.

Cables are covered with plastic insulation which permits them to be buried directly into concrete or asphalt. Cold lead wires are attached to the heating cable. These lead wires must be long enough to reach a dry location for terminating.

Snow-melting systems are designed for average conditions. This means that during heavy downfalls the snow will accumulate slightly. You can minimize installation and operation cost by using two 18-inch-wide heat strips for the wheel tracks of your car, rather than a system to melt snow off the entire driveway. A mat 18 inches by 4½ feet costs approximately $30 without installation at the time this was written. Cost of two 18-inch-wide by 30-foot-long mats for a 30-foot driveway would be about $165. Cost of individual cables would be less.

You can install heating mats and lay individual cable yourself. A licensed electrician can wire and connect the units to the household electric supply. A reputable supplier of heating equipment can usually give adequate advice on the capacity needed for your situation and the method of connection. Manufacturers can also give helpful information.

The spacing of individual heating cables depends on the watts-per-square-foot required, which varies with the average number of hours and inches of snowfall per year in each area. Cable is usually rated at 10 watts per square foot. There are many variables involved in the cost of operation. Yearly operating cost in Chicago, for example, for a 30-foot-long driveway with 18-inch-wide mats for car tires, using a system consuming 40 watts per square foot would be about $26 at the time this was written.

When you install the cable, a lead wire must terminate at a junction box. The junction boxes can be placed in the slab where the cable is laid, or brought out to a main supply point. If boxes are exposed to weather they must be of the outdoor waterproof type as specified by the National Electric Code.

Wires can be laid when new cement or asphalt drives are built. To wire an existing asphalt drive, a cable-asphalt sandwich can be built.

hot fluid melting systems

An alternative to the electric cable method of melting snow from driveways and sidewalks, particularly for large homes and commerical use, is the hydronic pipe snow-melting system. Pipes are embedded in the pavement through which heated anti-freeze or oil circulates to melt snow.

The Hydronics Institute, 35 Russo Place, Berkeley Heights, NJ 07992, publishes a booklet containing information and procedure on installing a home hydronic system called *Snow Melting Calculation and Installation Guide for Residences* (No. S-40).

A standard system uses ¾-inch pipe on 12-inch centers buried within concrete, or on 9-inch centers in asphalt. These pipes are in S-shaped coils that can be connected by means of a supply and return main to a heat exchanger which is attached to the house heating boiler or auxiliary boiler.

Components needed for the system include a gas or oil-fired boiler, heat exchanger, heater pump, expansion tank, gauges, valves and controls, the pipe that circulates the liquid and the liquid. A boiler needed to melt snow on a 500-square-foot area would take up less space than a washing machine in your basement. Flexible polyolefin and rigid copper tube or wrought-iron pipes are among those used in the system. A thermostat is also suggested for heat control.

Some manufacturers provide a package arrangement including design, engineering, materials, labor, on-site inspection and a guarantee for installing the system. This package is the most trouble-free but also the most expensive. A homeowner who is handy could purchase needed materials and do his own installation for much less. However, it would be wise to employ a specialist for welding work if rigid pipe is used.

Secrets of cutting compound angles

BY WAYNE C. LECKEY

Compound cuts are made with both the blade and miter gauge tilted the required degrees. The blade guard has been removed for picture clarity

■ GETTING THE FOUR CORNERS of a "hopper"-style picture frame to fit is fairly easy, but determining the degree of bevel for a simple four-piece box with sides that slope, say 35°, can be puzzling. For example, the butt joints of the box appear to be 90°, when viewed from the top, but when they're viewed in a true plane, you'll find the "square" edges are less than 90°—actually 70½°. That's the tricky part of compound angles: The bevel does not show in a plan drawing, and even when you study the completed job, the angles are not what they seem.

Compound angles are required when sawing the parts of any pyramidal shape of four, six or eight sides, and are made with the blade (or table, as the case may be) tilted to cut a bevel and the miter gauge swung to cut a miter. Thus both the miter and the bevel are cut in one operation.

The chart on the next page takes all the guesswork out of setting your saw to cut a number of common compound angles. It gives the required tilt for the saw blade and the swing (tilt) of the miter gauge in degrees.

The fastest and most economical way to saw parts for sloping box or flared frame is from a long board which has been prebeveled along both edges. This is called strip cutting. The miter gauge is left at the same setting and the board is flopped after each cut. When the parts are individually cut from scrap, the miter gauge is turned around and used backward for the second cut so wide side of work is always against the miter-gauge facing.

The upper drawings on this page show four standard miter-gauge positions for strip cutting—A and B for cutting miter joints, C and D for butt joints. Here the blade tilts to the right.

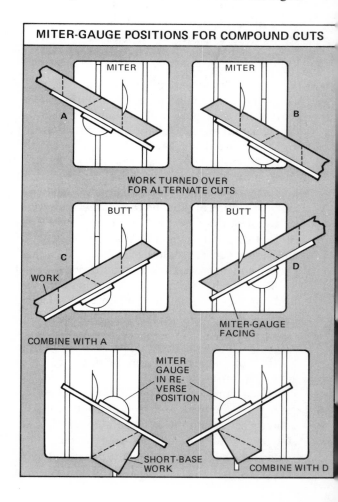

MITER-GAUGE POSITIONS FOR COMPOUND CUTS

MITER

MITER

A

B

WORK TURNED OVER FOR ALTERNATE CUTS

BUTT

BUTT

C

D

WORK

MITER-GAUGE FACING

COMBINE WITH A

MITER GAUGE IN REVERSE POSITION

SHORT-BASE WORK

COMBINE WITH D

The two sets of positions are pairs worked by shifting the miter gauge from one table groove to the other. Prebeveling the edges is done so the top and bottom edges of the pieces will be on a flat plane when assembled. If the box sides slope 35°, for example, the top and bottom edges are beveled 35°.

You can use any of the four miter-gauge positions shown when the work is not prebeveled. However, only two of these positions can be used when the work is prebeveled and the job calls for mitered joints at all four corners, as the bevel must bear against the miter gauge with the sharp corner facing up. When a peak is to be formed like the roof of a birdhouse, and cut from individual prebeveled pieces, the long side of the work must be held against the miter-gauge facing for both cuts; the bevel must face up for both cuts.

In the case of rough work, compound joints are simply butted and nailed or, for greater strength, glued and nailed. However, in finer work, splines are used. These are thin strips of wood cut to fit saw kerfs made in mating members.

When parts are cut individually from separate pieces, the first cut is made with the work held in the position shown above

To make the second cut, the miter gauge is turned around and used backward. The same miter-gauge setting is used

SAW-TILT AND MITER-GAUGE SETTINGS FOR COMPOUND ANGLES

FRONT VIEW — ANGLE

4 SIDES, BUTT JOINTS

4 SIDES, MITER JOINTS

6 SIDES, MITER JOINTS

8 SIDES, MITER JOINTS

WORK ANGLE	SAW TILT	MITER GAUGE	SAW TILT	MITER GAUGE	SAW TILT	MITER GAUGE	SAW TILT	MITER GAUGE
5°	1/2	85	44-3/4	85	29-3/4	87-1/2	22-1/4	88
10°	1-1/2	80-1/4	44-1/4	80-1/2	29-1/2	84-1/2	22	86
15°	3-3/4	75-1/2	43-1/4	75-1/2	29	81-3/4	21-1/2	84
20°	6-1/4	71	42	71	28-1/4	79	21	82
25°	10	67	40	67	27-1/4	76-1/2	20-1/4	80
30°	14-1/2	63-1/2	37-3/4	61-1/2	26	74	19-1/4	78-1/4
35°	19-1/2	60-1/4	35-1/4	60-1/4	24-1/2	71-3/4	18-1/4	76-3/4
40°	24-1/2	57-1/4	32-3/4	57-1/4	22-3/4	69-3/4	17	75
45°	30	54-3/4	30	54-3/4	21	67-3/4	15-3/4	73-3/4
50°	36	52-1/2	27	52-1/2	19	66-1/4	14-1/4	72-1/2
55°	42	50-3/4	24	50-3/4	16-3/4	64-3/4	12-3/4	71-1/4
60°	48	49	21	49	14-1/2	63-1/2	11	70-1/4

Figures are in degrees and are for direct setting to tilt scale and miter-gauge scale provided tilt starts at 0° and miter gauge at 90° in the normal position.

How to repair fancy picture frames

BY ROBERT S. TOPPER

When a fancy picture frame with corner overlays is broken, it doesn't need to be replaced. If one of the corners is good, you can repair it yourself

■ ORNATE PICTURE FRAMES with fancy overlays can be repaired even if much of the composition overlay is missing. All you need is one overlay intact or partially intact and repairable. The frame shown had corners which were badly damaged but one of them could be repaired by building it up with water putty so that a mold could be taken of it to recast the other three.

After the corner is repaired, it's surrounded with a wood form. I used InstaMold (available at craft stores) to fill the form. It's a powder you mix with water to a fairly thin consistency so it can be brushed into crevices and valleys of the overlay without leaving air pockets. It dries in approximately 30 minutes, after which the form can be removed. Remove the form first, then gently lift off the mold.

I used water putty which dries rock hard. I mixed it to a thick cream and poured it into the mold. Then I placed the frame corner upside down on top of the mold, pressed down to force out excess putty and left intact for 12 hours. When you lift off the mold, a facsimile of the missing overlay remains which is difficult to tell from the original.

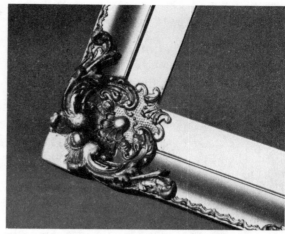
1 Rebuild the partially missing corner as close to the original as possible with water putty. Let this dry about 30 minutes

4 Chip off the old overlay to the bare wood. Then make undercuts with a chisel to help anchor the new overlay casting to the frame

7 If more than one corner needs to be replaced, continue to use the mold since it shrinks as it becomes thoroughly cured

2 Assemble a wood frame around the corner overlay. Fit it as close to the picture frame as you can and dam with wet paper wads

3 Mix casting powder with water, fill the mold, let it harden. Then carefully lift the casting from the frame overlay

5 Pour the water-putty mixture into the inverted mold level with the top. Mix the putty until it reaches the consistency of thick cream

6 Place the filled mold right side up under the face side of the frame corner. Press down into the wet putty to force out the excess

8 When this much of an embossed overlay is missing, the overlay must be replaced with a new casting. It's beyond repair

9 Coat the new overlay with a clear sealer (Deft), wipe the frame with a lacquer thinner, then spray the entire frame with a gold paint

This unit is half cold frame, half hotbed. Follow drawings (right) to build either side independently or a custom-sized frame to fit your specific gardening plans

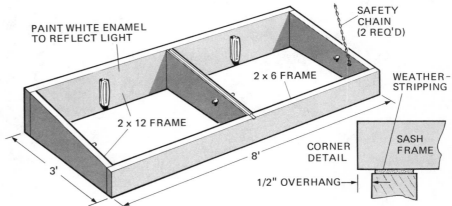

SAFETY CHAIN (2 REQ'D)

PAINT WHITE ENAMEL TO REFLECT LIGHT

2 x 6 FRAME

WEATHER-STRIPPING

2 x 12 FRAME

SASH FRAME

CORNER DETAIL

8'

3'

1/2" OVERHANG

120

Get a jump on summer with cold frames

■ THE MOST INEXPERIENCED wood-worker can build a cold frame suitable for the most experienced gardener. And if you like gardening, you'll find that a good cold frame is almost as useful as a small greenhouse, at a fraction of the cost.

The most versatile unit possible is really a combination of cold frame-hotbed. Separate storm sash and a center partition create two different areas. On the left is a cold frame heated by

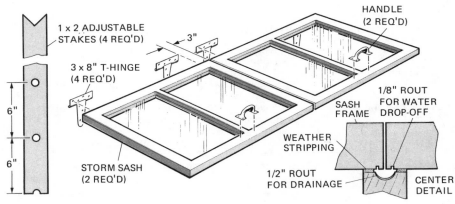

1 x 2 ADJUSTABLE STAKES (4 REQ'D)

3 x 8" T-HINGE (4 REQ'D)

3"

HANDLE (2 REQ'D)

6"

6"

STORM SASH (2 REQ'D)

SASH FRAME

1/8" ROUT FOR WATER DROP-OFF

WEATHER STRIPPING

1/2" ROUT FOR DRAINAGE

CENTER DETAIL

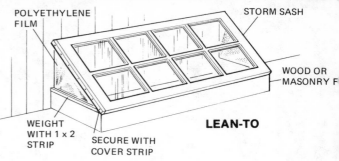

LEAN-TO

POLYETHYLENE FILM

STORM SASH

WOOD OR MASONRY F

WEIGHT WITH 1 x 2 STRIP

SECURE WITH COVER STRIP

This simple cold frame is ideal for the south side of a barn or garage. You can use a wooden or masonry frame at the bottom and plastic sheets along the sides

ORGANIC HOTBED

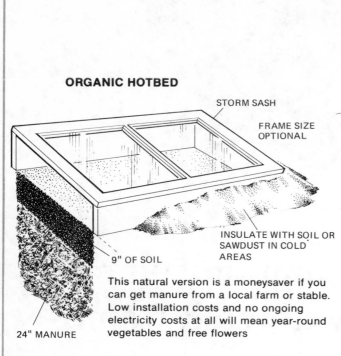

STORM SASH

FRAME SIZE OPTIONAL

INSULATE WITH SOIL OR SAWDUST IN COLD AREAS

9" OF SOIL

24" MANURE

This natural version is a moneysaver if you can get manure from a local farm or stable. Low installation costs and no ongoing electricity costs at all will mean year-round vegetables and free flowers

CLEAR FRAME

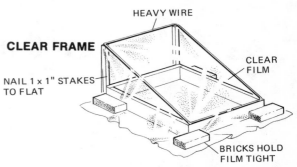

HEAVY WIRE

CLEAR FILM

NAIL 1 x 1" STAKES TO FLAT

BRICKS HOLD FILM TIGHT

No-frills model here, built with a minimum of time and money invested, will still get you satisfactory results

ELECTRIC HOTBED

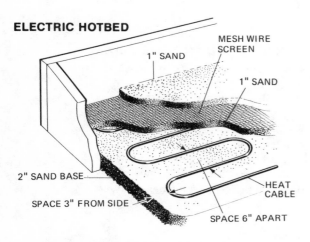

MESH WIRE SCREEN

1" SAND

1" SAND

2" SAND BASE

SPACE 3" FROM SIDE

HEAT CABLE

SPACE 6" APART

This year-round frame will do some gardening on its own by automatically controlling temperature level

RAISED FRAME

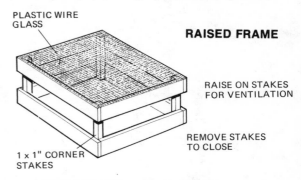

PLASTIC WIRE GLASS

RAISE ON STAKES FOR VENTILATION

REMOVE STAKES TO CLOSE

1 x 1" CORNER STAKES

Four corner stakes are used to raise and lower this primitive but functional model. Construction is so simple that it makes a great project for a child

YEAR-ROUND USES FOR COLD FRAMES

Early spring	Hardening-off plants—ease transition for young seedlings from greenhouse to garden.
Spring and summer	Seed sowing.
	Early start for hardy and half-hardy annuals and perennials.
Late spring and summer	Use sand or peat moss for propagation of cuttings.
Autumn	Seed sowing for dormant winter until early-spring germination.
Winter	Protection for newly started perennials.
	Growing tender bulbs.
	Storage for bulbs and plants to be forced.

VINYL DOME KIT ASSEMBLY

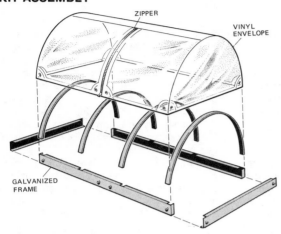

ZIPPER

VINYL ENVELOPE

GALVANIZED FRAME

Spring will arrive early at your house with this growth dome from Arrow Industries, 100 Alexander Ave., Pompton Plains, NJ. It provides 12 sq. ft. of heated space under a zippered vinyl envelope. The lightweight galvanized steel frame can be set up in 15 minutes and add 60 days to your growing season. The cost is about $17

COLD FRAME VARIATIONS

TYPES
Wooden frame and sash
Masonry frame and sash
Wooden frame and plastic cover
Organic hotbed and conventional frame
Electric cable hotbed and conventional frame
Kits, growing dome
Lean-tos, wooden sash and frame

ACCESSORIES
Thermometer
Electric-heat cable element
Lath (snow fencing) for summer sash
Safety chains

the sun's rays. On the right is a year-round hotbed with an auxiliary heat supply. Most garden supply centers sell heat cable in different lengths that can be snaked over a two-inch sand base. The wire has a built-in sensing switch that automatically calls for heat if the in-frame temperature falls below 74°. You can build either side of this frame as an independent unit, or build the double sash size as all cold frame or all hotbed.

a lot for a little

Keep construction simple and efficient. Depending on how enterprising you are, you can use scrap wood and used storm sash to help keep the price tag for the complete setup below $100 and as low as $50. A cold frame is simply a slant-sided box with a transparent, hinged lid. Take a total dimension for the storm sash and make the frame ½ in. smaller on all four sides. This gives you a nice overhang to keep rainwater from dripping inside the frame. It also gives you a margin for error. If you're not an experienced woodworker, don't worry; you're not building a finished cabinet and a little enamel paint will make this unit look pretty good. Most garden books recommend cypress or redwood. But you can save some money with fir or any scrap wood on hand. Soak it well with two coats of a preservative like Woodlife and finish with two coats of exterior white enamel. Here are some tips for a successful installation:

- Locate with sash facing south.
- Provide a windbreak on north side.
- Make sure site is well drained.
- Install a thermometer.
- Maintain a temperature range of 40° to 100° F. (85° optimum).
- Keep airtight; use weatherstrip.
- Prevent sash blow-over with safety chains.

We've outlined different cold frames you can build down to the simplest and most temporary varieties. You can even dig a hole and spread plastic across the top secured with a few rocks.

365 days of summer

You'll get your investment back from the extra harvest of vegetables and flowers you can start ahead of schedule with a cold frame. Check the seasonal chart for year-round advantages of hotbeds. With either organic or electric versions you can have fresh chrysanthemums on a Thanksgiving table or a centerpiece of poinsettias for Christmas morning. The next stop in year-round gardening is a greenhouse.

Ten clever shop tips

1 With a spacing jig attached to the miter gauge, it's a simple trick to cut a perfect-fitting box or finger joint on your own table saw. The jig is little more than a wood fence screw-fastened to the gauge and fitted with a small projecting block which uniformly spaces a series of notches across the width of the work. The notches are made with a dado cutter, and their width and depth are generally equal to or slightly less than the thickness of the stock. With ½-in.-thick stock, the notches would be ½ in. wide, ½ in. deep and ½ in. apart.

To make the joint, stand the two pieces to be joined against the fence so the edge of one piece is even with line A and the edge of the other is even with B. Push the work across the cutter, then shift it so the notch just cut sits over the spacing block, and make a second notch. Place the second notch over the block and make a third notch and so on. Repeat the step until notches are made the full width of the work.

It is important that the two pieces of stock are held in the same position throughout the notching. This is assured when the spacer block projects far enough to catch both pieces. If desired, the two pieces can be clamped together with a small C-clamp. Adjustments can be made by moving either the spacer block or the fence itself to give you the perfect fit on your joint.

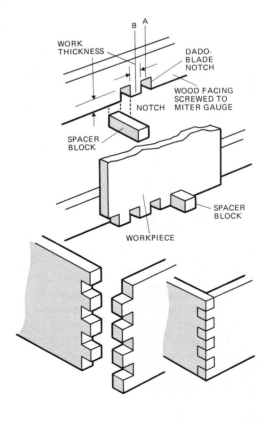

WORK THICKNESS

B A

DADO-BLADE NOTCH

WOOD FACING SCREWED TO MITER GAUGE

NOTCH

SPACER BLOCK

SPACER BLOCK

WORKPIECE

2 If you want to dish a disc, but don't have a lathe, there's another way to form a saucer-like cavity—with your table saw. All you need is a V-notched board clamped to the saw and positioned so it centers the blank directly over the vertical axis of the blade. With blade running below the table and the disc face down in the V-notch, crank up the blade ⅛ in. into the work and slowly rotate the disc 360°. You should begin to feel the blade cutting into the wood. Raise the blade another ⅛ in. and repeat the same procedure.

By taking a number of light cuts and slowly rotating the work each time, you'll produce a perfectly concave dish requiring very little sanding. If you want a cut which has a smaller diameter, try using a smaller blade. Remember, the sharper the blade, the better cut you will get.

Saucer-like cut in the underside of a wood disc is made by rotating the work over a saw blade. V-notched board is clamped to the table so it positions directly over the blade

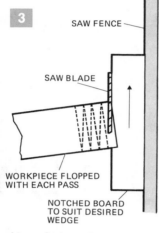

SAW FENCE

SAW BLADE

WORKPIECE FLOPPED WITH EACH PASS

NOTCHED BOARD TO SUIT DESIRED WEDGE

3 If you must cut a lot of wedges, you can mass-cut them in jig time by using a notched board. The board is notched as shown to suit the desired taper, and the saw fence is set so the blade just clears the jig as it's passed along the fence. Sawing is done with the grain after the stock is first crosscut from wide material.

As each wedge is cut, the stock is flopped in the notch. Like slicing cheese, the jig is pushed forward, then withdrawn with the wedge in the notch. Select stock free of knots and with straight grain. If you use a hollow-ground combination blade, there will be no need to sand the wedges. Width of the stock from which the wedges are cut must equal the length of the notch so the wedges will have chisel points. If blunt points are wanted, make the notch in the board deeper.

Notched jig pushed along a fence provides a fast way to mass-produce wedges on a bench saw. The work is held at an angle in the jig and is flopped over after each cut

4 How do you bore a hole completely through a board edgewise that's 2 in. or so wider than the bit is long? You bore from opposite edges. In doing so, there's a trick to keeping the two holes aligned and here's how:

Clamp a scrap board to the drill-press table and bore a hole in it ½-in. deep. Then lower the table and bore a hole 3 in. deep in the edge of the work. Replace the bit with a long dowel of the same size. Align the dowel with the hole in the wood table by lowering the chuck, then lock the table. Put the original bit back in the chuck, insert a short dowel pin in the hole in the wood table, place the work over the pin and bore down from the top edge to meet the first hole. If you have carefully followed the correct procedure, both holes will be on target and align perfectly.

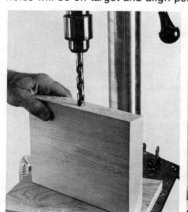

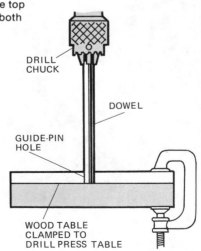

DRILL CHUCK

DOWEL

GUIDE-PIN HOLE

WOOD TABLE CLAMPED TO DRILL PRESS TABLE

5 You can buy a tenoner that slides in the groove of your saw table and has a special clamping fixture to hold the work, or you can make one that rides the fence and uses a common C-clamp as shown here. Both are used to make the cheek cuts on a tenon after the shoulder cuts have already been completed.

When a single blade is used, the work can simply be turned edge for edge to make a second cheek cut. If you use two blades with a spacer between, one pass is all that is necessary and you're done. If your saw's fence is a simple box channel like the one shown in the photo on the right, the tenoner is made to fit it like a saddle with scant clearance to ride without binding and without play. Waxing the inside will help it slide easier. In following the dimensions, note that the tunnel is dimensioned for a 1-in.-thick fence and will vary in size with the particular fence you have. Note too that the vertical stop against which the work is placed, then clamped, must be at a right angle to the base to give you a properly cut tenon to fit your project.

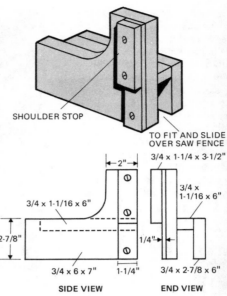

SHOULDER STOP

TO FIT AND SLIDE OVER SAW FENCE

3/4 x 1-1/4 x 3-1/2"

3/4 x 1-1/16 x 6"

3/4 x 1-1/16 x 6"

2"

2-7/8"

1/4"

3/4 x 6 x 7"   1-1/4"   3/4 x 2-7/8 x 6"

SIDE VIEW   END VIEW

6 While you can set blade height by the saw's built-in scale, it's often quicker to do it with a stepped gauge block comprising a number of 1/8-in. thick plywood strips glued together in a stack. Each strip is 1/2 or 3/4-in. shorter than the next. To use the block, you place it over the blade and crank the blade down (or up) until the block rests flat on the table. For example, if you want to set the blade 3/4 in. high, you pick the sixth step.

7 The best-holding glue dowels are dowels which have a spiral kerf. Not only does the kerf help line the hole with glue from top to bottom, but it affords an escape for glue trapped in the bottom of the hole when clamps are applied. To kerf a glue dowel on a bandsaw, tilt table 15°, clamp the miter gauge to it and slowly rotate the dowel as the blade cuts a 1/16-in.-deep kerf. Don't attempt this with a short length of dowel.

8 The first thing to make after you buy your first table saw is a push stick to have handy when you're ripping work narrower than 4 in. It is both for convenience and for safety. A wooden coat hanger will provide you with two ready-made push sticks which require only notching, although it's simple enough to make a push stick from scratch with scrap wood. The fence-straddling pusher is another type for use when the shape of the rip fence permits. Its D-grip handle keeps the hand securely in place and safe from the blade. Make it to ride the fence freely and not bind anywhere.

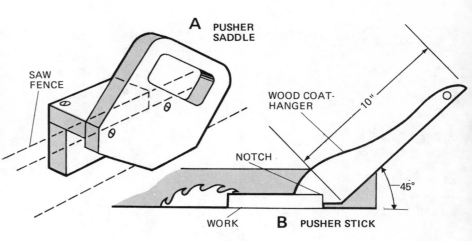

A PUSHER SADDLE
SAW FENCE
WOOD COAT-HANGER
10"
NOTCH
45°
WORK B PUSHER STICK

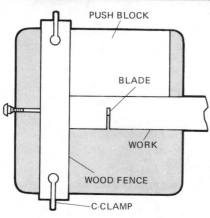

PUSH BLOCK
BLADE
WORK
WOOD FENCE
C-CLAMP

9 While a bandsaw is primarily for cutting irregular shapes, it still has other potential. Here it is being used for quantity cutoff work even though it has no fence or a groove for a miter gauge. As shown in the setup above, a scrap of wood is clamped to the table to serve as a fence and a wood block pinch-hits for a miter gauge. In use, narrow stock is guided squarely through the blade by the backup block used as a pusher. To maintain a high level of accuracy it is suggested that you make the block as perfectly square as is possible.

10 When work must be held in close contact with the fence for the entire length of a cut, the spring action of a spring board can often prove to be much better than the hand. It's simply made by sawing a 60° angle at the end of a hardwood scrap. Then rip several closely spaced "fingers" one-third its length. To use it, clamp it to the saw table. As you feed the wood through the saw the fingers will hold the piece to be cut in contact with the fence by bearing lightly against the wood.

The sweeping elegance of this luxurious platform is matched by its versatility. Full-length storage drawers slide out easily on casters, and convenient end tables can be placed at any point along the 1-in. aluminum rails

Dream stuff: handsome platform beds

■ ONE OF THE BEST FEATURES of this king-sized platform bed is that hidden beneath the elegant styling and generous proportions is more easy-access storage than you are likely to find in most closets. When you first look at this bed it may seem to be too luxurious for your bedroom. But when you begin to study the plans you will see that every decorative detail is built to serve an important purpose. Notice that the platform part of the bed has a significant over-hang. It is designed this way to create a floating effect that makes a large piece of furniture seem less imposing in your bedroom. But the design also puts to use one of the biggest dust collectors of all time—the dead space under a conventional bed. Here are the full-size drawers, bigger than you will find in any dresser. They are made with casters on the bottom to roll out easily on a hard floor or even on a rug.

KING-SIZE BED

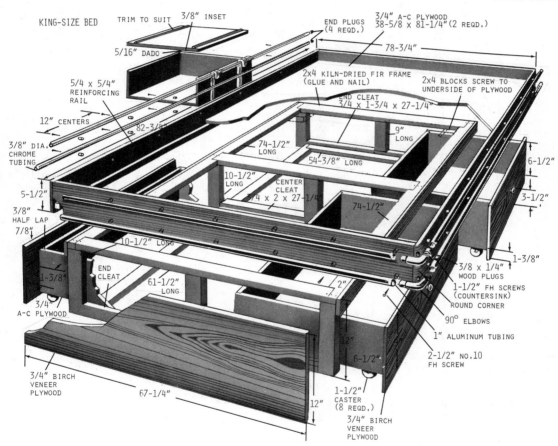

The Simmons mattress we used is about 6-in. thick. Allow ½ in. between the mattress and the side rail to accommodate bedcovers

A plywood jig with nails supports the aluminum tubing for marking the screw holes. Sliding drawers (far right) have casters on the front and Teflon glides at the rear

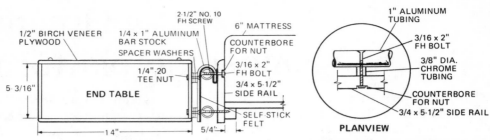

1/2" BIRCH VENEER PLYWOOD
1/4 x 1" ALUMINUM BAR STOCK
SPACER WASHERS
2-1/2" NO. 10 FH SCREW
6" MATTRESS
COUNTERBORE FOR NUT
3/16 x 2" FH BOLT
3/4 x 5-1/2" SIDE RAIL
SELF-STICK FELT
1/4"-20 TEE NUT
END TABLE
5-3/16"
14"
5/4"

1" ALUMINUM TUBING
3/16 x 2" FH BOLT
3/8" DIA. CHROME TUBING
COUNTERBORE FOR NUT
3/4 x 5-1/2" SIDE RAIL
PLANVIEW

END TABLE DETAILS

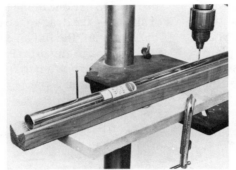

A grooved 2x2 will support the 1-in. aluminum tubing during drilling

A block with a 1½-in. hole and a simple pipe tee guide the rail bending

With this jig, the aluminum bar stock can be bent by stages in the vise

Self-stick felt lines the inside of the bar stock where it rests against the rails

movable end tables

The interesting and attractive rails on the sides of the bed are made from 1-in. aluminum tubing with compression-socket elbows connecting the straight lengths. The rails are attached to the side with screws and spacers every 12 in. as is shown in the details above.

The end tables are designed in keeping with the free-floating design of the total bed by hooking onto the side rails. Aluminum bar stock is used and bent like an upside down ''J'' to hook over the top rail and bear against the bottom one. The straps securely hold the end tables at convenient right angles to the bed. But the design of the straps lets you freely move the tables to any point along the rails. Since the tables are supported without any permanently fastened hardware, you can move them aside for better access to the drawers or for a more convenient position. Since the siderails run around the foot of the bed as well, you may even want to move one of the tables around to the end of the bed to support a TV set.

construction tips

We strongly suggest that you use kiln-dried 2x4s for the frame of the bed. This dimensionally stable wood won't shrink and tighten up the drawers. To keep the drawers sliding and operating smoothly, install Teflon guides at the back corners of each to reduce friction against the support cleats. Much of the construction of the bed is in the supporting members and won't be seen. Devote the most attention and time to critical areas like the side rail corners. If you cut carefully with a good sharp saw blade, a simple butt joint is all that's needed.

You should first clamp the joint in place and

then counterbore for the screws and plugs. Then carefully drill pilot holes through the joint so the screws will seat firmly without splitting the ¾-in. end grain. Take the joint apart to apply some glue, then tighten up the screws in the predrilled holes. If you cut plugs (the same size as your counterbore) from your railing material, they'll be unnoticeable when you finally sand them flush.

the single sleeper

You may already have a good double bed for yourself and don't want to attack the project described above. But how about the kids? Couldn't one of them use a single, smaller version of the platform bed? Our small platform bed is a less challenging project that you can probably build in an afternoon. Study the plans carefully that are shown below. The simple base is made from plywood panels that are reinforced for strength and stability at each of the corners. Carriage bolts and wingnuts hold the pieces together. This means that the bed can easily be taken apart for moving.

sleep on a dream

Both of these beds are designed not only for good sleeping but to add style to the bedroom. Begin working on one of them today and you'll be sleeping on a dream before you know it.

You can build this simple platform bed for about $50, including the foam mattress. The solid platform is surrounded by pine rails, mitered at the corners and reinforced with 5/4-square kiln-dried strips. The support platform is made of plywood and painted to suit. Pull out the eight carriage bolts and bed will store flat

SMALL PLATFORM

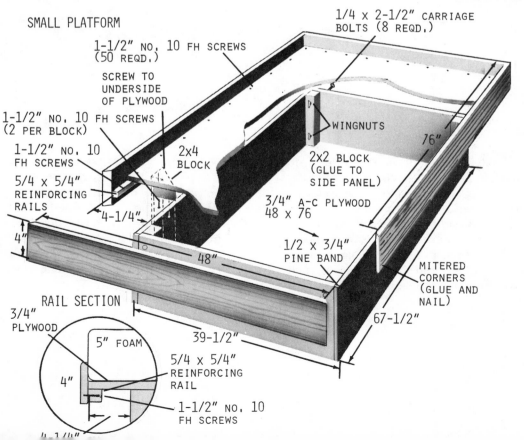

SMALL PLATFORM

1/4 x 2-1/2" CARRIAGE BOLTS (8 REQD.)

1-1/2" NO. 10 FH SCREWS (50 REQD.)

SCREW TO UNDERSIDE OF PLYWOOD

1-1/2" NO. 10 FH SCREWS (2 PER BLOCK)

1-1/2" NO. 10 FH SCREWS

5/4 x 5/4" REINFORCING RAILS

2x4 BLOCK

4-1/4"

4"

48"

WINGNUTS

2x2 BLOCK (GLUE TO SIDE PANEL)

3/4" A-C PLYWOOD 48 x 76

1/2 x 3/4" PINE BAND

76"

MITERED CORNERS (GLUE AND NAIL)

67-1/2"

RAIL SECTION

3/4" PLYWOOD

5" FOAM

4"

5/4 x 5/4" REINFORCING RAIL

1-1/2" NO. 10 FH SCREWS

39-1/2"

The fine art of layering wood

Laminating is the process of combining two or more woods into a project. By using this method, everyday objects can take on a striking new look as you can see in the six handsome projects shown on these pages

BY PENELOPE ANGELL

■ COMBINING TWO or more woods into laminations can produce surprising patterns and color blendings. Laminating also offers a chance to experiment with small amounts of exotic woods that would ordinarily be too expensive.

To prepare the laminate, glue the wood pieces together with a thin, even coat of liquid hide, epoxy resin or other wood glue. Clamp the wood tightly with bar or pipe clamps to form a "blank." Place scrap wood on either side of the blank to protect it from clamp marks.

After the glue has cured, plane the blank smooth and saw, carve or lathe-turn it to form the object. Sand it smooth with coarse, medium and fine sandpaper, then apply your finish.

Be sure all mating surfaces are smooth and totally free of imperfections and dust. Purchase dressed lumber.

Here the author is using a wood rasp to shape the laminated salad scoops

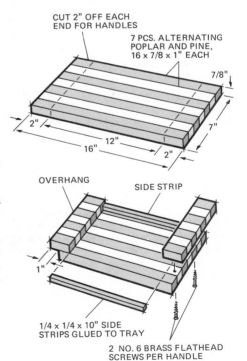

1. Fancy tray

The handles of this poplar and pine tray are cut from the ends of the tray blank to give a continuous pattern effect. The sides are strips of poplar.

Materials: 4 pieces of poplar and 3 pieces of pine, each 16 x ⅞ x 1 in.; 2 strips of poplar, each 10 x ¼ x ¼ in.; glue; 4 No. 6 brass flathead screws, 1⅛ in. long; sandpaper (3 grades); vegetable oil.

Method: Prepare the laminated blank with alternating 16-in.-long pieces of wood as explained on the facing page. After the glue has dried and the wood is planed smooth, saw 2 in. off both ends of the blank for the handles. Attach the handles to the tray with screws by predrilling two holes in the underside of each handle approximately 2 in. from each side. The handles should have a 1-in. overhang. Mark screw placement 2 in. from both sides on the underside of the tray, then countersink them. Glue the poplar strips to the tray sides. Sand smooth, then finish with oil.

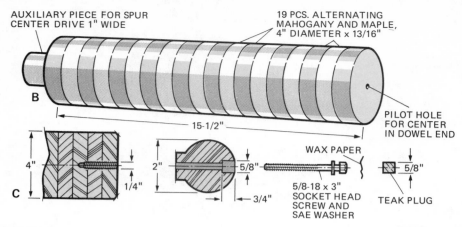

AUXILIARY PIECE FOR SPUR
CENTER DRIVE 1" WIDE

19 PCS. ALTERNATING
MAHOGANY AND MAPLE,
4" DIAMETER x 13/16"

2. Rolling pin

B

15-1/2"

PILOT HOLE
FOR CENTER
IN DOWEL END

4"

C

1/4"

2"

5/8"

3/4"

WAX PAPER

5/8-18 x 3"
SOCKET HEAD
SCREW AND
SAE WASHER

5/8"

TEAK PLUG

Use a dowel as an axle while you are sanding the discs

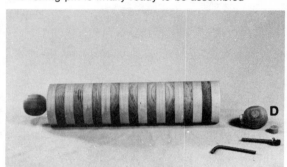

A

The rolling pin is finally ready to be assembled

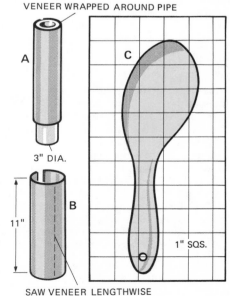

D

This rolling pin is made of maple and teak discs turned on a lathe.

Materials: 10 maple and 9 teak discs each 4 in. in diameter by ¹³/₁₆ in. thick; 2½-in.-square teak stock about 8 in. long; glue; ¼-in.-diameter dowel; 2 sockethead screws ⅝-18 x 13 in. and SAE washers; sandpaper; wax paper; peanut oil.

Method: On a jigsaw cut out the 19 discs. Drill a ¼-in. center hole in each (A). Using a dowel as an axle, individually sand the disc edges. Cut the dowel to equal the combined thickness of the discs plus 1-in. Slide the discs onto the dowel and glue together with an auxiliary piece of wood to serve as the spur center drive (B). (You may want to enlarge the disc holes to ⁹/₃₂ in.) When dry, lay out

the center on the drive piece, mount and turn. Remove the auxiliary spur drive and clean the glue from the rolling pin end. Turn the teak stock to a 2-in. diameter and saw crosswise in half for the handles. Drill pilot holes through both handles and make a ⅝-in.-diameter counterbore in one end of each handle ¾ in. deep. Drill pilot hole to ¹¹/₃₂ in. on each handle. Cut two teak plugs ⅝ in. diameter by ¾ in. deep. Drill ¼ in. by 2 in. deep into each roller end and make a ⁵/₁₆-18 coarse thread tap (C). With a cotton swab place five-minute epoxy glue into the threads in the roller ends, being careful not to get any on the outside face. Add wax paper over the screwheads or the roller may not rotate. Assemble using PVA (polyvinyl acetate) glue for the plug (D). Finish with oil.

3. Salad scoops

These salad scoops are made with five layers of reddish Padouk veneer.

Materials: 5 pieces 9x11-in. veneer ¹/₂₈-in. thick; casein glue; lead pipe about 3-in. diameter and 11 in. long (or other cylindrical form); rubber strips for clamping (from an inner tube or rubber gloves); 2 6-in. pieces of leather lacing; vegetable oil.

Method: Cut the veneer pieces, then sponge with water until pliable. Glue them together with an even coat of glue. Clamp the veneer around a pipe, securing it with the rubber bands until the veneer is dry. It will form a nearly complete cylinder (A). Remove from pipe and saw into two equal pieces (B). Trace the full-size pattern (C) on a veneer piece and saw to rough shape with a coping saw. Trace pattern on reverse side of paper as guide for second scoop to produce a right and left-hand scoop. Refine with wood rasp. Sand, then oil. Drill holes for leather hangers.

VENEER WRAPPED AROUND PIPE

A

3" DIA.

C

B

11"

1" SQS.

SAW VENEER LENGTHWISE
IN EQUAL PIECES

4. Breadboard

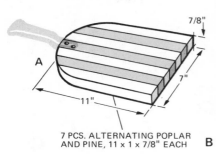

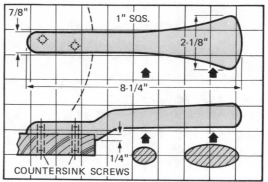

This poplar and pine breadboard has a handle carved from walnut.

Materials: 4 pieces of poplar and 3 pieces pine, each 11 x 1 x ⅞ in.; 1 piece of walnut 10 x 2½ x 2¾ in.; glue; sandpaper; 2 No. 6 brass flathead screws 1⅛ in. long; mineral oil.

Method: Prepare laminated blank with alternating wood pieces. After the glue has dried, plane smooth. Rough-shape the handle end of the board with a saw (A), and sand smooth. Rough-shape the handle with a saw (B). Round with a ½-in. wood gouge and a wood rasp. Sand smooth. Join handle and board by carefully predrilling screw holes in the underside of the handle, marking off screw placement on the underside of the board and countersinking them. Finish with oil.

---

5. Striped bowl

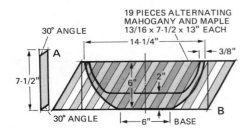

Rectangular blank is bandsawed to form thick disc equal to outside diameter of bowl top (14¼ in.) plus ½ in.

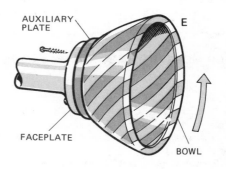

Angled mahogany and maple pieces form a striking pattern.

Materials: 10 mahogany and 9 maple pieces, each ¹³/₁₆ x 7½ x 13 in.; sandpaper; glue; peanut oil.

Method: To prepare the laminated blank, mark and saw off at 30° angles the ends of the wood on the 7½-in. dimension (A). Glue alternate types of wood together and clamp. The laminated blank will not have vertical sides

(B). Saw off the slanted sides to form a rectangle (C). Locate the center of the blank. Mark off both center auxiliary faceplate circle and top outside bowl diameter (14¼ in.) plus ½ in. on the blank. Use a bandsaw to form a thick disc the diameter of the bowl top plus ½ in. (D). Attach auxiliary plate to faceplate and screw to bowl. Mount on lathe and turn the outside of the bowl. Reverse and turn inside of bowl (E). Sand, then oil.

6. Duck

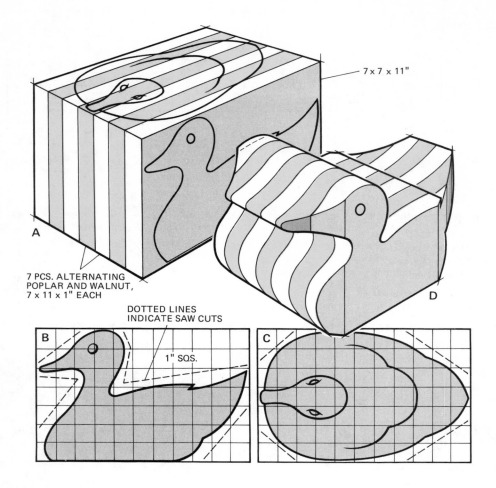

7 x 7 x 11"

A

7 PCS. ALTERNATING
POPLAR AND WALNUT,
7 x 11 x 1" EACH

D

DOTTED LINES
INDICATE SAW CUTS

B

1" SQS.

C

This poplar and walnut duck is a reward for a craftsman.

Materials: 4 poplar and 3 walnut pieces each 7 x 11 x 1 in., glue; 15-in. square plywood; 2 screws; ¾ and ½-in. wood gouges; rasp; sandpaper; linseed oil; butcher's wax.

Method: Prepare the blank and plane smooth. Draw the duck on the blank (A). Form the side of the duck by cutting with a saw (B). Secure the duck to the work surface. Fasten it to the plywood square with screws and clamp the plywood to the work surface. Refine sides with gouges. Redraw and form top (C) with saw and gouges. The rough shape should look similar to the drawing (D). Work toward the back and shape tail. Level bumps and gouge marks with rasp. Sand smooth. Apply three coats of oil. Remove excess oil and apply wax.

FOR MORE INFORMATION ON LAMINATING

Books
■ Glenister, S.H., *Contemporary Design in Woodwork,* Vols. 1, 2 and 3, John Murray, London, 1968.
■ Nilsson, Ake R., *Woodware,* Drake Publishers, Inc., New York, 1973.
■ Piepenburg, Robert E., *Designs in Wood,* Bruce Publishing Co., New York, 1969.

Organizations and schools
■ American Crafts Council, 44 West 53rd St., New York, N.Y. 10019; maintains Museum of Contemporary Crafts at 29 West 53rd St., New York.
■ National Woodcarvers Assn., 7424 Miami Ave., Cincinnati, OH 45243; for amateur and professional woodcarvers; publishes bimonthly bulletin.

■ The Woodsmith's Studio, 142 East 32nd St., New York, NY 10016; classes in woodworking, wood finishing and carving.

Sources of exotic woods and tools
■ Albert Constantine and Son, Inc., 2050 Eastchester Rd., Bronx, NY 10461.
■ Craftsman Wood Service, 2727 South Mary St., Chicago, IL 60608.
■ Sculpture House, 38 East 30th St., New York, NY 10016.
■ Woodcraft Supply Corp., 313 Montvale Ave., Woburn, MA 01801.

Wood manufacturers' tour
■ Kennedy Brothers, 11 Main, Vergennes, VT 05491; specializes in wood wall hangings. Gift shop; factory open to 4 p.m. weekdays.

Two stowaway tables for the outdoors

The table above can be opened on one or both sides for serving and closes to only 7 inches wide. Table below breaks down into four separate parts for easy storage

■ IMAGINE HAVING a Christmas display on your lawn 12 months of the year simply because it is too big and bulky to put away! You can liken this to a bulky picnic table that sits around from one summer to the next, too large to stow away come winter, a headache to move each time you must mow around it. And before long, its ap-

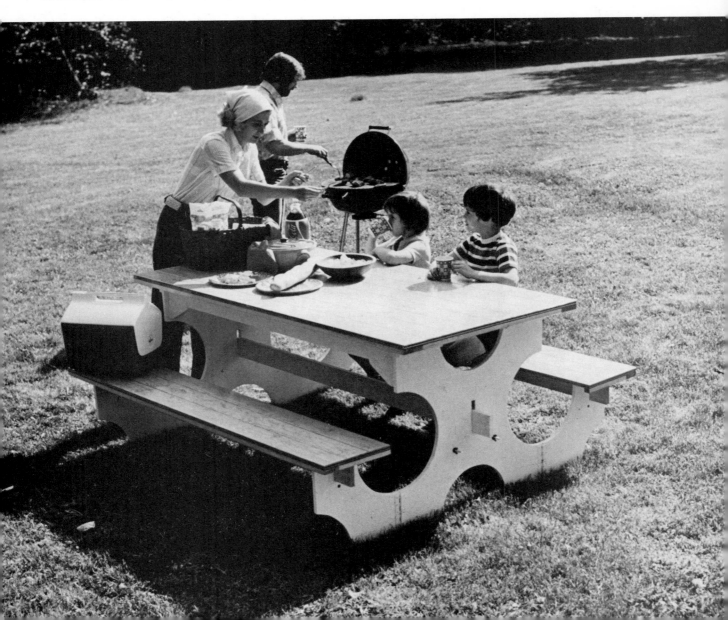

pearance starts disintegrating from constant exposure to the elements.

Not so with the two unique tables shown on these pages. You can take them apart, close them up, move them indoors if you wish, or park them in the garage in a minimum space.

The 3x6-ft. table in the large photograph on page 137 breaks down into four parts—two benchtops, stretcher and a table that folds flat. To set it up, you place the table face down and open the wood turn-buttons which hold the legs in tow and the metal ones which anchor the leg braces. Lift one leg, back off the wingnuts, swing open the twin bench legs and insert the stretcher part way in its slot. Then lift the opposite leg, swing out the bench legs, raise both side braces, shove the notched stretcher in place and pull up on it to lock it. Turn the table right side up, open the notched rails on the underside of the benchtops and fit them into the notches in the legs. This procedure may sound complicated but once your family gets used to it you will be surprised how quickly the table will be ready for your picnic.

two sheets of plywood

It takes two 4x8-ft. sheets of plywood (with some waste) for the legs, table and benchtops, and 1x2, 1x3, 1x4 and 2x4 lumber for the rest. You'll need 20 3-in. plain butt hinges, four wingnuts and bolts, six metal turnbuttons and about six dozen 1¼-in. No. 8 flathead screws,

along with some water-resistant glue. A couple coats of a marine-type spar varnish inside and out give good protection for the plywood table and benchtops. We used Zip-Guard by Star Bronze Co., Box 568, Alliance, OH 44601. Two coats of acrylic latex house paint will keep the legs in good condition and will add some color to the table.

You'll need a saber saw to cut the legs, but it's worth the small extra charge to have the lumberyard saw your plywood into the nine individual pieces required. This way, there won't be much cutting to be done and a handsaw will handle what's left. Kerfing of the table and benchtops adds to the looks, but is optional. The kerfs are easy to cut if you have a router or portable circular saw.

It's important that the leg hinges at the top fit flush in their rabbets so the side braces will pass over the barrels when moved up or down. Note too that the end-view drawing shows a ¾-in.-sq. block added to the tops of the bench legs to bear against the underside of the benchtops for added support.

the second table

The fold-down table is light enough to carry to a deck or yard and elegant enough to use inside, too. It doesn't look like a plywood table (even though the panels are) because the edges are banded with ¾-in. solid stock. You can use any hardwood from mahogany (which we used to get

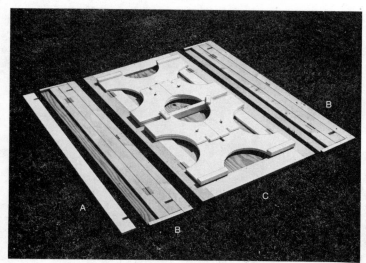

The four parts of this collapsible table are the stretcher (A), benchtops (B), and table (C). The bench and the table legs hinge to the tabletop. Use the cutting diagrams (right) to minimize waste

CUTTING DIAGRAMS

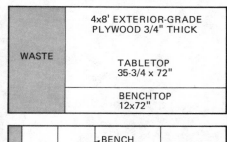

4x8' EXTERIOR-GRADE PLYWOOD 3/4" THICK

WASTE

TABLETOP 35-3/4 x 72"

BENCHTOP 12x72"

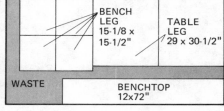

BENCH LEG 15-1/8 x 15-1/2"

TABLE LEG 29 x 30-1/2"

WASTE

BENCHTOP 12x72"

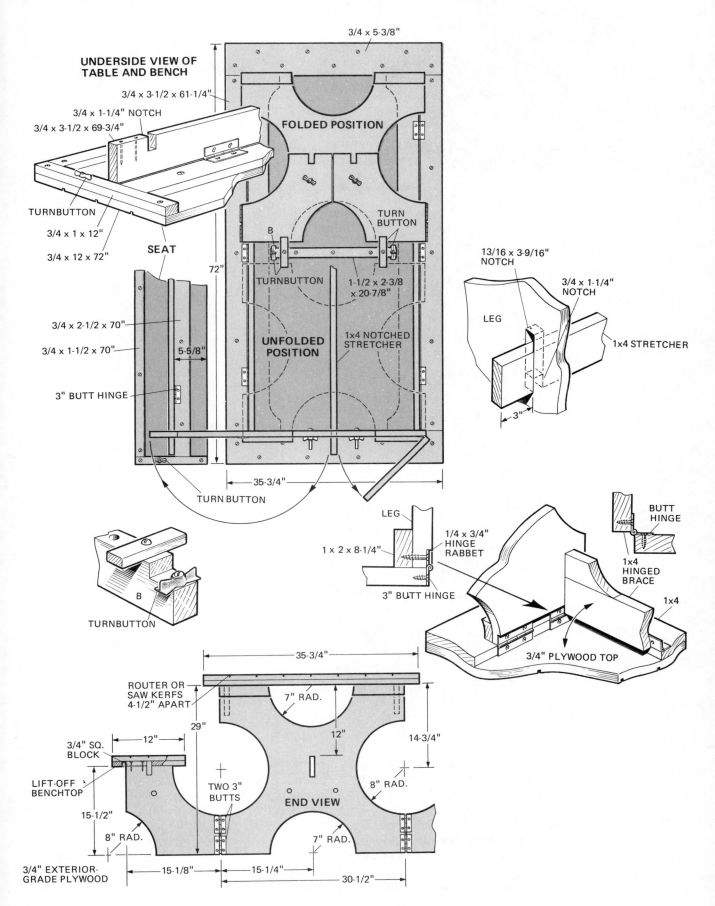

UNDERSIDE VIEW OF
TABLE AND BENCH

3/4 x 5-3/8"

3/4 x 3-1/2 x 61-1/4"

3/4 x 1-1/4" NOTCH

3/4 x 3-1/2 x 69-3/4"

FOLDED POSITION

TURNBUTTON

3/4 x 1 x 12"

3/4 x 12 x 72"

SEAT

72"

B

TURN BUTTON

TURNBUTTON

1-1/2 x 2-3/8
x 20-7/8"

3/4 x 2-1/2 x 70"

3/4 x 1-1/2 x 70"

5-5/8"

UNFOLDED
POSITION

1x4 NOTCHED
STRETCHER

3" BUTT HINGE

TURN BUTTON

35-3/4"

13/16 x 3-9/16"
NOTCH

3/4 x 1-1/4"
NOTCH

LEG

1x4 STRETCHER

3"

B

TURNBUTTON

LEG

1 x 2 x 8-1/4"

3" BUTT HINGE

1/4 x 3/4"
HINGE RABBET

BUTT
HINGE

1x4
HINGED
BRACE

1x4

3/4" PLYWOOD TOP

35-3/4"

ROUTER OR
SAW KERFS
4-1/2" APART

7" RAD.

29"

12"

14-3/4"

3/4" SQ.
BLOCK

12"

LIFT-OFF
BENCHTOP

8" RAD.

TWO 3"
BUTTS

END VIEW

15-1/2"

8" RAD.

7" RAD.

3/4" EXTERIOR-
GRADE PLYWOOD

15-1/8"

15-1/4"

30-1/2"

139

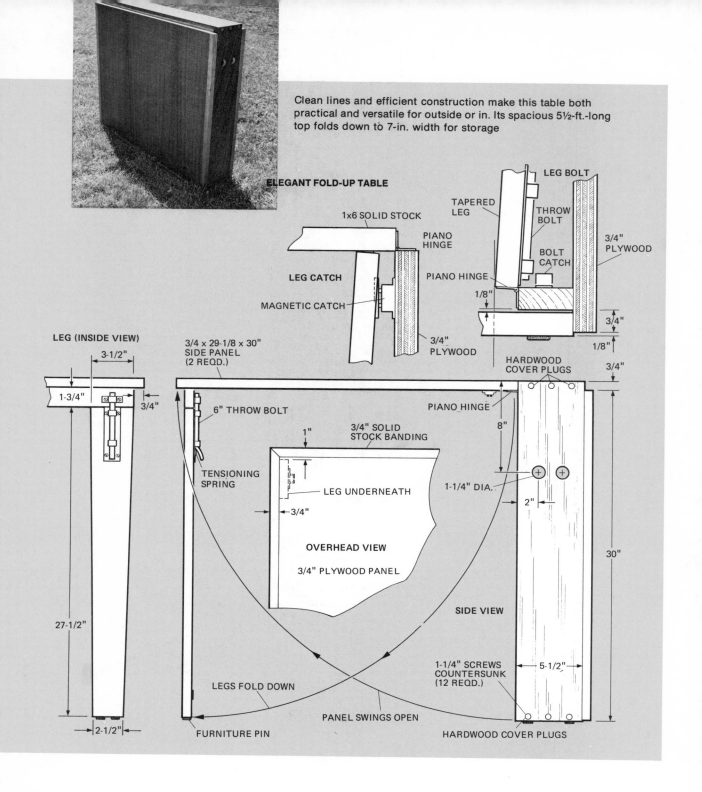

Clean lines and efficient construction make this table both practical and versatile for outside or in. Its spacious 5½-ft.-long top folds down to 7-in. width for storage

ELEGANT FOLD-UP TABLE

LEG BOLT

TAPERED LEG

THROW BOLT

1x6 SOLID STOCK

PIANO HINGE

BOLT CATCH

3/4" PLYWOOD

LEG CATCH

PIANO HINGE

MAGNETIC CATCH

1/8"

3/4"

3/4" PLYWOOD

1/8"

HARDWOOD COVER PLUGS

LEG (INSIDE VIEW)

3/4 x 29-1/8 x 30" SIDE PANEL (2 REQD.)

3/4"

PIANO HINGE

3-1/2"

1-3/4"

3/4"

6" THROW BOLT

8"

1"

3/4" SOLID STOCK BANDING

TENSIONING SPRING

LEG UNDERNEATH

1-1/4" DIA.

2"

3/4"

OVERHEAD VIEW

3/4" PLYWOOD PANEL

30"

SIDE VIEW

27-1/2"

1-1/4" SCREWS COUNTERSUNK (12 REQD.)

5-1/2"

LEGS FOLD DOWN

PANEL SWINGS OPEN

2-1/2"

FURNITURE PIN

HARDWOOD COVER PLUGS

a rich, dark tone) to a light birch. You'll need a sharp blade (carbide tipped is ideal) to cut the panels without damaging the edges. A plywood blade also will do the job nicely.

Assemble the center frame first. For good, tight construction, cut a ¼ x ¾-in. rabbet along the edges of the vertical center boards and lock in the horizontal members with glue and screws. Contrasting wood plugs are inserted into the

countersunk holes. Let them extend ¹/₁₆ in. to assure a smooth, flush finish when you do the sanding. Furniture pins in the bottom of the legs help steady the completed table. We used teak oil for a lustrous finish. It's made by Watco and is available from Woodcraft Supply Corp., 313 Montvale Ave., Woburn, MA 01801. Whichever table you build, it will be there when you need it and fold out of the way when you don't.

Build a stack of swingers

BY ROSARIO CAPOTOSTO

■ THIS ROLL-ABOUT stack of swinging trays offers handy storage for the hobbyist and the man with a home office. I made it for about $20.

The nine trays are made of ¼-in. fir plywood, butted, glued and nailed together. They swing open on a length of thinwall conduit. Use a smooth-cutting blade to mass-produce the tray parts. Use a fairly hard wood such as poplar, birch or soft maple for the tray corner blocks. Dress a square length, bevel one corner, then slice it into 3-in. pieces to project ¼ in. above the tray edges. Sand the blocks and glue in place.

Holes in the blocks must be bored squarely and identically so the trays will align and swing out evenly. Clamp a flat board to your drill-press table and two stop blocks at one corner. Hold each tray firmly against the blocks as you bore and stop when the bit's point pokes through. Turn the tray over to complete the hole. Half-inch conduit is $^{11}/_{16}$ in. o.d. (outside diameter).

Assemble trays with glue and ⅝-in. (20-ga.) brads, being careful to drive them straight. Cut parts from flat plywood

Ease all sharp corners of assembled trays with a block plane, then sand outside surfaces

Protect outside corner with a notched 90° block when gluing and clamping pivot blocks in right front corners of trays

Clamp two stop blocks to wood drill-press table to assure identically bored holes in the corner blocks of all nine trays

Coat holes with sanding sealer, then sand lightly when dry. Cotton on stick makes swab. Follow with a coat of candle wax

Slide trays over conduit post. Wax coating inside holes and on tops of corner blocks assures smooth-swinging trays

Bore holes for conduit in top and bottom sections of cabinet before final assembly. Glue the bottom section in place first

Attach free-swinging, swivel plate casters to the four corner blocks. Wheels should extend about 1 in. below the sides

When the holes are bored, paint trays and insides of holes with sanding sealer, then sand lightly when dry with 220-grit paper, holes and all. Rub a wax candle in the holes and across the tops of the blocks.

Make the outer cabinet shell from ¾-in. fir plywood. Drill a ¼-in.-deep hole in the top of the base section and in underside of the upper section, and nail and glue the base section in position. Insert the conduit in the hole in the base and place the upper section over the top of the con-

duit. Then glue and nail the top section in place.

Now turn the unit upside down and install blocks in the corners for plate-type swivel casters.

A facing of ¼-in. plywood is attached to all surfaces except the top edges of the upper compartment. These edges are faced with ¼ x 1-in. solid pine. Ease (round slightly) all corners with a block plane and sand. You'll find the wild grain pattern of fir plywood can add an interesting effect when finished natural.

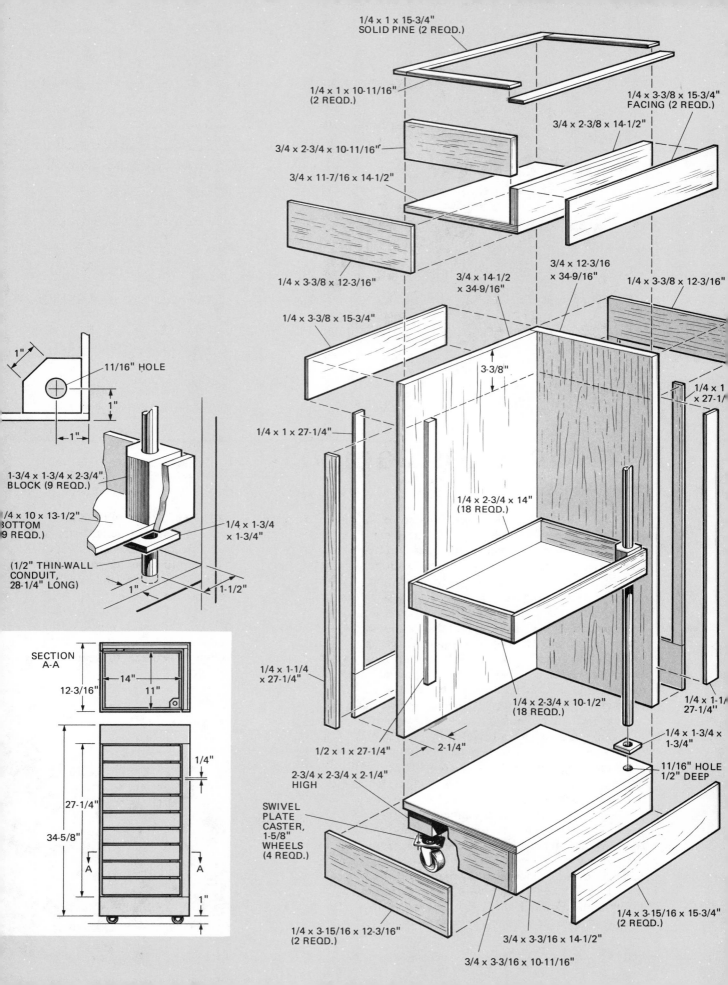

1/4 x 1 x 15-3/4" SOLID PINE (2 REQD.)

1/4 x 1 x 10-11/16" (2 REQD.)

1/4 x 3-3/8 x 15-3/4" FACING (2 REQD.)

3/4 x 2-3/4 x 10-11/16"

3/4 x 2-3/8 x 14-1/2"

3/4 x 11-7/16 x 14-1/2"

1/4 x 3-3/8 x 12-3/16"

3/4 x 12-3/16 x 34-9/16"

1/4 x 3-3/8 x 12-3/16"

3/4 x 14-1/2 x 34-9/16"

1/4 x 3-3/8 x 15-3/4"

3-3/8"

1/4 x 1 x 27-1/4"

1/4 x 1 x 27-1/4"

1/4 x 2-3/4 x 14" (18 REQD.)

1" HOLE — 11/16" HOLE

1"

1"

1-3/4 x 1-3/4 x 2-3/4" BLOCK (9 REQD.)

1/4 x 10 x 13-1/2" BOTTOM (9 REQD.)

1/4 x 1-3/4 x 1-3/4"

(1/2" THIN-WALL CONDUIT, 28-1/4" LONG)

1"   1-1/2"

1/4 x 1-1/4 x 27-1/4"

1/4 x 1-1/4 x 27-1/4"

1/4 x 2-3/4 x 10-1/2" (18 REQD.)

1/4 x 1-3/4 x 1-3/4"

11/16" HOLE 1/2" DEEP

SECTION A-A

12-3/16"

14"

11"

27-1/4"

1/4"

34-5/8"

A   A

1"

1/2 x 1 x 27-1/4"

2-1/4"

2-3/4 x 2-3/4 x 2-1/4" HIGH

SWIVEL PLATE CASTER, 1-5/8" WHEELS (4 REQD.)

1/4 x 3-15/16 x 12-3/16" (2 REQD.)

3/4 x 3-3/16 x 14-1/2"

1/4 x 3-15/16 x 15-3/4" (2 REQD.)

3/4 x 3-3/16 x 10-11/16"

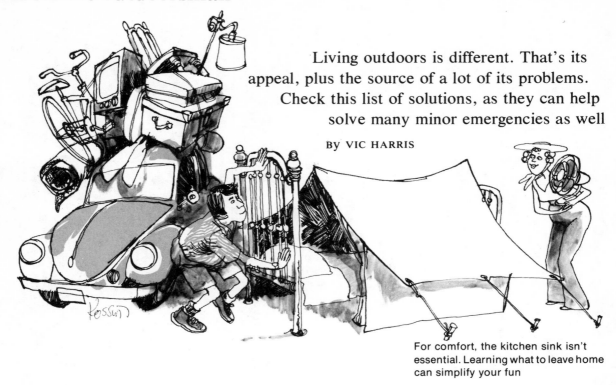

Living outdoors is different. That's its appeal, plus the source of a lot of its problems. Check this list of solutions, as they can help solve many minor emergencies as well

BY VIC HARRIS

For comfort, the kitchen sink isn't essential. Learning what to leave home can simplify your fun

Answers for campers

■ **1. WHERE TO CAMP.** For first-timers, there's a special apprehension about where they'll end up for the night. At the start, pick a spot close to home, call or write for reservations, try to arrive early for a better choice of location. A letter to the tourist department of a state should get you a list of public and private campgrounds. Buy the Rand McNally (about $6.95) and Woodall (about $6.95) guides at camp and sporting goods stores. Use their rating systems with caution, however; a recommended campground may mean floodlit volleyball until midnight. Ask the advice of other campers.

2. What to take. Though recreational vehicles now make it possible to travel with everything *and* the kitchen sink, that can make for cumbersome camping. For a start, find a rental outfit or borrow basics from a friend. Keep two lists: one of items to take along and another of gear you see and wish you had. Add equipment you really want, but except for first-aid kit, safety and foul-weather needs, leave home items you'll never use.

Select quality gear and study mail order catalogs like Herter's, Cabela's, Recreational Equipment, Eddie Bauer, L.L. Bean, EMS, Laacke & Joys and others.

3. A good night's sleep. Almost all the problems of the day can be handled better after a restful night in bed. For kids and backpackers, that means at least a hip-to-shoulder pad under blankets or sleeping bag. Some adults prefer a cot that keeps them off the ground.

Avoid camping on rocky, sloping or swampy ground, and unless you are sure there will be no discomforts, consider taking along a tent or RV, bug spray, and enough bedding to keep you warm and comfortable.

4. Keeping warm. Even on a mid-summer desert or tropic seashore, a raw chill can set in after dark. Best answer is the layer system: You add or remove a wool shirt, sweater, down jacket, wind shell, knit cap, extra socks and gloves to keep comfortable without sweating. Sleep in any or all of them if necessary.

Down gives the most insulation per ounce, stows most compactly, is most expensive, hardest to wash and dry out. Polar Guard and Fiberfill synthetics approach down's warmth-keeping ability, dry much more easily, cost less.

5. Keeping dry. Match your gear to your climate. Campers from the southwest find it hard to believe the occasional nonstop rain of the northwest or east. Boating foul-weather gear is too heavy, and light plastic wear will shred during your first walk through the woods. Choose a large medium-weight poncho or rain jacket and chaps. Watch out for "waterproof" gear; such clothing will make you sweat and a tent could drip condensation and restrict air for breathing if tightly closed. Note how experienced campers rig rain flies over tents, tables, storage areas.

6. How to beat crawlers and fliers. Few things can turn off camping fun like a cloud of no-see-ums, sand flies or mosquitoes. Avoid sheltered campsites during bug season, and take shelter behind screens and mosquito netting, long-sleeved shirts and pants and even a head net and gloves if the bugs are bad. Foggers, smudge coils, sprays and creams are getting better.

Hornets, ticks, wasps and yellow jackets can be discouraged by strong sprays, but avoiding

For a peaceful sleep from real and imagined discomforts, pick a level spot and protect it from bugs.

them is best. Good housekeeping with food and garbage well covered helps you keep from attracting flies, squirrels, raccoons, and other unwanted guests. Snakes are rare but should be avoided. Putting a hand or foot under a rock ledge or a fallen log is looking for trouble.

7. Gadgets to go. Many campers buy the best in lights, stoves, heaters, tents and fully equipped recreational vehicles and then don't try out the gear until they camp for the first time. "I was afraid it would flare up in the kitchen," they explain. Modern gear shouldn't flame up anywhere. Learn ahead of time how to replace a mantle, assemble the stove, prime a burner, charge batteries, fuel up, or replace an LP tank.

Carry backup items like a few stubby candles for light, warmth and cooking heat. A small LP catalytic heater can also supply safe heat.

RV owners should do particular homework with the instruction manuals for all their rolling appliances. Experience shows they should know how to service their plumbing, cooking, heating and lighting systems.

8. Camp cookery. What to take to eat and drink becomes more simple with experience. Except in deserts, good water is usually available at most campsites, but it's wise to carry an emergency jug. Wilderness travelers and backpackers, however, should use water purification tablets.

Firewood is seldom supplied, and burning campground trees is the worst form of vandalism. Bring a campstove instead. LP gas is easiest and safest to use; gasoline is cheapest; the little alcohol and heat tablet burners are compact for packers; charcoal is inconvenient for every meal cooking. You can choose the same foods you favor at home, repacking them into a grub box if space is limited. For backpackers, light freeze-dried precooked meals are convenient—but expensive.

9. Emergencies. Outdoor problems are half-solved when you figure good answers in advance. Get a doctor's checkup and any necessary prescriptions before you leave. Carry a well-stocked first-aid kit, and note the nearest telephone location.

Consider, also, the new advantages of carrying along a Citizens Band radio. Though limited in range, it can often reach someone who can relay a telephone call for aid.

10. The unknown. Uncertainty is often the most worrisome problem for today's camper. Experience and a healthy respect for the wild are the basic answers.

How to pick a pack

BY RICHARD DUNLOP

■ YOU DON'T HAVE to be an equipment freak to be concerned about the pack for your back. The wrong one can yank you backward just when you want to lean forward into a hill to let gravity help you on a steep climb, and it can catch in the brush and hang you up. A poorly fitted pack can give you more varieties of backaches than you ever imagined existed, and make you wish you'd stayed home. On the other hand, you don't have to take a money's-no-object approach to achieve backpacking comfort. The idea is to match the kind of pack you use to the kind of backpacking you plan to do.

There is always controversy over the pros and cons of soft packs, packs with frames, and which designs of each are best. You'll hear a lot of talk about inside versus outside framing, contour frames and flexible frames. Almost every one of the nation's 5-million backpacking enthusiasts seems to have his own surefire suspension theory. A little common sense discussion of the facts may help.

the ancient art of backpacking

From the first North American use of a pack frame by Sioux and Cheyenne Indians—even back to the vineyard workers of Europe carrying baskets of grapes—it was obvious that the frame distributed weight more evenly across the back and shoulders. As Mic Mead, president of Adventure Pack at El Cajon, CA, explains, "It provides fixed points to attach the load to the wearer." Eventually recreational hikers took up the pack frame of the mountain men. As long ago as 1878, Henry Merriam constructed a pack and frame with good hip-suspension.

In 1922, Trapper Nelson, a Seattle hiker, began to manufacture a pack frame made of spruce covered with a tightly laced piece of canvas to act as a back pad. This frame, and countless frames copied from it during the twenties and thirties were popular until immediately after World War II when A. I. Kelty invented the arc-welded contoured aluminum pack frame with padded shoulder straps. To go with the frame, Kelty created a nylon pack with easy-to-get-into pockets, compartment design allowing for variable load placement and a waist that would help distribute weight more evenly on the hips. A Kelty, or a not-too-different Camp Trails, frame pack is lightweight and allows a load to be carried high and close to a backpacker's center of gravity so that he doesn't have to lean forward like a Neanderthal when he walks. These packs soon became the most popular designs used on North American trails, and they remain among the favorites today.

stay loose, says one designer

"Modern pack designers, however, always overlooked one critical factor," says Murray Peltz, director of research and development at JanSport in Everett, WA. "The human body does not remain rigid while walking. Merriam had made this simple observation when he designed that 1878 pack so that the bag and frame could move independently on the hiker's body."

One answer to the rigidity problem was the soft pack. The Germans invented the rucksack. A good rucksack fits the body well and moves with it. Eventually it replaced the American knapsack because it was suspended from the strongest part of the shoulders and thereby put less strain on the back. With most of the load on the shoulders, nevertheless, this meant muscle fatigue not only in the back but in the legs as well.

Today's rucksack is fashioned of tight canvas to make it light in weight, but since it is only a sack with a draw cord to bring the top together, its interior is usually a jumble of articles. And since it is close-fitting, it also is often too warm on the back during a hot day's hike. Pack it properly, or sharp and hard objects inside can poke and rub against your back.

frame up

A pack frame makes it possible to ignore placement of objects in the pack except for the usual necessity of placing heavy objects high and close to the body. Most backpackers today find the frame pack invaluable for long-distance hikes because it keeps its shape well and is easy to live out of. Not everyone agrees about its superiority, however, because soft packs are now available that control the distribution of the weight through compartmentalization. Lawrence Horton of Rivendell Mountain Works, Victor, ID, is an advocate of the soft pack, and is blunt in his criticism of the frame pack:

"The idea of a frame was originated for the purpose of carrying heavy, awkward-shaped objects too hard, sharp or bulky to carry against one's back. They are ideally suited for carrying giant loads—75 pounds and up. In fact, if one is not carrying at least this much weight, or something like oxygen tanks, gasoline drums, or maybe pig iron, the advantages of a frame pack are questionable. They are bulky, cumbersome, heavy, fragile and expensive. Current designs, loaded with gadgetry, tend to become more and more cumbersome."

inside job

To Horton, it appears that the backpacking public has become so conditioned to the necessity of a frame that "when confronted with a soft pack, they have no idea where to put their sleeping bag—no frame extends below the pack!"

The soft pack began its present popularity rise in the early 1960s when Don Jensen, a Harvard student with a penchant for climbing Alaska's peaks, worked out a design for a pack that transfers much of the load directly to the hips. It is a compartmentalized shaped pack which fits snugly into the contours of the back. Its adherents say that its weight seems to become part of the hiker's body and that the pack does not move

or sway. On the negative side, because it hugs the body so closely, it can be hot on a torrid day.

It is limp when unloaded and gains vertical shape only when it is stuffed. Many long-distance backpackers say it can be hard to live out of. Whatever its drawbacks, however, it has been widely imitated. Rivendell Mountain Works makes the original in four lengths to insure proper fit to a hiker's back. The first Jensen pack was built to carry about 50 pounds comfortably, and held approximatley 3100 cu. in. Now there is also a Giant Jensen with 4400-cu.-in. capacity, designed to carry upward of 75 pounds.

The internal frame pack is also popular with many, particularly for relatively short backpacks. It does not hug the back as well as the Jensen soft pack, but it keeps vertical shape better when it is empty.

adjustable fit

Recently there has been a strong trend toward pack frames that employ adjustable fittings on the shoulder level cross bar instead of arc-welds in order to make the frame more flexible. JanSport, a leader in the manufacture of frame packs employing this kind of frame, and the firm that first introduced it in 1967, claims that the "mechanically secured joints allow the frame to flex with the body's motion while hiking." High Touring, the Salt Lake City backpack manufacturer, also makes its frames adjustable.

"If the trail is long, points of wear on your body must be constantly changed to prevent sore spots. The more points of adjustment, the better," comments Frank Cunningham Jr., of High Touring.

Lowe Alpine Systems of Boulder, CO, also makes a flexible frame that is winning much

Packs for every purpose range from daypack rucksack (left) and soft-stuff sack pack (center) to a full frame pack (right). Three shown here are sew-it-yourself pack kits which are available from Frostline

favor from veteran backpackers. LAS claims that "for the average backpacker who sticks only to established trails, the rigid design is fine. But for the advanced hiker, the extreme lack of versatility and flexibility of a rigid frame may outweigh its few advantages."

When it comes to strength, JanSport refers to multicycle torque tests performed by Ron Barstad and Dr. Stanley Chen of the Engineering Department, Arizona State University, that indicate their frame had not failed when the test was halted at 500 cycles, while the next strongest frame failed at 350 cycles. The Alpine Designs Adjustable Frame was also tested at Arizona, and was the only frame rated superior in quality of material and construction, excellent-superior in design and comfort. Alpine Designs in Boulder also reports that its new mini Flexpack is so adjustable that it can perform as an adult ski touring pack during the winter and a child's frame pack during the summer. To would-be customers for the full-sized Flexpack, Alpine Designs says, "Lift the frame over your head and crash it to the floor as hard as you can."

picking the perfect one

With something like 35 United States manufacturers offering better than 300 kinds of backpacks, selecting a pack for your own use can be mystifying. At least it can be said that the frames of reliable manufacturers are all reasonably well made. The weight range of the frame is not too important. Heliarc welding is considered the strongest, but eutectic welding holds up just about as well. Aluminum fittings are satisfactory, too.

Frame contour has been found to be important. Let the frame bend forward at the top and it moves the center of gravity forward. The hold-open-bar carries much of the weight of the load and should be attached to the frame and not, as in some of the inexpensive models, used in a fabric pocket.

The belt is another key feature of a pack that should be checked. A good hip-suspension system distributes the weight evenly over as much of the hips as possible and keeps the load in close to your body. It should, at the same time, allow the back to adjust to the pack when making a steep climb or descent. This will reduce back and leg fatigue as well, while providing better balance and a feeling that the pack is secure. Some hikers claim that only the single piece belt permits the frame to ride smoothly on their hips. Others favor the two-piece belt.

BACKPACK SOURCES

Among major companies in this field are the following. Some can supply names of dealers while others offer mail-order catalogs, services.

Adventure Pack
656 Front St.,
El Cajon,
Calif. 92020

Alpenlite
115 S. Spring St.,
Claremont,
Calif. 91711

Alpine Designs
6185 East Arapahoe,
Boulder,
Colo. 80303

Camp Trails
Box 14500,
Phoenix,
Ariz. 85063

Cannondale
37 Pulaski St.,
Stamford,
Conn. 06902

Coleman
250 N. St. Francis,
Wichita,
Kans. 67201

Frostline Kits
452 Burbank,
Broomfield,
Colo. 80020

Gerry
5450 N. Valley Hwy.,

Denver,
Colo. 80216

High Touring
1251 E. 2100 S.,
Salt Lake City,
Utah 84106

Holubar
Mountaineering
Box 7, Boulder,
Colo. 80302

JanSport
Paine Field Park,
Everett,
Wash. 98204

Kelty
1801 Victory Blvd.,
Glendale,
Calif. 91201

Lowe Alpine Systems
1752 N. 55th St.,
Boulder,
Colo. 80301

Recreational Equip.
Box 22090,
Seattle,
Wash. 98122

Revendell
Mountain Works
Box 198,
Victor, Idaho 83455

---

choose quality

Examine not only the frame but the shoulder straps to see how well padded they are and whether they are wide enough so they won't bite into your muscles. Cheap ones skimp on pad material and sometimes use easily frayed nylon belting that can slip through buckle fasteners.

Stitching should be of durable nylon or cotton-wrap nylon, with stitches small, straight and even. Several companies provide do-it-yourself backpack kits at lower prices. Double stitching is required over pockets, and stress points must be reinforced. Zippers should be made of materials that will not jam in cold or damp weather.

There is a bewildering variety of pack compartments available. Most lines include a single-compartment model plus various dividers. In some you can unzip the floor of the upper section to make one big bag for large items. Others unzip around the outside for access to individual pockets. Somewhere there's a pack to best suit your purpose.

These poppers produce good results. Here the author's son has used one to land a good-sized striped bass

Head and tail ends are rounded on a belt sander. The shaft is smoothed with hand sanding

Bottom hooks were omitted on some plugs for easier casting and improved balance

A hollow head for making the plug pop is easily routed into a concave cup with a spherical file bit in drill

Plugs are painted several coats. One or two treble hooks are then placed in screweyes

Finished plugs are dressed with bucktail streamers of deer-tail hair tied on treble hooks

Make your own poppers

BY GEORGE LINNANE

■ WHEN MY SON cast the surface popper into his first school of bluefish, the strike was so vicious that it caught him unprepared. He fumbled with the antireverse lever and the blue lunged to the surface and broke off the line. It was hard to lose a king-size fish and even worse to see a $3 popping plug go with him. Homemade poppers might be the answer.

For basic material, we used ¾-inch birch dowels. An electric drill, mounted in an inexpensive drill press stand, and sanding discs are the only power-tool necessities, but since my shop has a table saw and belt sander, we used them as well. After studying a number of successful plugs, we decided one 4⅝ inches long with a ¾-inch diameter would match a seven or eight-foot spinning rod with 10 to 15-pound test monofilament line. Heavier lures for bigger tackle were later made of ⅞-inch stock in five-inch lengths.

First step is to cut a 5½-inch length of dowel. Next, drill one end with a ½-inch bit ½-inch deep. Then route this hole with a spherical rotary

file bit, rounding it into the concave shape which causes the splashing and popping. We found this a critical operation that had to be done while the blank is held vertically with pliers in the drill stand. The blank can also be clamped in a vise and drilled freehand.

Before sanding, the hollowed end is cut at a 45° angle and then rerouted again with the rotary file bit to deepen the hole. The shaft can then be hand or disc-sanded. Weighting consists of drilling a ⅜-inch hole, ⅜-inch deep in the underside one inch from the tail end and filling it with molten lead. Total weight: about 1¼ ounces.

For painting, two coats of a flat oil-base primer proved necessary, plus three coats of acrylic spray or airplane dope. Metallic Christmas glitter was rolled into a final clear plastic coat. Three No. 214 ¾-inch zinc-plated steel screw eyes, one at each end and one 1¼ inches from the front lower lip are screwed into predrilled holes, with size 1 galvanized treble hooks secured to the back two. A white bucktail was tied to the tail hooks.

Protect your boat from the five big

Theft, fire, sinking, explosion or going adrift can be guarded against today by using electronic early warning devices strategically located on your vessel. They are well worth the cost

BY MORT SCHULTZ

■ THE STATISTICS are scary. According to Coast Guard figures for five recent years, there were 2038 pleasure-boat accidents that involved flooding and sinking, 737 fatalities, 146 injuries, and $4,973,200 in property damage. Fire or explosion of fuel aboard recreational craft caused 1705 accidents, 85 fatalities, 662 injuries and $13,845,000 worth of property damage. These figures are enough to scare and alert any pleasure-boat skipper.

"Early warning detection alarm systems can

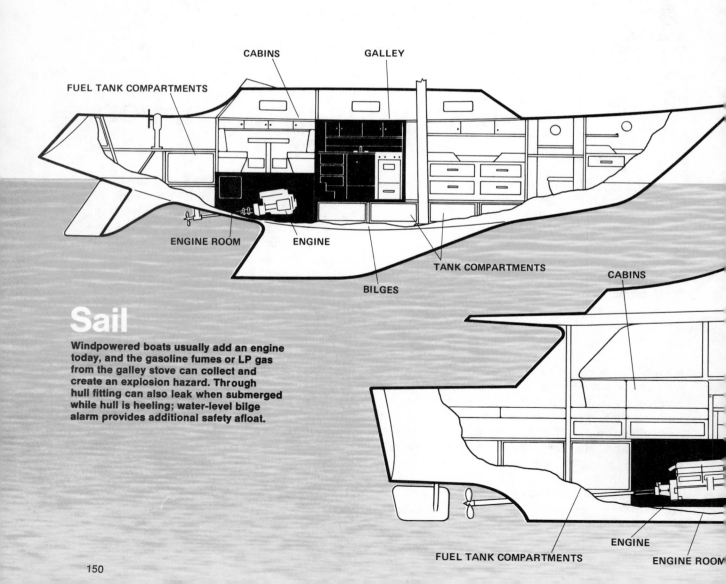

CABINS

GALLEY

FUEL TANK COMPARTMENTS

ENGINE ROOM

ENGINE

TANK COMPARTMENTS

BILGES

CABINS

Sail

Windpowered boats usually add an engine today, and the gasoline fumes or LP gas from the galley stove can collect and create an explosion hazard. Through hull fitting can also leak when submerged while hull is heeling; water-level bilge alarm provides additional safety afloat.

FUEL TANK COMPARTMENTS

ENGINE

ENGINE ROOM

hazards

prevent many accidents and deaths,'' states Lt. Frank Sambor of the Coast Guard's Boating Safety Branch on Governor's Island, NY.

By discovering with one of these alarms well in advance that danger is building up, a boat owner could ventilate an engine compartment to purge fumes, repair a gas leak, plug a leaking hull, or simply make for shore as fast as possible.

Though there is no law that requires a boat owner to outfit his craft with warning systems, in light of statistics it's clear that those who don't are flirting with danger. No one is immune to explosion, drowning or hypothermia (sudden loss of body heat from intense cold). The hazards of exposure to the cold are suspected of claiming the lives of hundreds who suddenly find themselves in the water, and the Coast Guard estimates that one-third or more of all drowning deaths result from this. It's apparent that bilge flooding and subsequent sinking and explosion or fire in the engine room are major threats to boat and passengers. Fortunately, highly sophis-

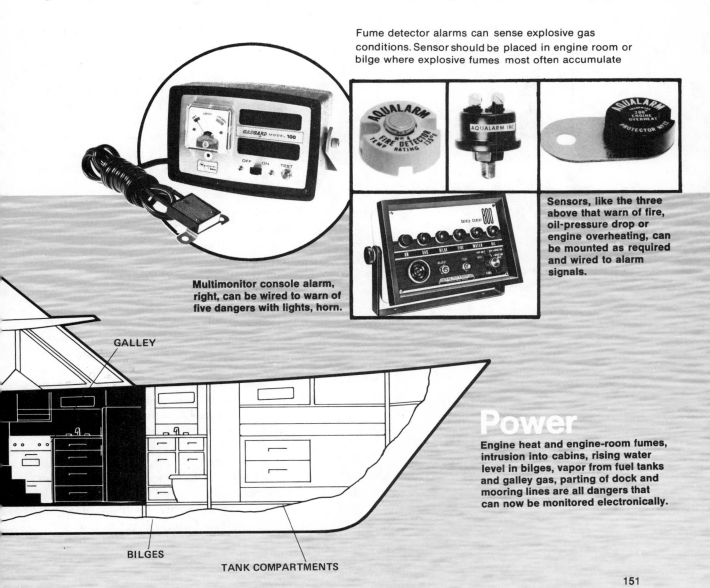

Fume detector alarms can sense explosive gas conditions. Sensor should be placed in engine room or bilge where explosive fumes most often accumulate

Sensors, like the three above that warn of fire, oil-pressure drop or engine overheating, can be mounted as required and wired to alarm signals.

Multimonitor console alarm, right, can be wired to warn of five dangers with lights, horn.

GALLEY

Power

Engine heat and engine-room fumes, intrusion into cabins, rising water level in bilges, vapor from fuel tanks and galley gas, parting of dock and mooring lines are all dangers that can now be monitored electronically.

BILGES

TANK COMPARTMENTS

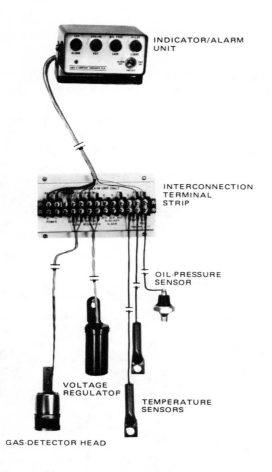

INDICATOR/ALARM UNIT

INTERCONNECTION TERMINAL STRIP

OIL-PRESSURE SENSOR

VOLTAGE REGULATOR

TEMPERATURE SENSORS

GAS-DETECTOR HEAD

Console monitors such as the one above can monitor a variety of hazards and even more sensors can be easily wired right into the indicator/alarm unit

ticated and reliable detection-alarm systems are available which monitor both. The problem is getting boaters to install and use them.

Alarm systems come either as single units that perform one function, or console models that monitor a number of functions. Single-unit systems are supplied to accommodate boat owners who need to monitor only one danger. For example, if your boat is powered by an outboard, has an open cockpit with no enclosed engine compartment, and there is no place for explosive fumes to accumulate, you purchase a simple bilge alarm system to warn of a leak. With enclosed engine and fuel-tank compartments, you would want a fume detector to warn of gasoline leaks or spills as well.

Although not as dramatic as a bilge alarm system or vapor-detection unit, sensors that monitor engine oil pressure and temperature serve an important function. If trouble in one of these areas goes undetected, your powerplant will be ruined. Detectors which monitor engine temperature and oil pressure are simple sensors like the ones you have in your car. Afloat, they are wired to an alarm bell or indicator light installed in a strategic location so they are easily heard or seen.

burglar alarms, too

There are also available as single units or in consoles with other detectors fire and intrusion (burglar) alarms. Fortunately, most pleasure boats are small and open enough so that passengers and crew can spot fire in its early stages. If you wish the protection of a fire-alarm system and none is offered by your marine supply store, you can investigate equipment made for the home. Most are detectors that sniff smoke created during the initial stages of a fire. Marine alarms, though sometimes more expensive, are desirable, however, since they are constructed to operate dependably in the moist and often corrosively salty atmosphere found around boats.

With an increase in boating thefts, an intrusion alarm may be worth considering. It warns when unauthorized persons board your boat while it is docked. For the most part, these are pressure-sensitive devices that are activated when stepped on, setting off a loud alarm bell or horn.

There are also magnetic devices screwed to the inside of cabin doors. When the magnetic field is interrupted by someone breaking into the cabin, a loud alarm sounds. These alarms can be rigged to indicate if mooring lines have been cut, untied or chafed free.

how they work

Bilge and explosive vapor detector systems are basically simple mechanisms consisting of a sensor mounted in the area being monitored. In the case of a bilge alarm, the sensor is a float device which rises as the water rises. When the float reaches a preset level, it activates the alarm, giving you time to start pumping, head for shore, and attempt repairs.

In the case of a good-quality vapor detector, the sensor has a platinum (active) filament that's exposed to the atmosphere of the compartment in which the sensor is placed. This filament is the main part of what is called an electrical Wheatstone bridge circuit. When no explosive vapors are present, the circuit has the same current flowing in its active and reference filaments, which "equalizes" the current and keeps the alarm in a passive state.

When explosive fumes come in contact with the active filament, there is a change in resistance owing to a rise in temperature of the platinum wire. The temperature increase is a chemical reaction of platinum when it's exposed to explosive gas fumes. The resistance produces an imbalance in the circuit which is proportional to the amount of vapor present, causing the current to flow through the alarm circuit and produce a warning.

The warning indicator is usually mounted in or near the cabin or at the helm position, and may be a horn, bell or light. Console units may have a set of lights with labels that indicate which form of trouble is occurring. Better models will also have some test arrangement so you can be sure the lights and bells will function in an emergency. Simple single systems may cost as little as around $10, while the more elaborate multiple-warning consoles run about $200 or more, plus charges for extra sensors.

buying tips

There are several important points to keep in

Bilge alarm is triggered by rising water which pushes up a float to activate a bell in time to start pumping

mind as you shop for and install the alarm systems you need.

1. Even though your boat may be equipped with an automatic bilge pump, don't discount the need for a bilge alarm. Bilge pumps can fail, or a leak can develop a larger capacity than the pump can handle. It is always better to be safe with an alarm than sorry with a sinking boat.

2. An alarm system generally works off the boat's electrical system although many have batteries. In any event, a low power drain is necessary—1.0 amp. or less is ideal.

3. Alarm systems should possess stainless-steel hardware to withstand corrosion.

4. Installing an alarm system is a relatively simple task, requiring only basic tools. If you want to find out how easy this is, write the maker first for instructions.

5. Explosive fume detectors should be mounted low enough in the engine compartment or bilges to sniff gas fumes which are heavier than air, but sensors should not become submerged in bilge water.

6. Install as many vapor detectors as needed, and remember the galley as well where bottled gas may be used for cooking and refrigeration.

7. Use No. 16 or larger wire when splicing in detectors.

8. You can test sensors by placing 10 drops of gasoline or lighter fluid in a two-pound coffee can. Let vaporize by covering it for several minutes, remove lid and lower in sensor. Your alarm should sound.

Make priceless photos last for generations

BY DAVE SAGARIN

■ THOSE TREASURED PHOTOS we hope our grandchildren will also cherish may be long gone unless we're careful. But there are ways to make our photos last, whether we process them ourselves (by far the best way), or send them out for processing.

Either way, photos will spend most of their lives outside the darkroom. Here, the enemies they face are light, moisture, heat and chemicals.

■ **Light** is the least of our problems: Most photos are kept in darkness anyway, and even for prints on display, light seems to be a problem only for color materials. You can slow the fading of color prints by displaying them where direct sunlight or window light (rich in ultraviolet) won't strike them—or, better yet, in rooms that get no direct sunlight. You should also file transparencies or negatives from which the prints were made, so you can replace them when they fade, as eventually they must. (Stored color transparencies and negatives fade more slowly.)

■ **Moisture** accelerates mildew and most chemical processes that age photographs. So don't keep your photos in damp parts of your house. Too little moisture, though, can menace prints, making them stiff and brittle as they dry out.

■ **Heat** accelerates chemical action and drying; if a damp basement's no place to keep your pictures, neither is a summer-baked attic.

■ **Chemicals,** alas, are all around us: in the air, in storage shelves and wrappings, and even in our photographs themselves. The chemicals within our photos must be handled in processing—or in a later refixing and rewashing of photos whose processing you're unsure of. There's not much you can do for yourself about air pollution, though you can avoid pollutants within your house. (Don't, for example, store photos near darkroom or other chemicals.)

But common storage aids carry chemicals, too. Avoid stained, unpainted or bleached wood shelves, or shelves whose paint is less than a month old; avoid glassine or paper wrappings (except those made of acid-free paper designed for archival storage) and most adhesives. Polyethylene, vinyl and cellulose acetate materials seem to be okay, as are the black papers (but not the boxes) that wrap enlarging papers.

■ **Albums and framing** can lengthen or shorten print life, too. I'm leery of photo albums that don't state whether they're made from acid-free or 100-percent rag paper. Alternatives include albums that hold prints under clear plastic (but discard their pages' paper liners if they're not acid-free or rag); stitched (not glued) albums of 100-percent rag paper put together for you by a

The archival dryer shown below is from East Street Gallery. You can make your own of wood and plastic screening

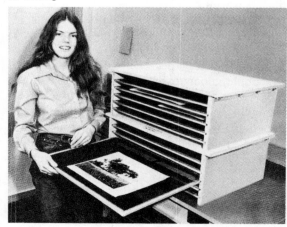

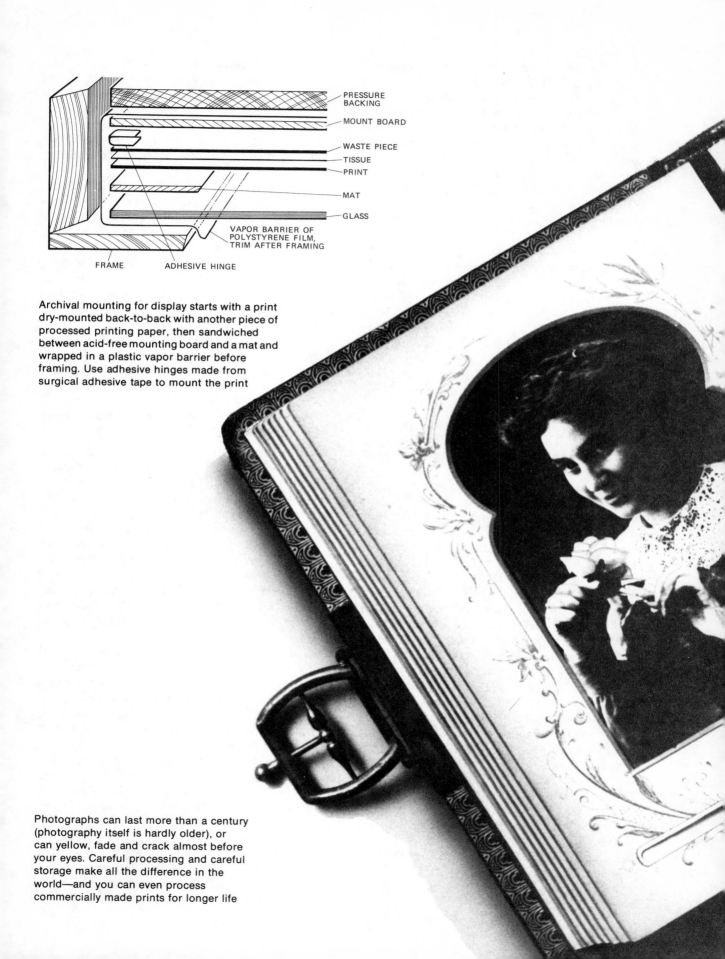

PRESSURE BACKING

MOUNT BOARD

WASTE PIECE

TISSUE

PRINT

MAT

GLASS

VAPOR BARRIER OF POLYSTYRENE FILM, TRIM AFTER FRAMING

FRAME   ADHESIVE HINGE

Archival mounting for display starts with a print dry-mounted back-to-back with another piece of processed printing paper, then sandwiched between acid-free mounting board and a mat and wrapped in a plastic vapor barrier before framing. Use adhesive hinges made from surgical adhesive tape to mount the print

Photographs can last more than a century (photography itself is hardly older), or can yellow, fade and crack almost before your eyes. Careful processing and careful storage make all the difference in the world—and you can even process commercially made prints for longer life

binder; prints dry-mounted back-to-back and plastic-bound by a commercial bindery; and portfolio boxes of dry-mounted prints.

If you're going to hang or display your print, dry-mount it back-to-back with another piece of the same kind of printing paper (a scrap print will do) that's also been archivally processed. Attach the mounted print to a piece of acid-free mount board with adhesive hinges made from surgical adhesive tape. Then overmat the print with another piece of museum-quality board, as shown.

This sandwich of mat, mount and photo should be wrapped in a vapor seal of plastic sandwich wrap. Working in a cool, dry area wrap the sheet around the print sandwich before inserting it in the frame, and hold the vapor barrier in place with pressure from a board behind. The frame itself should be metal—if it's wood, paint it carefully with a two-part epoxy paint to seal it. The frame's glazing should be glass, not plastic (which can absorb moisture, and which scratches easily).

■ **Processing your own photos,** you can insure them a long life with very little more time or expense than you'd spend insuring them a short one.

Prints should be made with at least an inch of blank paper all around the image area, if your easel allows this, so destructive processes starting at the edge will take longer to reach the image. Try to time print exposures so the print takes at least the recommended 1½ minutes (more won't hurt) to develop; developer should be no warmer than 68° F. (20° C.). After developing your film or print, use a fresh acetic-acid stop bath, agitating for 30 seconds.

■ **Fixing is critical:** Too short a fixing time, or use of exhausted fixer, leaves silver salts in the emulsion, eventually causing stains. Too much fixing risks bleaching out the image (especially in very light grays), or saturating the paper fiber so that the fixer is virutally impossible to wash out.

The best technique is to use two fixing baths. Fix in the first bath for no more than two minutes, increasing the time gradually to four minutes as you approach the solution's rated useful limit. Then fix for two minutes in the second fixer. When the first fixer is exhausted, dump it, move the second in its place and mix a fresh second bath.

Commercially developed prints and films have had at least some fixing; so two minutes in unexhausted fixer should be all the additional care they need there.

■ **Washing is another story.** All photos should be washed, after fixing, in a hypo-clearing solution (such as Hustler bath, available in photo stores) for several minutes before regular washing.

Thorough washing involves soaking the print in clean water, draining the water off and replacing it until there's no residual hypo in the print or its paper backing.

The best print washer around is made and distributed by the East Street Gallery in Grinnell, IA. (It also puts out an excellent book of information on archival processing, treatment, storage and formulas.)

You can wash very well in a tray, but it takes more effort. Use a tray one size larger than the largest print you're washing, wash no more than 12 prints at a time, and fill the tray just deep enough to easily cover the top print.

With prints face up, slide the bottom print out, drain it outside the tray, and set it face up on top of the stack. Continue to do this until the print that was originally on the bottom is now on top for the second time. Drain the water, refill the tray, and start over. Repeat every five minutes for an hour.

■ **The best way** to dry prints is first to squeegee excess water off the print with a rubber blade or roller used *only* for prints that have been archivally washed as described above—other prints might leave chemicals on the squeegee. Air-dry prints face down on neoprene or fiberglass screening bought at a hardware store. Stretch the screening over frames for flatness, then stack them, with air spaces between, in a box like East Street's dryer or hang the frames in a stack from your ceiling—not in your darkroom, where chemical dust is in the air. Prints dry flattest in warm, humid air.

New, plastic-coated RC printing papers soak up less chemicals, take less time to process (about 40 percent less fixing, 80 percent less washing, and 25 percent less developing) and will probably last longer than conventional papers. Dry RC papers face up; don't stack them until totally dry.

■ **Protective solutions** such as gold, sulfer or selenium toners, or Kodak's GP-1 solution, are a further precaution for long print life. Large photo stores usually stock toners or books that tell you how to make them.

■ **Color prints** are most stable when processed correctly; you can also rewash commercial prints and soak them in their appropriate stabilizers (look behind the print to find which paper was used, then use the stabilizer made for it).

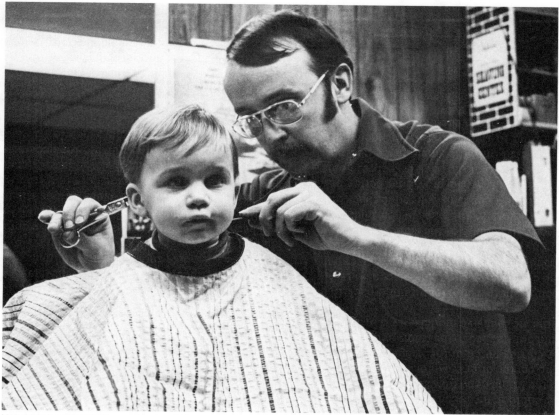

Neighborhood activities make good picture possibilities you'll enjoy in later years—especially if your own family is participating. But click off enough frames to let people get used to your shooting

Doing their own thing in their own homes, your subjects feel more at ease—and the home environment supports the picture. We still have the afghan Grandma made here

Family photos can be more than snapshots

BY DAVID SAGARIN

■ DON'T SNEER at the snapshot. It's a quick response—aim and shoot. But when everything works right, there's a wonderful freshness and reality to it. If you're not quite ready, though, or something isn't working, you're out of luck, and the moment passes.

A formal photograph, with properly adjusted lighting, carefully determined exposure and traditional posing, generally comes out all right but without much individuality. Sometimes you feel

Stand back when shooting people in activities—but just far enough to make the activity and the people's relationship to their environment clear. There's not much doubt about where this activity is taking place

Get in close and fill your frame with your subject. You don't even need a "portrait" focal-length lens: This shot was taken with a normal 55-mm lens at about 2½ feet from the subject. You should experiment with your camera to determine the best distance for this kind of portrait

more comfortable giving traditional photos, but there's a quality to a really good candid shot you can't get any other way.

What's a candid? It's a *planned snapshot,* made by predicting the course of spontaneous action and preparing yourself to take the best advantage of it.

Your planning needn't be complex—it can't be. Just try to picture in your mind what the finished print or slide will look like: Relate the situation to other times you've shot in similar light, or with similar backgrounds. If there's something you weren't happy about then, change it now. Maybe direct sunlight caused a squint, or a background of tangled foliage was confusing. Or maybe every time you're at the beach you overexpose (or, with metered cameras, underexpose).

You can control these things by moving around, by getting higher or lower, or by fudging the exposure settings in the direction you think they should go. You also gain control from prediction: Move to get a good background—*not* for the action as it's happening now, but for the action where you judge it will be happening by the time you've finished moving.

And instead of trying to keep action in focus as it moves, prefocus where you know the action's going, and shoot just as it gets there.

When the kids are doing something great, don't worry that if you take the time to change position you'll lose your shot. Shoot quickly where you are, then shift and shoot again—film is cheap, but memories are priceless. And once you start thinking of positions as you shoot, you'll find yourself already in a good position when the best action starts. Not only that, but as you get into what you're doing, you'll be less of a distraction to the people you're trying to shoot.

You might think it's easier to shoot good informal portraits of people you know well, but it's harder: The relationship gets in the way. A very fine professional photographer I know always took awful pictures of his wife—awkward, ugly, harassed. But that was his view of her; they're divorced now, and he takes lovely pictures of his new girl friend.

As long as you're aware of this problem, you can fight it. Just deal with those close to you as objectively as you can in the shooting situation. Concentrate on trying for good pictures, and they'll *be* good pictures.

Shooting kids in low-light situations or indoors? Get them involved in activities where slow shutter speeds and slow focusing won't be problems. And don't feel that you have to show a face in every shot

An unusual pose and activity kept my subject's interest alive, for a livelier expression. By getting above the subject I was able to get a simpler background than if I had shot her against the branches of the tree

Art and technique are blood brothers, not enemies. The more confident you are in the technical aspects of photography, the more forethought you've lavished on them, the more attention you'll be able to give to the situation, people, composition . . . *pictures*. When you see a photo you really like, think about how it was made: Where was the photographer in relation to the subject? What lens was used—telephoto, normal, wide-angle? What would the effect have been if another lens or viewpoint had been used? What's the relationship between photographer and subject?

Look hard at lighting, too. Compare your memories of good pictures with the lighting you're about to shoot by: Your lighting can usually—and easily—be improved. In bright sunlight, the first consideration is to lighten the shadows and soften the modeling of features with reflected "fill" light. A light wall (not a bright color, unless you're shooting black-and-white) will serve; so will a white card or cloth. Better yet, work in open shade to minimize skin texture. With black-and-white film, increase the ASA rating about 50 percent and double the development time. This will increase contrast

enough to offset the flat light and lighten skin tones (which also helps make blemishes disappear).

Indoors, you get more natural results with bounce flash or available light, but the same basic principles hold: Keep lighting contrasts reasonably low, and fill in shadows that contain important subject detail.

But indoors or outdoors, plan your snapshots as you shoot, and they won't be just snapshots—they'll be photos you'll be proud to show as photos, as well as captured memories.

Getting good candids often means shooting a lot of film—but it does not mean showing lots of pictures. Even within the family, too many shots don't preserve memories; they dissipate them. So once your shots have been developed, edit ruthlessly until you've come up with the one or two shots that best show the people and the situation (but don't be afraid to do a mini picture story of several related, but unduplicated shots).

You can edit parts of pictures, too, either cropping as you enlarge or trimming off unwanted details from store-bought prints. But better yet, think as you shoot—and edit in your viewfinder.

BY IVAN BERGER

Film loaders and accessories include (clockwise from upper left): Premier, Prinz 66, Western, Watson, unbranded model, Prinz standard. In the front row are empty cartridges, bulk film and the new Whitehead Cinek self-loading spools still in pilot production stage

Load your own 35-mm film cartridges

■ WHAT'S THE BEST photo equipment investment you can make? If you use a 35-mm camera, the answer is a bulk loader. Fill it up, use its contents once, and it has paid for itself. It will keep on cutting your film costs a third or more. And you'll be able to use some special-purpose films you just can't buy by the roll.

Here's how the economics work out: With a loader costing between $6 and $20, plus 18 empty cartridges (less than a quarter each—and they're reusable), you can turn a 100-foot roll of film into 18, 36-exposure cartridges. An under-$50 bulk roll of Ektachrome, for instance, gives you 18 rolls at less than $3 each, including cartridges, a saving of well over a dollar a roll, or about $20 total.

Exact costs vary. Discounts are available on both factory loads and bulk rolls. The number of uses you can get from a cartridge depends on how carefully you (or the lab you send your film

to) open them, and how free you keep them from dust. You can even reuse factory-loaded cartridges—except for Kodak's, which must be pried, not popped open, and can't be reused.

You can bulk-load quite a number of the films you now buy in cartridges—plus several that don't come in factory loads. There are black-and-white films from Kodak, Ilford, Luminos and Supreme, plus the super-sharp, almost-grainless H&W Control films. In color, you can get Kodak Ektachromes and Vericolor II (but not Kodachrome or Kodacolor).

Most well-stocked photo stores carry at least some bulk films (usually Kodak's), as do such mail-order shops as Spiratone (135-06 Northern Blvd., Flushing, NY 11354), Porter's (Box 628, Cedar Falls, IA 50613) and 47th-Street Photo (36 East 19th St., New York, NY 10003).

Bulk rolls come in lengths of 100, 50 or 27½ feet. The large, economy-size 100-footers are really the most economical, but you may prefer shorter rolls of films you use less often.

Today's loaders are light-tight and require darkness only for the few moments it takes for you to put the bulk roll in. If you lack a darkroom, you can use a light-tight changing bag; in a pinch, you can even do it at night under the covers of your bed or in a closet.

Actually, there are two light-tight compartments in these loaders: The large one holds the bulk roll, and the smaller, with its own door, holds the cartridge. Connecting them is a light-tight slit, the light trap, designed to let the film be drawn out of the big compartment.

To load a cartridge, you first open it and remove its spool, then attach the spool to the film end protruding through the light trap. With the film coming from your right, the spool's long end should point toward you.

Reassemble the cartridge around the spool, insert it under the crank in the loader, close the light-tight door, and wind till you have enough film in the cartridge. Then open the door, remove the cartridge, and cut and trim the film end. Some cameras will require that you trim your leader like those on factory loads or 27½-foot rolls, and you can get trimming templates for this. Most cameras will do nicely with a short, diagonal cut as shown below.

There are two basic types of loaders: Inexpensive, under-$10 ones, such as the small Prinz (and the unbranded model shown) use felt-lined slots as light traps. The felt works, but the longer you own the loader, and the more you use it, the greater the chance that a sharp bit of dust will embed itself in the felt and scratch your film.

More expensive models (still under $20), such as the Watson, Western, Premier and Prinz 66, have light traps that can't scratch the film because they never touch it. Instead, a door clamps tight against the film when you open the cartridge compartment, but opens wide to pass the film through freely when the cartridge-compartment door is closed. Interlocks prevent opening the cartridge compartment till you've closed the light trap; but you must remember to open the trap when you wind the film to prevent scratches.

These models also have counters that click off the number of exposures you've wound; felt-trap models usually just have charts telling how many crank winds correspond to what number of exposures.

Most models of the same type work about equally well, though the tiny, light unbranded model would chew film if you set its lid at the wrong angle, and the Premier had the best interlock, but the worst crank.

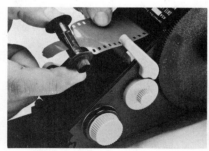
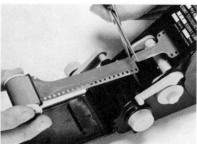

Short 27½-foot rolls have a precut tongue to fit slotted cartridge spools (left), a film leader and a new tongue every 36 exposures. Longer rolls save you more

Longer, 100-foot and 50-foot rolls must be taped to the film spool (left) and cut at the end of each roll (center). The leader must also be cut in the end (right)

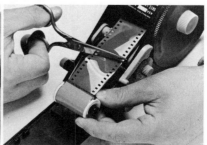

Interesting CB installations include a center-mounted set with a telephone-type handset hooked handily over the rim of the dashboard padding (top); a set hidden in the glove compartment (above) to elude thieves (but don't leave a microphone clip nearby as a tip-off; this mike is magnetically mounted); a small set in the shift-lever notch (right) of a mini-truck (but make sure to leave enough room to shift easily)

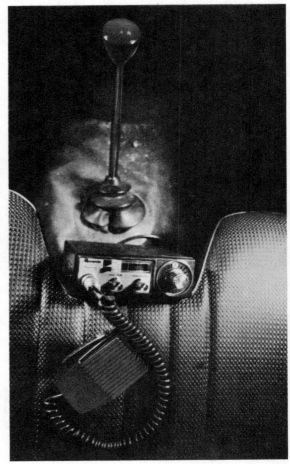

The best spot for your CB

BY ANTHONY R. CURTIS

■ BIG BOPPER, a Pennsylvania CBer whose wife goes by the name of Chantilly Lace, goofed when he mounted a Citizens Band radio in his car. Figuring his wife would like to talk on the radio from her side of the front seat, he placed the set under the dash on the passenger side. But one snowy day last winter, when Bopper was driving alone, he reached over to twist the channel selector and didn't see a car blocking his way. There was just time to avoid it by skidding to a stop against a hillside—and losing a tooth on the steering wheel.

The moral? Safety and convenience, *in that order*, are the main considerations when you're placing a CB transceiver in your car. The set has to be where you can operate it without looking away from the highway, and where you won't bang your head or knees on it when getting in and out or in a sudden stop. But since safety usually means making life convenient for the driver, there's little conflict between the two goals.

Mount your set where the driver can reach it as in the homemade, overhead-van console above, or under the dash near the center (other photos here). Where both a scanner and a CB set are used (upper left), the CB should be near the driver, since its controls need more attention. Microphone hangers can be attached to the CB set's mounting bracket, as shown above, or wherever else on the dash you find convenient. The most important things to keep in mind when mounting your CB are the safety and convenience of the driver

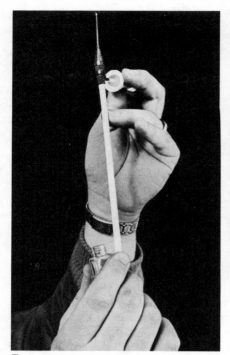

To protect your set, you can mount it in a sturdy, strongly installed locking device (above right) with a strong padlock to secure it. Use cardboard to protect it against scratches during installation (right), and cover exposed metal parts of your antenna with colorless nail polish to prevent weather damage. Check periodically, and if the polish is worn, apply a fresh coat to the antenna

Mobile radios have been mounted in every conceivable corner of a car. For example:

- Behind the front seat in the rear passenger compartment.
- Sitting loosely on the seat or dash.
- In the glove compartment.
- Under the front seats.
- Between driver and front passenger seats.
- Above the windshield.
- Above, on, in or under the dashboard.

Let's compare them, one by one.

In the rear-seat area might be a good location in a chauffeured limousine, where only the passengers would use the set. If the driver is going to use it, though, a radio mounted in back of the seat, with the microphone cord snaked around to the front, may look classy, but it can hardly be safe when you turn around to change channels.

Unattached radios sitting on the front seat, tunnel hump or dash will slip around as you maneuver the car or adjust the radio controls. Such units can distract the driver and possibly become flying hazards in a panic stop or collision.

"Invisible" locations in the glove compartment or under the seat are awkward for the driver to reach, as Big Bopper found out. They're not that theftproof, either, since thieves can guess there's a CB somewhere as long as you leave your antenna on the car.

Between the front seats, all controls are easily within the driver's reach—but since he can't see the dial without twisting half-way around in his seat, he'll have to select channels by counting the clicks. (It might help to cement markers of different shapes at the most commonly used channel positions.)

Above the windshield is where you find many CB sets in vans or trucks (cars usually lack sufficient headroom for this). This is actually a variant of a dashboard mounting; it turns the over-windshield area into a second dash.

Both driver and passenger can have easy access to an overhead set, depending on how far across the car you put it. And if you don't want to build your own roof-mounted console, you can buy ready-made mounts. But be sure the mike cord doesn't dangle in the driver's line of sight or jiggle distractingly in the corner of his eye. And since a sharp-cornered radio can be a hazard in a crash, make sure it's above head level and that everyone's well belted in.

Another roof-mount technique is to hang the set from a van's roof right behind the front seats. This makes the controls more accessible to the driver than hanging it from the back of his seat, but still means that he'll have to tune by touch—or turn away from the road to find his channel. And with controls facing forward, the rear passengers have no access to them.

The dashboard is the best and most common mounting point. Here, the radio can be visible and accessible to both driver and front-seat passenger, there is easy access to 12-volt power and the connections can be inconspicuous.

A few CB sets, mostly combinations that include commercial broadcast radio and/or tape, fit in the dash, like factory-installed car radios. The location is convenient, and an in-dash set is hard to steal; but it's hardest to install, too.

Atop the dash is where the tuning dial is easiest to read and the controls are often nearest at hand. But a radio here can also block the driver's view ahead, or cause head injuries in an accident. And holes that are cut into the top of its dashboard may reduce a car's resale value. Also, since the speakers are located at the bottom of most CB-set cabinets, an on-dash mounting may muffle the sound somewhat.

So most sets are slung beneath the dash, using the brackets that come with them. For increased rip-off protection, you can substitute a locking bracket (make sure the lock is hefty and the bracket's mountings strong and solid) or a slip-on bracket that lets you remove the set without having to undo all its connections individually.

Connect your set's power line to a handy 12-volt source and snake the coaxial cable lead-in from the antenna to the radio or vice versa, depending on which end of the wire has the thinner plug.

Antennas mounted in the front cowl or fender have shorter cables that can be passed through the firewall directly into the dash area.

Make sure the plug at the radio end of the antenna cable matches the radio's antenna socket. If not, you can cut off the old plug (as close to the cable's end as possible) and mount a new one; but since coax connectors are no fun to install, you may prefer to buy a ready-made cable with connectors attached if your antenna's cable is removable.

When all connections have been made, and the bracket mounted, you're ready for the last two steps. Stick on your radio the FCC-required Transmitter Identification Card (FCC form 452-C, usually supplied with your radio) with your name, address and call sign.

You may also wish to engrave your driver's license number and state inside the cabinet, to help you recover your set should it be stolen. (Social Security numbers aren't as good, since federal privacy laws make them harder to trace.)

The other necessary step is to mount the microphone hanger. Most radios are supplied with hangers that are designed to be screwed to the dash or the radio's bracket (which may have pretapped holes to hold it in place).

Where to get your CB's 12-volt power

Before looking for a power source for your mobile CB, consider whether you want to use a circuit that's always on (so the set is always available, should an emergency arise), or one that's switched off when you turn off the ignition (so there's no chance of accidental battery drain if you leave the set on, and to prevent unauthorized use).

Both kinds of circuits are available under the dash and at the fuse block (which may be under the dash, on the firewall, or in the engine compartment).

Unless it's hard to reach, the fuse block is your best power source because it lets you wire your set to the battery side of the fuse where it won't add to the load of the car's fuse is already carrying (your set has its own fuse, either on its back panel or in its power cord). A ring, spade or hook-tongue connector soldered or crimped to your power cord will help you make a solid, secure connection to the fuse block; if its wires are buried, you can also push the tongue of a spade lug into the clip that holds the fuse.

Make sure your polarity is correct: Hot wire (usually red) to the positive (+) side of the line, ground wire (usually black) to the negative (−) side—even if the car's ground is positive. If your car has positive ground, you may also have to insulate your CB set from its mounting bracket.

Hatchbacks can take regular trunk-mounts like this Radio Shack one (above), but the angle may be wrong; one solution is to bend it (above right) or use Hustler's ball-mount (right)

Short antennas adapt to a variety of mounts (clockwise from top left): Breaker base-loaded trunk rim mount; telescoping, cowl-mount ''disguise'' antenna; Hy-Gain foldover adapter (for center-load antennas only; shown here on a base-load coil for demonstration); Antenna Specialists magnetic roof mount

How to add ears to your wheels

BY IVAN BERGER

■ IF THE THOUGHT of gashing up your car's bodywork to mount an antenna is what's been keeping you out of CB radio, you can stop thinking about it and get on the air. There's now a host of antennas that are easy to install—and to remove later with little or no trace.

Antennas are available in all lengths from 2 to about 9 feet, with hardware for permanent or temporary mounting on your fenders, bumpers, roof, rain gutters or trunk lid. And the shorter, more modern types are quickly supplanting the old, bumper-mount, 9-foot-tall whips.

These modern antennas are practical, but not ideal. The ideal—a good, old 9-foot whip mounted on the car roof—is hardly practical.

The impracticality is obvious: An antenna topping out 13 or 14 feet above ground would be a major inconvenience—while it lasted. But the

''ideal'' part demands a little explanation:

The antenna you buy is really half of an antenna. The other half is your car. So reception and transmission will be strongest in the directions where there's more of your car to help. As the diagrams on page 169 show, centering the antenna on the roof gives you even results in all directions (or as close as you can get without owning a circular car). A roof mount also gains a slight advantage from its height above the ground.

On a moving car, a 9-foot whip antenna ($20 to $35) will live up to its name—it will whip. According to some antenna authorities, this won't cause problems. But according to others, the whip effect changes efficiency as the antenna waves closer to or farther from the car's body, and the angle at which it polarizes the waves it transmits will seldom agree with the angle of the antenna trying to receive them, especially if that's another waving whip.

On the other hand, the whip's length, a quarter of a 27-MHz CB wave's, makes it more efficient than shorter types. And modern bumper mounts make it possible to install a whip without drilling holes. Those ''soft,'' five-mph bumpers can pose problems, though; you may have to run a ground wire from the mount to either the

Gutter mounts include a screwdriver-locking type (this one with built-in flipover to clear obstructions) and temporary clip-on; both are from Antenna Specialists

roof-top antenna a better bet, at least to some experts, than a longer one back at the bumper.

Though a permanent roof installation will require a hole in your roof, we've heard no complaints about antenna holes leaking—and when you sell the car, inconspicuous rubber plugs are available from Antenna Specialists and Radio Shack.

The tricky part is snaking the antenna cable down from the roof to the dash under the car's cloth or plastic headliner. If your car has a center dome light, it may be easier to remove the light temporarily and work from the opening it leaves.

Ordinarily, antenna cables are best snaked from the radio end, with its big plug, toward the antenna, since the plug at the antenna end, if any, is usually slender. Roof antennas are probably an exception; you might do better to cut off the plug (shortening the cable as little as you can), snake the cable from the top, and put on a new plug.

magnetic mounts

Easier to use are antennas with magnetic mounts. Just stick such an antenna to the middle of your steel roof, and snake the cable through a partly opened window, a vent, or through the opening between the door and frame, if there's enough foam gasketing around the door to keep the wire from kinking. This is an ideal solution if you want to hide your antenna between uses to keep it from attracting vandals or CB-set thieves. It's also ideal for travelers who want to use their CB sets in rental cars away from home.

Antennas designed for rain-gutter installation have spring clamps for temporary mounting, or are screwdriver-tightened for more permanent locations. But gutters on some modern cars are weak or nonexistent altogether. And one temporary clip-on couldn't stay upright on our test car's steeply curved roof; the Antenna Specialists Flipper shown, though, had an adjustment screw that kept it upright.

Because they're mounted to one side of the car, gutter mounts give asymmetrical results, stronger on the car's opposite side than on their own. Front-back symmetry is a function of how far back they're placed on the car.

trunk mounts

Trunk-lip mounts are an even better compromise in terms of installation ease and radiating pattern, especially on hatchbacks where they ride at the rear center of the roof and radiate in a sort of symmetrical, forward-projecting oval.

bumper's metal frame or to the car itself. Bumper mounting also reduces overhead clearance problems, though it won't eliminate them. For garaging (few garage doors open 10 feet high), you can tie down the antenna's tip with an inexpensive gutter clip (about $2); but as whips become less popular, the clips are getting harder to find.

Shorter antennas are less efficient than whips, but a technique called "coil-loading" minimizes this loss. If you need only a slightly shorter mast, Hustler makes 74-inch and 82-inch models (about $35) that are rigid to eliminate the whip's limber sway, and which fold down at about the height of the car's roof, for easy garaging. These can be strap-mounted on bumpers, or mounted through large holes in the car's side or deck.

But most of the antennas sold today are shorter, coil-loaded models, between about 2 and 4 feet in length and selling for about $20 to $25. Because of their small size, they offer a wide choice of mounting positions.

Mounted on the roof, an antenna produces a directional pattern that is roughly an oval, with a bit more response to the front and rear (desirable, where you're most likely to talk to other cars on the same highway), but plenty to both sides as well. That's enough to make a short,

Matching the antenna involves minor length adjustments (top) using an SWR meter like this Radio Shack model as a guide

No holes are required for such a mount: It fits over the lip of the rear-deck lid, secured in place by setscrews that also bite through the paint to ground it to the metal of the lid. (On the few cars where the deck lid isn't grounded to the body, an additional grounding strap or wire will be needed.)

The cable can be run from the CB transceiver under the floor mats and along the sides or center hump (or beneath the sill plates of cars without mats) to the rear seat. On sedans, it will then go under the seat, through a hole (drill it yourself, if need be) into the trunk; line the hole with a rubber grommet to protect the cable. In hatchbacks, there's no trunk partition to hole through, but you'll have to either feed the cable up under the headliner or fasten it to the headliner with some sort of cable clamp. Leave enough slack in the cable for the lid to open without pulling your connections out; any remaining excess can probably coil up under the back seat. Don't try to shorten the cable—its length has been calculated for the best possible match between transceiver and antenna.

Also available are trunk-groove mounts that attach to the rim of the trunk opening rather than to the lid. They're not as streamlined-looking as the lid mounts, though, and they do require a little drilling (two small holes in the groove), so they're losing popularity to the lid types.

the co-phased array

You'll see a lot of trucks (and some cars) sporting pairs of matched antennas that face each other across the vehicle's roof, trunk or back bumper. These are "co-phased" so that they reinforce each other's output toward the front and rear. That puts more of your signal on the road ahead of and behind you.

For best results, co-phased antennas should be just about 9 feet apart, which makes them better performers on trucks and motor homes than on cars. And to work properly, they must use special, co-phased cable sets, usually provided with the antennas, though they're also available for use with matched pairs of whatever antenna you choose.

If you want to keep you car's CB a secret, you might consider an antenna that mounts on the cowl, where one would expect a regular car-radio receiving aerial. Cowl mounts, however, pick up ignition noise, and their pattern of coverage, as shown on page 169, is not the most useful. Besides, a decent CB antenna will still have a loading coil to show what it is. But straight masts that look like (and double as) regular car-radio antennas will severely compromise CB performance; regular car-radio aerials used for CB will be even worse.

For any antenna to operate at its best, its impedance and that of its cables must match that of the CB set. But since half of the antenna system—your car and the antenna's location on it—is beyond the manufacturer's control, he can't guarantee a perfect match.

But you can. Most antennas can be tuned for best results, by adjusting either the position of the antenna shaft, or a piece of it, within a setscrew collar, or by moving an element near the tip.

To make sure your adjustments are improvements, you can use readily available, inexpensive meters to measure standing-wave ratio (SWR), output signal field strength, or both. For best results, tune the antenna for the lowest possible standing-wave ratio, (anything lower than 1.5:1 is good, anything higher than 2:1 is pretty bad), double checking with field-strength meter as you go, to make sure you're increasing, not decreasing your output. Try to borrow, rent or share such meters if you can, rather than buying them outright; you won't need them often. In fact, you may not need one at all, save for reassurance: When I checked out my own hatchback installation (the one at the bottom of the right column on page 166), the needle of the SWR meter barely twitched, indicating that I'd done better by luck than I could have done on purpose.

center-load or bottom-load?

Coil-loading, the antenna-shortening technique mentioned earlier, takes several forms. Antennas can be loaded by coils concentrated at their center, top or bottom, or distributed along their entire length.

Continuously loaded antennas are less critically tuned than others; this makes them easier to install, though they're not as efficient as some other types.

Top-loaded antennas are most efficient, but harder to match, and their characteristics change as they move in relation to the car—a problem worsened by the tendency of topweighted masts to sway. This design also puts the most fragile part of the antenna, its coil, where it's most likely to hit something.

Center-loaded antennas are one of the two most popular coil-loaded designs, because they radiate efficiently—up to 2 dB better than base-loaded types. But the coil bulge halfway up the mast increases wind resistance and, possibly, sway; and it makes any damage from overhead obstructions costlier than replacement of a simple, replaceable shaft.

Base-loaded types, which seem to be most popular on the roads, have their coils at the bottom. This does reduce efficiency a bit, but it also presents only an inexpensive rod to bend or break, and offers a slender profile to the wind. Base-loaded types are also a bit less susceptible to noise pickup from the ignitions of passing cars. And base-loaders are more tolerant of low capacitances between the car and the ground—which makes them better for small cars. With cars shrinking, it's likely that the market for base-loaders will expand.

Antenna directional patterns:

Where you mount it counts

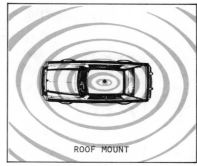
ROOF MOUNT

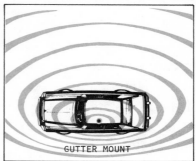
GUTTER MOUNT

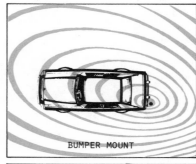
BUMPER MOUNT

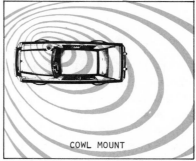
COWL MOUNT

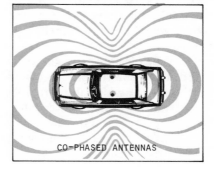
CO-PHASED ANTENNAS

Antenna placement doesn't affect range so much as how that range is distributed; extra signal projected in one direction will be at the expense of the signal sent in others. Overall range depends on many factors: antenna, CB set, terrain

169

Record care: it pays to be tender

A little care can extend the life of your records. Here's a look at some of the products on the market for keeping your records and stylus clean

Track your records clean with (from top): Audio-Technica AT-6002, $10; original Watts Dust Bug, $7; conductive Decca Record Cleaner, $15, controversial Lencoclean which keeps grooves wet, $13

■ DON'T BLAME YOUR RECORDS if they're full of noise, warps and scratches—blame yourself. Long record life is up to you.

It doesn't cost a penny to store your records properly (on edge, packed firmly together but not tightly squeezed), or to be sure you put them back in their dust jackets as soon as you've played them. And take care never to touch the recorded grooves—your fingertip oils will glue down airborne dust.

A dust cover for your turntable will keep records from getting dirtier while you play them and will slow down the rate at which the turntable collects dust it can transfer to the records later.

What's left is getting the records clean to start with. Shown here are a variety of tools for record cleanliness: devices that clean records as you play them, tracking along the grooves just as the tone arm does (above); gadgets to clean the discs just before you play them; devices to get dust off your stylus and to remove static electricity that attracts falling dust; plus a new lubricant.

Some of the best, shown here, are the Zerostat, the Discwasher, the Decca Record Cleaner, the Manual Parastat and Sound Guard.

Polishing cloths don't clean down in the grooves where the dirt matters; and I suspect them of leaving dust-catching residues on the record surface. Record sprays are even more likely to catch dust.

One possible exception to this is Sound Guard, a new, dry lubricant which does actually seem to reduce record wear in lab tests.

Most of the cleaners shown on the next page

Record cleaners vary in design: 1. Schweizer Designs Hydro Cleaner ($10) has a built-in fluid atomizer.
2. Decca Record Brush has conductive bristles to avoid static, also a stand with a built-in bristle
cleaner ($15). 3. Watts Parastat ($15) has bristles in the center to loosen dust and plush ends to pick up dust.
4. Discwasher ($15) has one-way slanted bristles and a pocket to hold the solution bottle. 5. Watts Preener
($4) is moistened by an internal wick. 6. Ball Brothers Sound Guard is a dry lubricant

are used damp—but *not* wet—the better to pick up dust without building up static. Europeans, though, swear by devices like the Lencoclean, which soaks the grooves as the record plays; but some experts feel this makes the record noisier if you play it dry thereafter; so if you start wet, stay that way.

To clean dirty styli, try: Schweizer Designs No. 210 (rear, $3); Audio-Technica AT-607 (center, $3); Watts Stylus Cleaner (right rear, $1.25); Discwasher cleaner with inspection mirror ($6)

Under the microscope, you can see thin shavings worn by even a fresh stylus (above, left), accounting for some of the fuzz that gathers on the stylus. But lubricated with Sound Guard (above, right) the record appears fuzz-free. The grooves on the record shown average 0.003 inches in width

To kill static attracting dust, try the Staticmaster 500 brush with a 1-year Polonium ionization strip ($15)

The Zerostat gun ($30) generates ions as you squeeze and release the trigger. These eliminate static

The tester measures line voltage and checks outlet wiring (see table below). Designed for three-wire grounded outlets, it can also check three-wire adapters used in two-wire outlets; here, yellow light shows that the "ground" screw isn't really grounded

Build an electric outlet checker

BY RUDOLF F. GRAF and GEORGE J. WHALEN

Are your grounded outlets really grounded? You can use this easy-to-build electric outlet checker to find out and
check your line voltage at the same time

CONDITION	METER READING	LAMPS
PROPERLY WIRED OUTLET	NORMAL LINE VOLTAGE (U.S. AVG. 117 VAC)	I_1 ○ ○ I_3 I_2 ●
OPEN GROUND	NORMAL LINE VOLTAGE	I_1 ● ○ I_3 I_2 ●
OPEN HOT WIRE	ZERO	I_1 ● ● I_3 I_2 ●
OPEN NEUTRAL WIRE	ZERO	I_1 ○ ● I_3 I_2 ●
HOT-NEUTRAL REVERSED	NORMAL LINE VOLTAGE	I_1 ● ○ I_3 I_2 ○
HOT-GROUND REVERSED	ZERO	I_1 ○ ● I_3 I_2 ○

LEGEND: ○ LAMP ON ● LAMP OFF

PARTS LIST

I1, I2, I3,—Set of three neon indicator lamps with built-in dropping resistors (Set: Radio Shack No. 272-338).

M1—0-150-v.a.c. voltmeter (Calectro D1-926 or equivalent).

Misc.—Phenolic case with 5⅝ x 2⅞ x 2-in. panel (Calectro J4-717); three-wire line cord with U-ground plug; solder.

■ ARE YOUR GROUNDED OUTLETS really grounded? Will the center screw of your ungrounded outlet be a safe connection for the pigtail ground wire of a three-wire adapter plug? Is the outlet's polarity correct? And what's your line voltage? Plug in this easy-to-build checker and you'll have all the answers.

Like commercial testers, it has three lights to indicate polarity. But because it also has an extension plug, you can read it easily even when your outlet is difficult to see or reach. And it checks voltage, too.

Parts are all readily available, and construction is simple. Take care when making the holes in the case. For the meter hole, drill a ring of small holes first, then carefully chip out the material between them. Holes for indicator lamps are first drilled small, then carefully reamed to size to avoid cracking the panel.

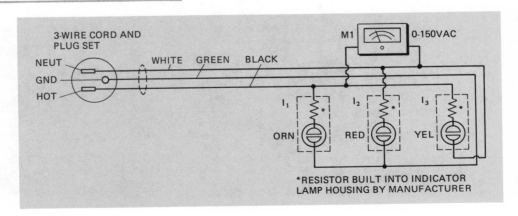

*RESISTOR BUILT INTO INDICATOR LAMP HOUSING BY MANUFACTURER

Here's back-yard summer fun

■ KIDS LIKE ALL KINDS of presents from the most complicated and expensive to the simplest and cheapest. But they're happiest when they know that you made the present yourself. The four games on these pages are easy to build, and one of them will suit your boy or girl (and some grownups if they get a chance to play), no matter what their age. You won't need any special tools to construct the stilts, swing, tetherball or basketball hoop. Since these games are played outdoors, you have to build them to withstand the weather. Make the swing out of solid oak stock and protect the pieces with two coats of spar varnish. All wood joints should be assembled with a waterproof glue or construction adhesive and all nails should be hot-dipped galvanized to prevent rust. For screws, use brass or aluminum.

The most complicated project, the basketball hoop, is worth the effort because the backstop adjusts to any height. The detail drawing (next page) shows how the heavy plywood backstop weights down the upper frame to get a clamping action between cross ties and 4x4 support posts. The cam action is so tight that 2x4 chocks under the cross ties on opposite sides of the posts will

Your kids are sure to enjoy the swing and stilts shown as much as the children in these photos are. Both projects have been made of durable hardwood for years of heavy, outdoor use

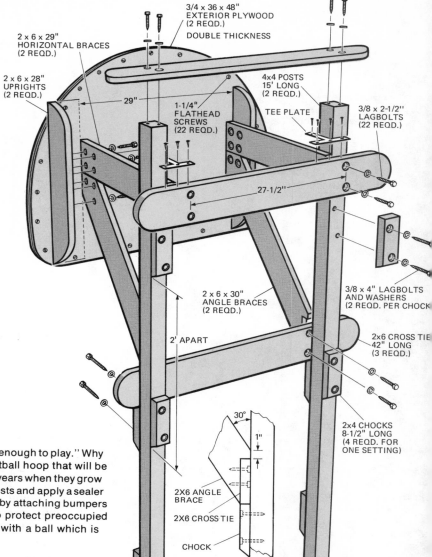

3/4 x 36 x 48"
EXTERIOR PLYWOOD
(2 REQD.)
DOUBLE THICKNESS

2 x 6 x 29"
HORIZONTAL BRACES
(2 REQD.)

2 x 6 x 28"
UPRIGHTS
(2 REQD.)

29"

4x4 POSTS
15' LONG
(2 REQD.)

TEE PLATE

3/8 x 2-1/2"
LAGBOLTS
(22 REQD.)

1-1/4"
FLATHEAD
SCREWS
(22 REQD.)

27-1/2"

3/8 x 4" LAGBOLTS
AND WASHERS
(2 REQD. PER CHOCK)

2 x 6 x 30"
ANGLE BRACES
(2 REQD.)

2' APART

2x6 CROSS TIE
42" LONG
(3 REQD.)

2x4 CHOCKS
8-1/2" LONG
(4 REQD. FOR
ONE SETTING)

30°

1"

2X6 ANGLE
BRACE

2X6 CROSS TIE

CHOCK

TREAT WITH
CREOSOTE

SET 3'
IN CONCRETE
BELOW GRADE

Basketball hoop

"Come back in a few years when you're tall enough to play." Why wait? You can build this adjustable basketball hoop that will be perfect for your kids right now and in a few years when they grow taller. Be sure to sand the edges of the fir posts and apply a sealer to eliminate splinters. Make the game safe by attaching bumpers (foam rubber in vinyl) around the posts to protect preoccupied players. Smaller players will want to start with a ball which is smaller than a basketball and work up

support the whole assembly. This system lets you raise the hoop as your kids get taller.

A pair of stilts is a great toy to develop balance and coordination. Use a hardwood like oak or maple for the stock and base pad. Exterior-grade plywood is fine for the foot platform that will easily support a 75-lb. child. For larger kids, add the alternate brace detailed in the drawings. To preserve the stilts and keep scrapes and bruises to a minimum, tell the kids to stay off hard surfaces.

Tetherball (page 177) is normally for two players. Each takes half of an imaginary circle around the center post for his court and tries to hit the ball past his opponent until the cord is completely wrapped around the pole. It's not easy because the other player is trying to do the same thing in the opposite direction. A metal sleeve, slightly larger than the pole, can be set in concrete at grade level so you can remove the pole to mow the grass or for winter storage. Your yard will be a special place for the kids after you've built one of these toys.

Child's swing

Whatever the object, kids will try to swing from it if it's possible. This good-looking design, assembled around a continuous rope loop, eliminates screwed joints that may split open under stress. The guard rails lift up along the ropes for easy access (you can face in either direction) and slide down to make an accidental fall next to impossible. Use nylon rope for a safer ride

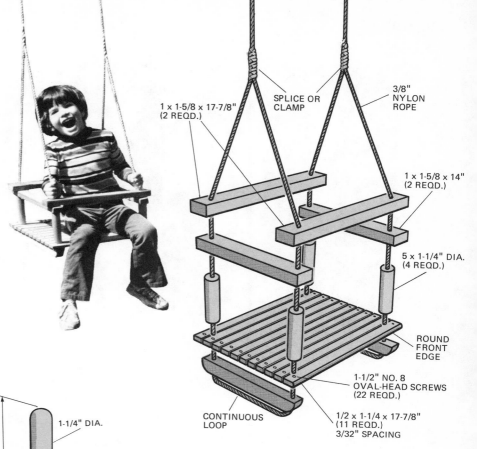

SPLICE OR CLAMP

3/8" NYLON ROPE

1 x 1-5/8 x 17-7/8" (2 REQD.)

1 x 1-5/8 x 14 (2 REQD.)

5 x 1-1/4" DIA. (4 REQD.)

ROUND FRONT EDGE

1-1/2" NO. 8 OVAL-HEAD SCREWS (22 REQD.)

CONTINUOUS LOOP

1/2 x 1-1/4 x 17-7/8" (11 REQD.) 3/32" SPACING

Stilts

We tested this design, and the foot platform held up after rough use by a 150-pounder. To play safe, use the alternate brace for anyone over 75 lbs. This pair is sealed with clear varnish, but you can decorate yours with bright enamel colors or contrasting wood stains

1-1/4" HOLE X 2-1/2" DEEP

1-1/4" DIA.

3/4"

1/4"

2"

2 1/2"

ALTERNATE BRACE

1/4"

46-1/2" LONG

2-1/2" NO.8 SCREW (2 REQD.)

2" NO. 8 BRASS FLAT-HEAD SCREW

1-7/8 x 1-7/8 x 16" HARDWOOD

4-3/8"

7/8 x 3/4" GROOVE

4-3/4"

3/4" EXTERIOR PLYWOOD

PAD

3-1/8"

2-9/16"

3/4" COUNTERSINK 3/8" DRILL

Tetherball

The toughest part of this project is locating a ball with a moulded loop on it. A 6-in.-diameter, concrete filled hole makes a strong, permanent base. Setting an oversize sleeve in the concrete will make the pole demountable. Tetherball is a game the whole family will enjoy

2" DIA. PIPE

CONCRETE BASE 6" DIA.

OPTIONAL SUPPORT SLEEVE

1/2" EYE BOLT

NUT

LOCKWASHER

THREADED C

LOCKWASHER

NUT

A champ's design for a home gym

BY MIKE McCLINTOCK

■ WHEN ARE YOU going to get in shape? Every year millions of Americans solemnly vow to remove excess inches from their bodies. Half an hour is reserved each evening for sit-ups, push-ups and jogging, but somehow, after a few short days of aching muscles, the resolution fades. Well, here's how to get (and keep) a shape-up habit.

We went to Bruce Jenner, world record holder and Olympic gold medalist in the decathlon, for expert advice on keeping the whole family in shape—and having fun while doing it.

"One reason I was able to keep training day in and day out was that I really enjoyed it. Even though I'm retired from competition, I still work out every day."

The room we planned with Bruce is small and simple enough to be a reasonable renovation project. Once you set it up, your family will enjoy using it every day.

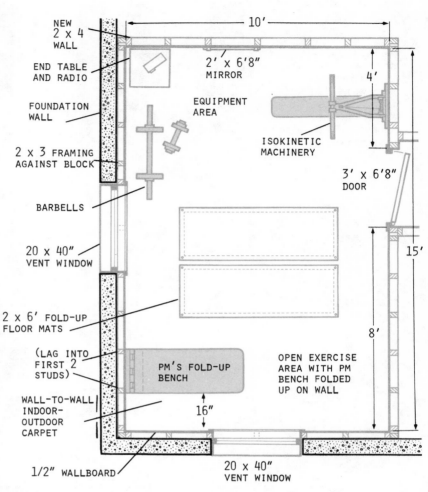

NEW 2 x 4 WALL

END TABLE AND RADIO

FOUNDATION WALL

2 x 3 FRAMING AGAINST BLOCK

BARBELLS

20 x 40" VENT WINDOW

2 x 6' FOLD-UP FLOOR MATS

(LAG INTO FIRST 2 STUDS)

WALL-TO-WALL INDOOR-OUTDOOR CARPET

1/2" WALLBOARD

10'

2' x 6'8" MIRROR

EQUIPMENT AREA

ISOKINETIC MACHINERY

4'

3' x 6'8" DOOR

15'

8'

PM'S FOLD-UP BENCH

OPEN EXERCISE AREA WITH PM BENCH FOLDED UP ON WALL

16"

20 x 40" VENT WINDOW

SHAPE-UP ROOM PLAN

Our plan (10x15 ft.) is small enough to fit into a corner of your basement, but big enough to hold the features recommended by Bruce. Among them are a padded floor (we used indoor/outdoor carpeting), and exercise bench, isokinetic machines, barbells, a mirror and a radio. If possible, choose a room with a ceiling that is high enough for lifting the weights

A low basement ceiling (typical in many new homes) does not rule out weightlifting. Even if you are as tall as Bruce (6-foot-2 and 190 lbs.), you can adapt the way he did by lifting from a sitting position. For general conditioning, he advises a lot of bar motion covering many exercises, with a low weight total on the bar. Don't strain muscles by trying a few big lifts

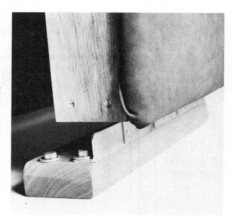

The heavy-duty wall attachment (near right) lets you fold the bench up and out of the way. A 1-in. foam pad (far right) is wrapped with a layer of Naugahyde to make a comfortable, long-lasting and attractive top for the bench

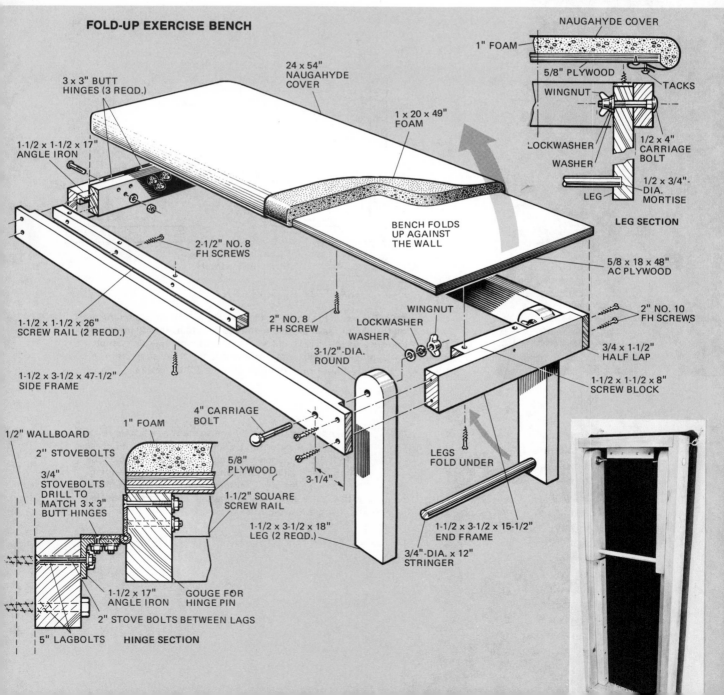

FOLD-UP EXERCISE BENCH

NAUGAHYDE COVER

1" FOAM

5/8" PLYWOOD

TACKS

WINGNUT

LOCKWASHER

WASHER

1/2 x 4" CARRIAGE BOLT

LEG

1/2 x 3/4"-DIA. MORTISE

LEG SECTION

3 x 3" BUTT HINGES (3 REQD.)

24 x 54" NAUGAHYDE COVER

1 x 20 x 49" FOAM

1-1/2 x 1-1/2 x 17" ANGLE IRON

BENCH FOLDS UP AGAINST THE WALL

5/8 x 18 x 48" AC PLYWOOD

2-1/2" NO. 8 FH SCREWS

2" NO. 10 FH SCREWS

1-1/2 x 1-1/2 x 26" SCREW RAIL (2 REQD.)

WINGNUT

LOCKWASHER

WASHER

2" NO. 8 FH SCREW

3/4 x 1-1/2" HALF LAP

1-1/2 x 3-1/2 x 47-1/2" SIDE FRAME

3-1/2"-DIA. ROUND

1-1/2 x 1-1/2 x 8" SCREW BLOCK

4" CARRIAGE BOLT

1/2" WALLBOARD

1" FOAM

2" STOVEBOLTS

5/8" PLYWOOD

3/4" STOVEBOLTS DRILL TO MATCH 3 x 3" BUTT HINGES

1-1/2" SQUARE SCREW RAIL

1-1/2 x 3-1/2 x 18" LEG (2 REQD.)

3-1/4"

LEGS FOLD UNDER

1-1/2 x 3-1/2 x 15-1/2" END FRAME

3/4"-DIA. x 12" STRINGER

1-1/2 x 17" ANGLE IRON

GOUGE FOR HINGE PIN

2" STOVE BOLTS BETWEEN LAGS

5" LAGBOLTS   **HINGE SECTION**

STAYING IN SHAPE

Overhead presses can be made from a sitting position. A barbell set (like the one that we purchased from Sears for use in these photos—about $40) is a valuable workout tool. You should start with a low weight total and gradually work your way up

Squat lifts strengthen a lot of muscles simultaneously. Standing, load the bar on your shoulders and balance it with your hands. Bend your knees (head and shoulders erect) until you touch the bench seat. Then return to a standing position

Specialized gym equipment is not essential, but isokinetic devices (like the one shown above) are good for all ages. Bruce suggested the mirror and radio. They'll make your room more attractive and more fun so you will want to spend more time there

About the biggest mistake you can make is to set up a crushing schedule of exercises and jump right into them. Your body (and your mind) isn't ready for the shock.

Tip No. 1: Start your shape-up program with a *short* series of *simple* exercises. Bruce says consistency is the key to getting in shape. "Just walking up and down the stairs 5 or 10 times is good for you—as long as you do it every night. Granted, it'll take you a few months to see results if that's all you do, but even a simple routine *will* get you in shape.

You can sneak yourself into a shape-up program by making an exercise out of some routine you do daily. Whether it's picking up mail or cooking dinner, you can find a minute to jog 50 steps in place or lift a frying pan over your head 10 times. It may sound silly, but if you do it regularly you'll start feeling and looking better. So don't start with 50 sit-ups—your stomach won't like it.

Although Bruce went through specific exercises for each of the 10 decathlon events, he also trained for general conditioning and stamina.

Tip No. 2: Bruce told us that "for general conditioning, do *more* of something *easy*, rather than a *little* of something *tough*." You'll be more likely to stick to your exercises if you can do

Sit-ups are a crucial part of staying in shape. Bruce says, "Sit-ups are really essential. They strengthen your stomach and your lower back." For the best results, you should hook your feet underneath the bar and bend your knees

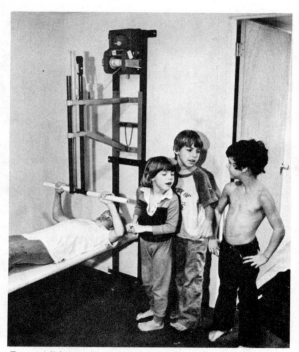

Even children will want to use your new exercise room. It's never too early for them to learn the importance of exercise for good health. We found that they wanted to give all of the equipment a try

them at home. If you rely on jogging to keep in shape, a few weeks of bad winter weather can put a crimp in your conditioning.

You don't need a lot of building experience to set up your own exercise room. Our plan (10x15 ft.) is easy to build and will fit nicely into a corner of your basement (see page 183 for construction details). Here are guidelines Bruce gave us on how to set up your room and enjoy it.

■ Keep it at a comfortable temperature. It should have some ventilation, but doesn't need special heating or airconditioning.

■ The floor should be resilient—working out on a concrete floor will be hard on your feet. Our plan calls for indoor/outdoor carpeting to cushion your feet and make the room look attractive. Bruce told us, "A padded floor is fine as long as it's firm—you shouldn't sink into it."

■ You should have an exercise bench. You can use it for bench presses, sit-ups, squat-lifts and other exercises. Our bench is simple and inexpensive to build. The whole assembly is hinged to a wall so you can fold it out of the way. You can leave the legs tucked up and fold the bench down to the floor for inclined sit-ups.

■ A barbell set is a good investment. For overall conditioning, Bruce says, "The idea here is not to lift a lot of weight, but to carry some weight through a range of motion. That's a lot more interesting than repetitive bench presses." Don't try for a big lift right off. Always warm up with some jogging in place or calisthenics.

■ For family fitness, *isokinetic* exercises are ideal. We tried one isokinetic device (Mini-Gym, made by Mini-Gym, Inc., Box 266, Independence, MO 64051). You tension your muscles by pulling on a counter-weighted rope. The resistance will depend on how hard you pull, so it's just as good for a 10-year-old as for a 50-year-old.

■ There are a few "extras." Bruce suggested a radio and mirror. After we mounted a mirror in the room, everybody who went in managed to take a quick look at himself. "One of the most important parts of any exercise program is to see some progress. When nobody's looking, you check those muscles—seeing some results really keeps you at it."

EXERCISE ROOM CONSTRUCTION

We boxed in the basement furnace with standard 2x4 walls covered with ½-in. wallboard. You can simplify the job by framing one of the inside walls under a basement girder. This way you can also box the lally column. Cut the 2x4 shoes (wide side on the concrete) to notch around the bottom of the columns

Use 2x4s for the new interior walls. Rather than nail on 1x2 strips that can cause leaks, we used 2x3s against the outside walls. Nail studs to a 2x3 shoe on the floor and another 2x3 plate nailed on the flat to the first floor joists. No special tools are needed

Cellar vent windows can be boxed in with 2x3s. Extend the casing flush to the inside of the new wallboard. Narrow, ½-in.-thick trim and a coat of paint finish the job

Recess the exposed lines like the wire below. Protect them as shown from nails

The "deadman" (shown below) is simply two pieces of 1x2 stock nailed in a tee and cut about ¾ in. shorter than the height from the floor to the joists. It supports one end of the unwieldly wallboard for the ceiling while you nail the other end

Fun with a doodling engraver

A fine ballpoint pen is used to form a design on cardboard taped to a wood wheel. For scribing metal, use a diamond stylus

BY WALTER E. BURTON

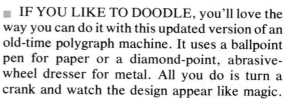

■ IF YOU LIKE TO DOODLE, you'll love the way you can do it with this updated version of an old-time polygraph machine. It uses a ballpoint pen for paper or a diamond-point, abrasive-wheel dresser for metal. All you do is turn a crank and watch the design appear like magic.

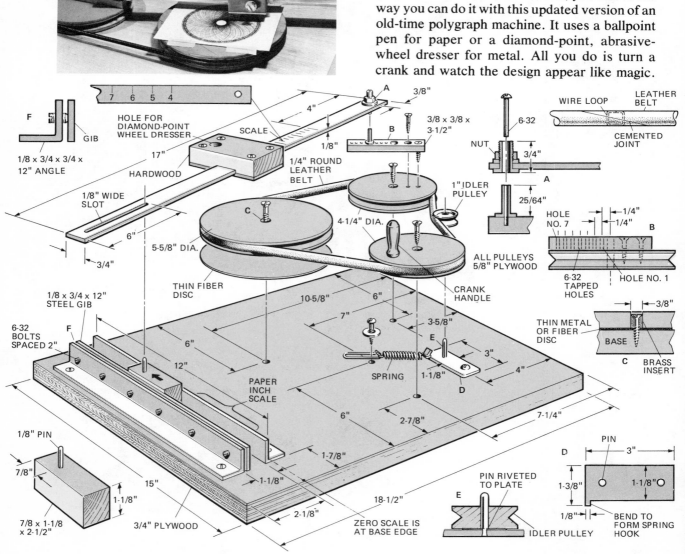

F — GIB
1/8 x 3/4 x 3/4 x 12" ANGLE

HOLE FOR DIAMOND-POINT WHEEL DRESSER
SCALE
HARDWOOD
17"
1/8" WIDE SLOT
6"
3/4"

4"
1/8"
3/8 x 3/8 x 3-1/2"
1/4" ROUND LEATHER BELT
6-32
NUT
3/4"
A
25/64"

WIRE LOOP   LEATHER BELT
CEMENTED JOINT
6-32

HOLE NO. 7
1/4" 1/4"
B
6-32 TAPPED HOLES
HOLE NO. 1

THIN METAL OR FIBER DISC
BASE
3/8"
C
BRASS INSERT

C
5-5/8" DIA.
THIN FIBER DISC
4-1/4" DIA.
1" IDLER PULLEY
ALL PULLEYS 5/8" PLYWOOD
CRANK HANDLE

1/8 x 3/4 x 12" STEEL GIB
6-32 BOLTS SPACED 2"
F
10-5/8"   6"
7"
3-5/8"
E
3"
D
4"
6"   12"   6"
PAPER INCH SCALE
SPRING
1-1/8"
2-7/8"
7-1/4"
6"
1-7/8"

1/8" PIN
7/8"
15"
7/8 x 1-1/8 x 2-1/2"
1-1/8"
3/4" PLYWOOD
1-1/8"
2-1/8"
18-1/2"
ZERO SCALE IS AT BASE EDGE

PIN RIVETED TO PLATE
E
IDLER PULLEY

D
PIN
3"
1-3/8"
1-1/8"
1/8"
BEND TO FORM SPRING HOOK

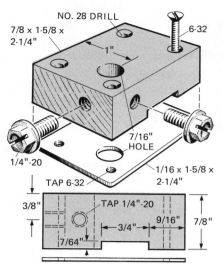

NO. 28 DRILL
7/8 x 1-5/8 x 2-1/4"
1"
6-32
7/16" HOLE
1/4"-20
TAP 6-32
1/16 x 1-5/8 x 2-1/4"
3/8"
TAP 1/4"-20
3/4"
9/16"
7/8"
7/64"

This handsome clock dial, an example of the use of metal designs, was engraved in wire-brushed aluminum

The circular design on this trinket-box lid was given a ground finish with abrasive grains and then inset in the lid

Basically, the machine consists of three plywood wheels connected by a leather belt. Bits of masking tape attach the item to be decorated to the wheel, which acts as a rotating "drawing board." As this wheel turns, a block carrying the stylus (diamond tool or pen) moves over it, guided by the stylus arm.

The rotating wheel draws circles; the stylus arm draws oval figures. The combination of these two kinds of curves forms a decorative, usually symmetrical, pattern. Patterns are easily varied by changing the position of the pin that guides the stylus arm, the position of the stylus block along the arm, or the distance of the pivot point from the center of the wheel that operates the stylus arm.

The relative sizes of pivot wheel and pattern-holding wheel, as well as distance of stylus from centerline of arm and effective arm length, also determine the pattern.

The machine's base is a piece of ¾-in. plywood. (Locations of the various parts are given in relation to bottom and right-hand edges when the crank wheel faces the operator.)

I turned the wheels from ⅝-in. fir plywood and grooved the edges for ¼-in. round leather belts.

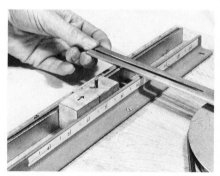

The index mark on the guide block is set by the inch scale

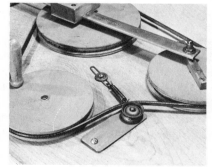

A spring-loaded idler pulley keeps the belt taut and slip free

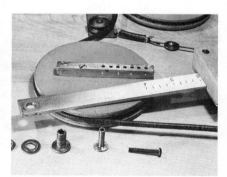

These are parts of the pivot assembly linking the stylus and the wood wheel

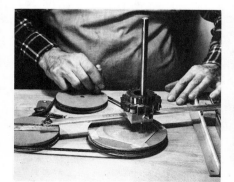

Light oil applied to the metal surface beforehand reduces stylus friction

Tabs of masking tape at the corners hold the metal plate flat

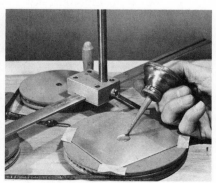

Added weight on the stylus arm lets the diamond cut the brass deeper

Each wheel bearing consists of a brass insert drilled to rotate snugly around a No. 6 wood screw. You can improve the wheel action by placing a thin washer of cardboard-like fiber between the wheel and the base.

I used a round leather sewing-machine belt, spliced the ends as shown and used Duco household cement and a wire-loop reinforcement to hold them in place. A coating of stick-type belt dressing will help to reduce the slipping.

A 1-in. idler pulley turns on a pin riveted to a thin steel plate, and a coil tension spring holds the pulley against the belt. An elongated wire loop clamped by a wood screw and washer anchors the spring.

The stylus has a ⅛ x 6-in. slot extending almost to one end. A ⅜-in. hole at the opposite end accepts the pivot assembly, which operates the stylus arm.

The steel crank bar has a series of 6-32 tapped holes on ¼-in. centers and is mounted so that hole No. 1 is ¼ in. from the wheel center. For small designs, an additional hole nearer the center is useful.

maple block holds stylus

A maple block grooved on the bottom holds the stylus. Depth of the groove is slightly less than arm thickness, so when the four 6-32 bolts are tightened, the block is locked securely on the arm.

Bore a $^7/_{16}$-in. hole almost tangent to the groove to accept a diamond-tipped, abrasive-wheel dresser. The block can hold other tools, such as a ballpoint pen if built up with a piece of rubber tubing.

The weight of the stylus arm and block is sufficient for holding a ballpoint pen in contact with paper. For engraving metal, additional weight is required. Milling cutters (which weigh about 1½ lbs.) slipped over the diamond-tipped rod will do the trick although any similar weight may be used.

The maple arm-guide block rests in a channel formed by two pieces of metal angle. A gib positioned between the block and left-hand angle is used to lock the block in a fixed position. One bolt enters a hole drilled about halfway through the gib to prevent endwise slippage.

The block's pin engages the slot in the stylus arm and is positioned somewhat nearer one end of the block than the other. Reverse the block and a greater range of pin position can be obtained in one direction. At the block's midpoint, on each side, is an index mark for positioning the block relative to a scale. An arrow on top of the block points normally to the rear edge of the base.

Three scales enable setting for repeat drawing of a particular design.

■ An inch scale 13-in. long is glued to the outer vertical surface of the right-hand metal angle 3 in. from the end for gauging the position of sliding block.

■ An inch scale, with ¼-in. divisions, is stamped along the top of the stylus arm, with the "0" position coinciding with the center of the pivot hole over the pulley. Only the portion from 4 to 8 in. is needed. The right-hand edge of the block is used as an index line in setting the position of the stylus.

■ A series of numbers—1, 3, 5 and 7—identify the tapped holes along the top of the steel bar. These numbers, with No. 1 hole near pulley center, indicate different positions of the stylus-arm pivot with respect to the axis of the pulley.

record design's 'formula'

Once a design has been worked out by trial, record its "formula" by writing down the three scale readings in left-to-right sequence. For example, 7, 5¾, 6 indicates that the guide block is at 7 in., the stylus-holding block is at 5¾ in. and the arm pivot is at hole No. 6. If desired, an arrow pointing upward for the "normal" position of the block, or downward for the reversed position, can be added to the formula.

Aluminum is easy to engrave; brass requires more pressure. Best pressure for various metals can be found by trial. Actually, when using a rounded diamond or other point, the "engraving" is more of a rubbing than a cutting action.

The metal blank should be flat. Its surface can be prepared in various ways, ranging from polishing to dulling by chemical etching or rubbing with a mixture of abrasive grit and water. For a ground-glass effect on aluminum, rub 180-grit aluminum-oxide grains mixed with water over the surface with a small metal block.

Fasten the blank with self-adhering tape and spread a thin layer of oil over the surface to reduce stylus friction. Bring the stylus against the blank with the arm elevated slightly above the guide block. Put additional weights in place, then turn the guide pulley slowly. Count the number of revolutions the wheel requires to create a pattern and record it along with the "formula." Best starting and stopping points for the stylus tip are on the smallest diameter of a pattern.

that spins. It can be built in a couple of evenings. Wing and tail sections call for 2 feet of ½ x 6-in. clear pine; about 14 inches of 1 x 6 are needed for the fuselage. Propeller pin and wheel axle call for 8 inches of ¼-in. dowel. All remaining parts can be made from scraps of ¾-in. stock. Follow the plans below for dimensioning and cutting each piece. Sand all edges until round to avoid splinters. The propeller is easily made on a drill press. A plain block jig, beveled to 45°, is clamped to the table as shown. The ¾-in.-sq. blank is then held against the bevel and run past a sanding drum on the drill-press spindle. Leave enough hub for a ⁵/₁₆-in. hole for prop pin and hub cowl. Assemble parts with brads and epoxy. The plane can be finished with clear finish or painted with a bright enamel.

■ THIS CHUNKY LITTLE BLOCK AIRPLANE for a chunky little aeronaut is a simple, nearly indestructible toy with just enough realism to excite his interest—including a prop

A toy plane for mini-pilots

BY H. R. HAGGERTY

This all-wood airplane will be a hit with any kid you give it to. It's made from pine and features a prop and wheels that really turn

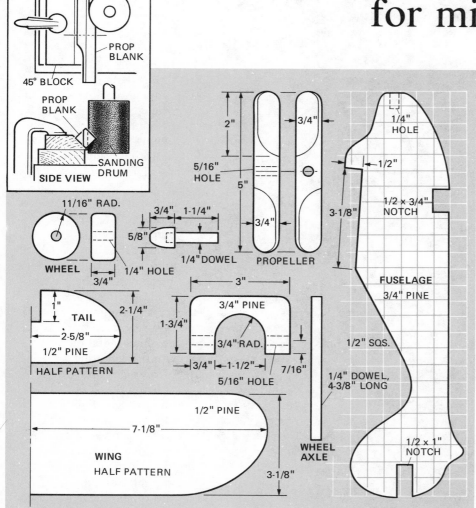

Make your Christmas bright

Wood-strip decorations

■ Wood shavings used in the peacock are made by running a plane over a soft pine board. Walnut and other wood veneers, as in the Christmas balls, are sold at lumberyards. We found the ½-in. width best to use. Both materials are shaped; then glued with white glue and held with tape (or bobby pins) until the glue dries. Wood shavings can be colored with water-base markers; they must be moistened before shaping.

Wood shavings (left) and wood trim are glued, then held in place with tape or bobby pins

Painted plywood

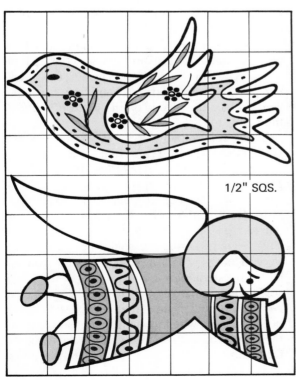

1/2" SQS.

■ You will need a jig saw with a fine blade for sawing intricate shapes in this project. A Dremel Moto-Tool is helpful.

Materials: Carbon paper, ¼-in. finished plywood, sandpaper, Plastic Wood, enamel undercoat and paints, fine paintbrush, clear decoupage finish, screw eyes.

Method: Draw the pattern to full size, trace it on the plywood and saw it out. Sand the edges and fill any holes with Plastic Wood. Apply the undercoat and let it dry. Do the same on the reverse side, then sand lightly. Paint the design you wish or follow our suggestions, having drawn or traced the design on both sides of the plywood. Use two coats of paint and sand between them.

After the paint is dry, twist a screw eye into the figure top and apply the clear finish. We hung the figure and applied finish to both sides at once. Three coats give a durable finish.

Metal stars

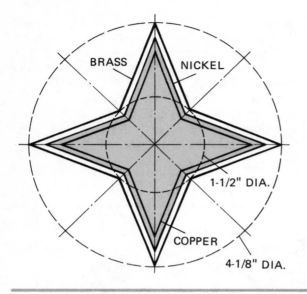

■ Metal stars are cut from nickel, brass and copper found in hobby stores and are glued with contact cement. Texture is made by hammering the metal on a wood rasp or by using an icepick.

To make the Bethlehem Star, cut the brass pattern twice and the nickel and copper ones four times each. Halve the nickel and copper ones vertically. Slit a brass piece from the top star point vertically to the middle; slit the other piece from bottom to middle. Slide the two together and glue. Position the nickel and glue. Do the same with the copper.

The pattern for the eight-pointed Star Flower is made by joining two 4¼-in. squares of copper together. Patterns for the brass and nickel designs are made using 3-in. and 2-in. squares respectively, and rounding the corners. The eight petals of the copper flower are based on 1-in. squares. You can use a sharp scissors or tin snips to cut the thin metal.

Stained-glass Poinsettia

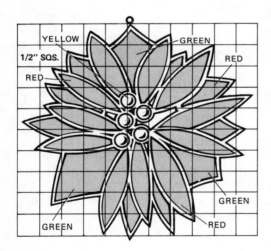

■ Make a poinsettia that glows next to your Christmas tree lights.

Tools: Glass cutter; breaking pliers to break off small glass pieces; groziers to remove excess glass bits; 25 to 100-watt soldering iron; hardboard work surface; safety glasses.

Materials: Five ⅜-in. yellow glass jewels; ½ to 1 sq. ft. each of red and green glass as thin as available; 1-lb. spool of $^{60}/_{40}$ solder; one roll $^{3}/_{16}$ or $^{7}/_{32}$-in. copper foil (depending on glass thickness); one 6-ft. strip of lead came with a ⅛-in. U-channel; flux (oleic or zinc chloride); kerosene; carbon paper; oaktag paper; burnisher.

Making the design: Draw the full-size pattern and make a copy on oaktag. Cut out each piece of the oaktag pattern; place them on the glass.

Cutting and breaking: Note: Before cutting the glass, practice on glass scraps. Dip the cutter in kerosene to lubricate it. Score the glass by drawing the cutter toward you in one firm stroke. Grasp the glass on each side of the score with thumbs and index fingers and make a fist. A quick up-and-outward motion will separate it on the score. To break small glass pieces, use breaking pliers; smooth leftover nubs with grozing pliers. Place the pieces on the pattern to check the fit.

Leading and foiling: Wrap the jewels in the U-channel of the lead came and cut it with sharp scissors so the ends butt together. Wrap the copper foil around the glass edges so an equal amount of foil is on both sides. Overlap foil ends ¼ in. Burnish the foil to the glass.

Soldering: Apply flux with a brush to the foil and lead; reapply during the soldering. Spot-solder several joints by heating solder with the iron and letting the solder flow along the copper foil. Then solder the copper on one side of the piece. Let cool, then solder the other side. At a strong point, solder a wire loop to hang the piece. Wash the poinsettia with soap. Supplies are available from Glass Masters Guild, 621 Sixth Ave., New York, NY 10011.

Index

The page number refers to the first page on which specific information can be found.